"Proceeding from the axiom that genuine understanding of the self, Ron Highfield sh of the self fail in this regard, because they ⟨ ...g⟩ ...u power in human terms and therefore in competition with God. To overcome this narrow, idolatrous image of both God and humanity, Highfield first deconstructs the modern self and then recovers the older, more profound, biblical, trinitarian understanding of human identity as grounded in God's love for humanity. Drawing with equal facility from theological sources both ancient and modern, the author unfolds a beautiful vision of human dignity, freedom, will and morality as participation in Christ, the true image of God and founder of our true humanity."

JENS ZIMMERMANN, Trinity Western University

"Henri Nouwen claimed that the most important question anyone asks is 'Who am I?' In a world where we define ourselves by performance, conformity and image, competing with one another and relying on the blessing of others to discover and live out of a healthy sense of self, Ron Highfield reminds us that it is when we embrace God's invitation that 'we become truly ourselves and live life to the full.' Dr. Highfield's solid scholarship, theological depth and inviting style allow us to wrestle honestly with the nature of God's love as we seek to be released from the bondage of the false, 'me-centered self.' We've needed this book for a long time, but it's been worth the wait."

CHAP CLARK, Fuller Theological Seminary

"Humans have great dignity. Yet from where does it come? How is it sustained and protected amidst the turbulence of life and ever-changing opinions? In Ron Highfield's philosophically informed meditation, he reminds us that a 'God-centered' identity is the only secure basis for our dignity. We are never as truly free, safe and whole as we are when we rest in the self-giving God of the gospel."

KELLY M. KAPIC, Covenant College

"For some people, God is far from being a solution to life. He is the problem. For how can I be a free, morally responsible agent if God ordains and orders the world? And what is the place of human dignity in a creation saturated with the presence of God? In this accessible and readable book, Ron Highfield engages with a host of thinkers in the history of ideas to show how we need to reorient ourselves from being 'me centered' to being 'God centered.' Only then, he argues, can we leave behind competitive views of our relationship to the Deity, in order to understand the dignity and freedom God bestows upon us as creatures."

OLIVER D. CRISP, Fuller Theological Seminary

GOD, FREEDOM & HUMAN DIGNITY

**EMBRACING A GOD-CENTERED IDENTITY
IN A ME-CENTERED CULTURE**

RON HIGHFIELD

IVP Academic

An imprint of InterVarsity Press
Downers Grove, Illinois

InterVarsity Press
P.O. Box 1400, Downers Grove, IL 60515-1426
World Wide Web: www.ivpress.com
Email: email@ivpress.com

InterVarsity Press® is the book-publishing division of InterVarsity Christian Fellowship/USA®, a movement of students and faculty active on campus at hundreds of universities, colleges and schools of nursing in the United States of America, and a member movement of the International Fellowship of Evangelical Students. For information about local and regional activities, visit intervarsity.org.

All Scripture quotations, unless otherwise indicated, are taken from the Holy Bible, Today's New International Version®, NIV® Copyright © 1973, 1978, 1984, 2010 by Biblica, Inc.™ Used by permission. All rights reserved worldwide.

Cover design: Cindy Kiple
Interior design: Beth Hagenberg
Images: Hand print: © GANNA RASSADNIKOVA/iStockphoto

ISBN 978-0-8308-2711-4

Library of Congress Cataloging-in-Publication Data
Highfield, Ron, 1951-
 God, freedom, and dignity : embracing a God-centered identity in a me-centered culture /
Ron Highfield.
       p.   cm.
   Includes bibliographical references and
   indexes. ISBN 978-0-8308-2711-4 (pbk)
   1. Identity (Psychology)—Religious aspects—Christianity. 2. Self (Philosophy) 3. Self. I.
Title.
   BV4509.5.H54 2013
   233—dc23
                                                                        2012041421

P	22	21	20	19	18	17	16	15	14	13	12	11	10	9	8	7	6	5	4	3
Y	33	32	31	30	29	28	27	26	25	24	23	22	21	20	19	18	17	16	15

CONTENTS

Preface 11

PART 1: THE ME-CENTERED SELF

1 HOW THE ME-CENTERED WORLD WAS BORN 17

Searching for Identity in a Secular Age 18

The Development of Inwardness 19

René Descartes and Disengaged Reason 20

John Locke and the Punctual Self 21

The Moral Space of Inwardness 22

Affirmation of Ordinary Life 23

John Locke and His Friends 25

The Moral Space of the Affirmation of Ordinary Life . . . 27

The Inner Voice of Nature 28

The Moral Space of the Expressive View of Nature 31

Realistic Expectations 31

The Self in a Culture Set Adrift 32

The Emotivist Self 32

The End of Ends and the Enlightenment Quest 33

Speaking of Christianity in a Post-Christian Culture 37

Looking Ahead 39

2 DEFIANCE: THE PROMETHEAN DIMENSION
OF THE MODERN SELF 40

Prometheus: The Myth 40

Prometheus: The Metaphor 42

3 SUBSERVIENCE: THE RELIGION OF IDOLS,
HYPOCRITES AND HIRELINGS 48

Default Religion 49

The Wish Reveals the Heart. 50

The Original Sin 51

The Unoriginal Sin. 53

Critics of Default Religion 54

The Bible 54

Modern Critics 59

A Medieval Critic. 61

4 INDIFFERENCE: A STUDY IN THOUGHTLESSNESS 64

The Idea and Practice of Indifference 65

Ways of Being Indifferent 65

    The Esthetic 65

    The Conformist 67

    The Celebrity. 70

    The Agnostic 74

The Indifferent God of Indifference 74

Retrospective on the Three Attitudes 76

5 THE GOD OF THE MODERN SELF 77

The Superhuman God 78

The Superhuman Being's Powers 84

Omnipotence Feared. 84

Omnipresence Dreaded 85

The Superhuman God's Inner Self 87

The Empty Self 87

The Self as Will. 88

6 THE SECRET ASPIRATIONS OF THE MODERN SELF . . . 90

What Is Freedom? 91

Self-Realization. 91

Self-Determination. 92

Self-Perfection 93

The General Idea of Freedom 94

Competitive Freedom 95

The Modern Concept of Human Dignity 96

Ambitions of the Empty Self. 100

**7 SOME UNWELCOME LIMITS ON FREEDOM
AND DIGNITY** 102

Freedom's Finitude 102

In Search of Dignity 107

The Fragmented Self 110

PART 2: THE GOD-CENTERED SELF

8 THE SELF-GIVING GOD OF THE GOSPEL 115

The Gift of Creation 116

The Sacrifice of Divine Love. 119

Divine Dignity. 121

The True Divine Self 123

9 THE IRONY OF DIVINE "WEAKNESS" 127

Misunderstanding God's Omnipotence 127

Divine Persuasion. 130

10 THE AWAKENING PRESENCE 139

Another Look at Power. 140

Presence 142

Divine Knowledge and Human Selfhood 143

Divine Knowledge and Self-Knowledge 148

A Backward Glance and a Forward Look 150

11 A NEW WAY OF BEING HUMAN BEING 151

The Temptations of Christ. 152

The Last Temptation 156

12 THE DIVINE ADOPTION 159

Our Father in Heaven. 160

Abba, Father 160

What Does Being a Child of God Mean? 161

Be Perfect as Your Father in Heaven Is Perfect 163

13 THE EMERGENCE OF GOD-CENTERED IDENTITY 170

The Self and Freedom. 171

The True Self and the "Other". 173

The Old and New Selves 173

Adam and Christ 175

The Inner "Other" 176

The Human and Divine Selves 178

Conclusion 179

14 THE FREEDOM OF THE CHILDREN OF GOD 181

Freedom Perfected 182

Freedom as the Power of a New Life 182

Freedom as a Gift 185

Freedom Here and Now 186

Christian Freedom as the Perfection of Freedoms 187

**15 GOD'S LOVE AS THE GROUND AND MEASURE
OF HUMAN DIGNITY** 191

Dignity in the Church Fathers and Medieval Theology 192

Dignity Without Limits 199

Pride and Shame 199

Dignity and Love 200

Human Dignity as a Relation to God 201

Dignity and Envy 202

16 THE RECONCILIATION OF HEAVEN AND EARTH 207

Competition Transcended 207

A Life of Faith, Hope and Love 210

The Modern Self Reborn 211

Prometheus Unbound 213

Religion Purified 213

    Stage-Three Religion 214

    Stage-Four Religion 215

Indifference Transformed 216

Conclusion 217

Subject Index 219

Scripture Index 229

PREFACE

If asked, most people will say they believe in God. When pressed, they will admit that their deepest desires and hopes depend on God for fulfillment. They may even insist that belief in God is "very important" to them. One might expect, then, that the thought of God would command their full attention, that their hearts would seek God above other things and that their lips would speak continually of God's greatness and grace. But as everyone knows, "belief" in God rarely translates into passion for God and action in response to God. The observation the great seventeenth-century spiritual writer François Fénelon made of his generation applies equally to ours: they seldom think of God, and when they do they imagine "something wonderful, far off and unconnected with us."[1]

Whence this irony, this contradiction between what we believe—or say we believe—and how we actually live? Why doesn't thought about God become life directed to God? Many possibilities come to mind. Our secular culture teaches us in a hundred subtle ways that God doesn't really matter. We dwell in large, anonymous cities where our sense of responsibility to each other is deadened by sheer numbers. Surrounded by machines, concrete and city lights, we lose touch with creation. We immerse ourselves in the practical business of living in a society that cares more about the quality of our cell phone than the substance of our character.

There is one factor, however, that I believe lies behind all others: even though they believe in God, many people have an uneasy feeling about God. If they could put it into words, they might express fear that God's existence

---

[1]François Fénelon, *Christian Counsel or Maxims on Divers Matters Pertaining to the Inner Life*, Christian Classics Ethereal Library, www.ccel.org/ccel/fenelon/progress.iii.i.html.

and activity in some way threatens their freedom and dignity. After all, we have been told from childhood that God fills all space and time, knows everything and exercises all power; that God made us, owns us and rules over all things. To some of our contemporaries God's all-encompassing will appears to restrict our freedom, and God's ownership and mastery over us seems to diminish our dignity. You can see why some of us take so little account of God and hesitate to seek and trust God wholly. Troubled by such thoughts, how could we *want* to think of God? The aim of this book is to calm these fears and remove these obstacles; it is to explain why God, far from posing a threat to our freedom and dignity, secures their foundation and brings their potential to glorious fulfillment.[2] More than this, I want to show why we should want to think about God and love God with our whole being and how we can give ourselves completely into God's care without losing anything conducive to our ultimate joy.

The book is divided into two parts, each of which is subdivided into short chapters. Part one, "The Me-Centered Self," comprising seven chapters, examines our distorted images of God and humanity. It raises questions that will be answered in part two, "The God-Centered Self." Chapter one draws on the work of Charles Taylor and Alasdair MacIntyre to paint a picture of the modern self. Our contemporaries tend to ground respect for others, hope for fullness and belief in their own dignity in the self, in its inward qualities, its ordinary life and its ability to express itself and impress itself on the world. They do not connect these human values and aspirations to God. Chapters two through four argue that, despite our reluctance to admit it, we are tempted to consider God a threat to our freedom and dignity. Some relate to God with defiance. Even in physical defeat they remain defiant in spirit. Others adopt a posture of subservience, figuring they will be better off in the long run to join the winning side. Still others invest themselves so much in the world that they become indifferent to God, losing a sense of self before God. Chapters five and six draw out the images of God and humanity implicit in these three attitudes of defiance,

---

[2]In the concluding chapter of his fine analysis of modern secular culture, Craig M. Gay calls for a "better theological account of individuality, freedom and personality than we have managed to give for quite some time" (*The Way of the (Modern) World Or, Why It's Tempting to Live As If God Doesn't Exist* [Grand Rapids: Eerdmans, 1998], p. 276). This book is in part a response to Gay's call.

submission and indifference. We imagine God to be a sort of superhuman being who is everything we would like to be. Despite the differences, we consider God and ourselves very much alike. We are both centers of desire and will, the difference being that God has the power to achieve God's desires and carry out God's will; we do not. Such a view of God provokes envy instead of love. Chapter seven makes explicit the views of freedom and dignity implicit in the competitive structure outlined in the previous chapters. I argue that the competitive view of freedom and dignity contradicts itself and collapses under its own weight. Separated from God, our freedom cannot attain the happiness it seeks and our dignity cannot find a secure foundation. This failure clears the way for a new approach to the divine/human relationship.

Part two probes the view of God and humanity brought to light in Jesus Christ. Chapters eight through ten explore the stories of creation and reconciliation in search of a noncompetitive image of God. The unselfish nature of God is demonstrated amply by the gift of creation, but even more dramatically in the self-giving of Christ. Through Christ we come to know that God is love. This God is not a lonely monarch but the Father who has always loved the Son in the Spirit. The gift of God's beloved Son for us sinners demonstrates that God's love is both costly and free. God's almighty power, omnipresence and comprehensive knowledge, which seemed so menacing when understood as attributes of a superhuman being, appear very different in light of the cross. God's power gives life and freedom, God's omnipresence opens a place for us and touches us with infinite love, and God's knowledge of us roots our identity in God's eternal life. We cannot think of God as a threat when we understand that God's very being is love and God's every act is giving.

Chapters eleven and twelve develop a noncompetitive image of humanity. We look again to Jesus Christ to find this picture, for Jesus is the son of Mary as well as the Son of God. As one of us, Jesus resisted the temptations hurled at him by the devil and finally gave up his life rather than abandon trust in God. In doing this, Christ pioneered the way to truly human life in which human beings achieve their deepest potential for freedom, dignity and joy. In the Sermon on the Mount, Jesus teaches us to think of God as our dear Father and of ourselves as our Father's beloved children. He enables us to participate in his loving relationship with his Father. According to Jesus, we were created to be children of God, and our life task is to mirror our Father's love for the world.

Chapters thirteen through fifteen explain how the Christian picture of humanity enables us to achieve true selfhood, perfect freedom and the highest dignity conceivable. In Christ we find an identity rooted not in others' changing thoughts about us but in God's eternal knowledge of us. Through the Spirit, God enables us to achieve the perfect freedom of life in harmony with our truest identity. Finally, chapter sixteen brings all these threads together in a harmonious reconciliation where God is fully and gloriously God and we are fully and gloriously human.

I wrote this book for students and teachers; ministers and laypeople; believers, searchers and skeptics; and for anyone interested in God, freedom, dignity and the search for self-understanding. In some ways its message is easy to grasp. It appeals to experience and intuition. It is not necessary to have read tomes of theology and philosophy to understand it. It makes one central point: God is not a threat to our freedom and dignity but their source and support. The volume is relatively thin, and its brief chapters divide the argument into manageable units of thought. In other ways it may prove demanding. I hope the book is thought provoking, for I intend it to challenge its readers to greater self-examination. It demands honesty and willingness to follow the argument, simple though it is, to its end. Though it teaches, I do not intend the book as an exercise in church doctrine. It is more meditation than dissertation, designed to inspire love as much as to instruct the mind.

I wrote the first draft of this book during the academic year 2006-2007. I moved back and forth from my undergraduate classes to my writing desk. As I wrote, I thought especially of young people who teeter on the edge of unbelief or indifference. I offer this book to them in the hope that it will encourage them to seek God and grow in their love for him, and that it will keep them from falling into unbelief or forgetfulness. I dedicate this book to all my students, over four thousand to date.

Part One

THE ME-CENTERED SELF

1

HOW THE ME-CENTERED WORLD
WAS BORN

As children we never questioned our identity or wondered about our place in life. Nor did we think of our "selves" as distinct from our relationships, activities and feelings. We just lived in the context we were born into and followed the natural course of our lives. But as we grew older we were encouraged to discover our own unique blend of preferences, talents and joys, and to create an identity for ourselves through our choices and actions. In contrast to previous ages, modern culture denies that one can become an authentic person or experience fulfillment in life by conforming to natural or socially given relationships and roles. Instead we are taught that our self-worth and happiness depend on reconstructing ourselves according to our desires. And the project of redesigning ourselves necessitates that we continually break free from the web of social relationships and expectations that would otherwise impose an alien identity on us.[1] I am calling this understanding of the self "me-centered," not because it is especially selfish or narcissistic but because it attempts to create its identity by sheer will power and rejects identity-conferring relationships unless they are artifacts of its own free will. It should not surprise us, then, to find that the modern person feels a weight of oppression and a flood of resentment when confronted

---

[1]Chap Clark documents the destructive effects of this understanding of human identity on contemporary teenagers in his book *Hurt 2.0: Inside the World of Today's Teenagers* (Grand Rapids: Baker Academic, 2011). According to Clark, two overarching negative motifs condition the lives of teens today: abandonment and loneliness.

with the demands of traditional morality and religion. In the face of these demands the me-centered self feels its dignity slighted, its freedom threatened and its happiness diminished.

In this chapter I draw heavily on the work of moral philosophers Charles Taylor and Alasdair MacIntyre to answer the following question: How, when and by whom did it come about that nature, family, community, moral law and religion were changed in the Western mind from identity-giving, happiness-producing networks of meaning into their opposites—self-alienating, misery-inducing webs of oppression?[2] How was the me-centered world formed?

SEARCHING FOR IDENTITY IN A SECULAR AGE

In his *Sources of the Self* (1989) and *The Secular Age* (2007), Charles Taylor argues that to possess an identity is to be located in a moral "space" whose coordinates are determined by certain goods and moral sources. The question Who am I? is answered by "knowing where I stand" in relation to these goods and moral sources.[3] As Taylor explains, "To know who you are is to be oriented in moral space, a space in which questions arise about what is good or bad, what is worth doing and what not, what has meaning and importance for you and what is trivial and secondary."[4] Oriented within this space I can know what I ought to do, what is valuable, worthwhile and admirable. Modern moral space possesses three axes that provide coordinates (x, y, z) within which to locate ourselves. Each axis represents a set of "strongly valued goods."[5] That is, these "ends or goods stand independent of our own desires, inclinations, or choices, that they

---

[2]Charles Taylor, *Sources of the Self: The Making of Modern Identity* (Cambridge, MA: Harvard University Press, 1989); Taylor, *The Secular Age* (Cambridge, MA: Belknap Press, 2007); Alasdair MacIntyre, *After Virtue: A Study in Moral Theory*, 2nd ed. (Notre Dame, IN: University of Notre Dame Press, 1984); MacIntyre, *Whose Justice? Which Rationality?* (Notre Dame, IN: University of Notre Dame Press, 1988); MacIntyre, *Three Rival Versions of Moral Enquiry: Encyclopaedia, Geneology and Tradition* (Notre Dame, IN: University of Notre Dame Press, 1990). I will also draw on the work of political philosopher Michael Allen Gillespie. See his *Nihilism Before Nietzsche* (Chicago: University of Chicago Press, 1995) and *The Theological Origins of Modernity* (Chicago: University of Chicago Press, 2008).
[3]Taylor, *Sources of the Self*, p. 27.
[4]Ibid., p. 28.
[5]Ibid., p. 31.

represent standards by which these desires and choices are judged."[6] They are (x) a sense of *respect* for and obligation to others, (y) a sense of *fullness* in life or what makes life worth living, and (z) a sense of our own *dignity* or what makes us worthy of respect (see fig. 1).

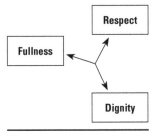

Figure 1

The shape of modern identity can be determined by coming to understand the way contemporary culture appropriates these fundamental values in contrast to the way premodern culture understood them. To give us historical perspective, Taylor traces in three trajectories how these strong values acquired their modern shape. He shows how (1) the growth of *inwardness* transferred moral principles from outside the human person to inside, (2) the Christian *affirmation of ordinary life* gradually led Western culture to focus on human flourishing in this world as the exclusive human goal, and (3) the development of an *expressive view of inner nature* produced a completely subjective view of the good. Taylor's three historical motifs provide the following outline. We will see how each of these trajectories adds to our understanding of the modern self's take on the strong values of respect, fullness and dignity.

The development of inwardness. In contrast to modern inwardness, ancient tribal and warrior cultures people found their identity in a moral space where respect, fullness and dignity were grounded in external things such as family status or war and the glory it achieves. Taking a first step toward inwardness, Plato (c. 428/27-347/48 B.C.) criticized the warrior morality, arguing that desire for glory and other unruly emotions must be subordinated to reason.[7] Reason's power of self-control centers the self and bestows the capacity for cool, deliberate action. But Plato does not locate all goods and moral sources within the self. For Plato, to reason is to see the natural order of the world and perceive the transcendent good to which it is directed. And one becomes a good human being by imitating the good thus revealed.

The Christian thinker Augustine of Hippo (A.D. 354-430) takes Plato's thinking further toward inwardness. When we turn our thoughts inward to

---

[6]Ibid., p. 20.
[7]Plato's thought on this issue can be found in the *Republic*.

consider our minds, we discover a vast mystery. The mind contains an endless universe of ideas and memories; it can even think about itself. Yet the mind cannot comprehend itself, explain its own powers or create the ideas it contains. Hence, Augustine concludes that our minds must be created and illuminated by an even greater mystery, a divine mind.[8] So Augustine finds humanity's greatest good revealed not in the natural order but in the divine truth seen by introspection. In contrast to Plato, Augustine denies that one can see the good just by turning to the natural order. We must also possess purity of heart, which only the grace of God can bestow. Here Augustine introduces a new function of the will, derived from Christianity, into Western thought. Right reason cannot function properly in a person who desires evil. We must *will* the transcendent good before we can see it clearly. Hence, the will must be liberated from evil desires before the mind can endure the truth. Even though Augustine's inward turn was revolutionary, he did not yet identify the human soul with the good and the true. The soul is merely the place where one can perceive the truth that transcends even the soul. Thinkers after Augustine followed his example in looking for the true good within the soul.

René Descartes and disengaged reason. The next step toward placing moral values wholly inside the self was facilitated by a revolution in natural science.[9] Galileo (1564-1642) is famous for using a telescope to spot Jupiter's moons; however, more enduring was his revolution of changing the metaphor for interpreting the physical world. Before Galileo, philosophers thought of the physical world as a combination of matter and form or idea. The world was a sort of living body, composed of matter and soul. In contrast, Galileo saw the world as a machine, as dead matter arranged by God in a certain order. The body of the world no longer possesses a soul. The French philosopher René Descartes (1596-1650) accepted Galileo's view that the world is a material machine bereft of soul. But he did not want to accept atheism or reduce everything to matter; hence, to preserve the existence of nonmaterial forms and purposes Descartes relocated them within the mind. The human mind does not get its ideas from the external cosmic order. In-

---

[8]Augustine's reflections on this subject can be found in book 10 of *Confessions*.
[9]Taylor understands Descartes as breaking the previously assumed connection between the human mind and nonmaterial forms that gave order and meaning to the material world.

stead, it imposes its internal order on the external world like God does. Notice the difference between Descartes and Plato. In Plato, the human mind humbly allows itself to be shaped by the natural order. For Descartes, mind—whether divine or human—asserts its superiority over the external world by imposing itself on it.[10]

Shifting from a passive to an active understanding of the mind's relationship to the world leads inexorably to a shift in human self-understanding and moral theory. For Descartes, our bodies are machines just like the rest of the world, so we can direct them and their emotions with reason in the same way we control the external world. The emergence of this dominating attitude toward the world and human nature indicates a profound change in Descartes's understanding of freedom. For Plato and the Platonic tradition, freedom can be attained only by bringing one's life into harmony with the ideal order that gives form and being to the world. For Descartes, freedom is the natural power to rule oneself as one chooses:

> Now freewill is in itself the noblest thing we can have because it makes us in a certain manner equal to God and exempts us from being his subjects; and so its rightful use is the greatest of all goods we possess, and further there is nothing that is more our own or that matters more to us. From all this it follows that nothing but freewill can produce our greatest contentment.[11]

In this framework, moral sources have been completely internalized within the mind. Our understanding of what is good and our power to attain it now must come from within, from "the agent's sense of his own dignity as a rational being."[12]

John Locke and the punctual self. John Locke (1632-1704) differed profoundly from Descartes in many ways, but he continued the path tread by

---

[10]Taylor explains Descartes's shift in these words: "The order of ideas ceases to be something we *find* and becomes something we *build*" (*Sources of the Self*, p. 144). In *The Secular Age*, Taylor contrasts the modern understanding of the self as "buffered" with the ancient concept of the self as "porous." The premodern person felt himself to be connected to an "enchanted" world and open to the influence of meanings, spiritual forces and demons. The modern person looks at the external, neutral world from the safety of an inner fortress (*Secular Age*, pp. 33-41).

[11]*Descartes: Philosophical Letters*, trans. Anthony Kenny (Oxford: Oxford University Press, 1970), p. 228; quoted in Taylor, *Sources of the Self*, p. 147.

[12]Taylor, *Sources of the Self*, pp. 151-52.

Descartes toward disengaging the self from the matrix of nature. Locke was radically antiteleological, that is, he believed that there are no inherent ends *(teloi)* toward which the world or human nature strives. Human nature does not possess "an inherent bent to the truth or to the good."[13] This rejection of teleology works a revolution in ethics. We cannot think of human nature as made for truth or love or any virtue. According to Locke, human nature inherently seeks only pleasure and avoids only pain. There is no inherent connection between essential human nature and moral good or evil that would guarantee that good always produces happiness and evil unhappiness. This connection must be established arbitrarily and extrinsically, by God or habit or tradition.[14] If we choose, we can disengage from this habitual connection and remake ourselves in any way we choose. Aristotle (384-322 B.C.) noted that a habit can be formed with or against the grain of nature. For Locke, however, there is no grain of nature, and a habit is a mere association of atoms of experience. As Taylor explains, "Habits now link elements between which there are no more relations of natural fit. The proper connections are determined purely instrumentally, by what will bring the best results, pleasure, or happiness."[15] For Locke, the self has no identifying attributes or relations or unchangeable structures. It is just an extensionless point, which Taylor calls the "punctual self."[16] On this reading, the modern self sits sovereign above the world, impressing its arbitrary will on a neutral external reality and reconstructing itself according to its whims.

The moral space of inwardness. Where does the history of internalization of moral sources locate modern identity on the three axes of moral space

---

[13]Ibid., p. 164.

[14]As you can see, Locke stands in the background to modern behaviorist psychology, which reduces seemingly meaningful patterns of behavior to stimulus-response mechanisms.

[15]Taylor, *Sources of the Self,* p. 171.

[16]Later in this book I will call this view of the self the "pure will" model. Along these lines Locke is forced to define personal identity in terms of consciousness: "For it is by the consciousness it has of its present thoughts and actions, that it is self to itself now, and so will be the same self as far as the same consciousness can extend to actions past and to come" (John Locke, *An Essay Concerning Human Understanding* 2.27, ed. and abridged Maurice Cranston [London: Collier-Macmillan, 1965], p. 194). Taylor calls this view a "radically subjectivist view of the person" (*Sources of the Self,* p. 172). I began using the term *pure will* before I discovered that Michael Allen Gillespie also uses it to describe the voluntarist view of God and humanity. See his *Nihilism Before Nietzsche* (Chicago: University of Chicago Press, 1995) and *The Theological Origins of Modernity* (Chicago: University of Chicago Press, 2008).

(see. fig. 1)? First, on the x axis of *respect*, if internalization and rational self-control mark the being of others we will see other people as individual autonomous agents and feel a special respect for their right to control their own lives. On the y axis of *fullness*, we will assume that fullness in life consists in ordering one's passions according to reason and imposing one's will on the external world. Perhaps living in this way brings about a sense of satisfaction at being in control of oneself and in exerting of power over nature. And on the z axis of *dignity*, one will find one's dignity in the inner integrity of one's being and in the power of self-control over passion and error. For the modern self, then, the most powerful reasons to respect others, the surest path to fullness and the clearest basis on which to assert our own dignity are internal to ourselves and others.

Affirmation of ordinary life. In traditional societies certain ways of living possess higher dignity than others do. In ancient warrior cultures a life of military glory and honor was to be sought above all others. But Plato criticized ambition for glory and advocated devoting oneself to wisdom. In his *Politics* Aristotle admits the necessity of living on the level of ordinary life, which Taylor calls the life of "production and reproduction."[17] But ordinary life is merely a foundation from which one can aspire to the truly good life. For Aristotle, one should seek excellence in contemplating the natural order and in deliberating with others about the common good of the political community one can achieve the good life in. The Stoic philosophers pronounced an even more negative judgment on ordinary life, urging that wisdom dictates that one detach oneself from the fluctuating passions of the body so one can devote oneself to the unchanging order of reason.

Christianity affirms the goodness of creation and ordinary life, but it also holds dear the ideal of a life dedicated totally to God. The monastic movements of the early centuries, though not denying that ordinary life was good and could be acceptable to God, sought a higher spiritual plane by sacrificing marriage, family, society and commerce. Accordingly, medieval Christianity developed a hierarchical theory of the Christian life. Some are called out of ordinary life into monastic orders and the priesthood. These Christians devote themselves to prayer and study, and they refrain from

---

[17]Taylor, *Sources of the Self,* p. 211.

marriage. They aim to achieve a higher level of holiness and merit before God, which can benefit the whole community. This system can lead to the idea that the laity need not concern itself with holiness and piety because these virtues are the province of monastic orders and clergy. Aware of this danger, medieval church authorities and reformers of various types attempted periodically to close the gap between the two levels. The Fourth Lateran Council (1215), one of the earliest of these efforts, required all Roman Catholics to participate in confession and Communion at least once a year.[18]

The sixteenth-century Protestant Reformation inspired a revolutionary movement aimed at collapsing the spiritual hierarchy and affirming ordinary life. The Protestant Reformers taught that salvation came by faith alone rather than by self-negating works, and that believers did not need the mediation of a priest to relate to God. The Protestant monarchs closed the monasteries within their lands and urged the clergy to marry and have children. Indeed, the Reformers came to see monastic life as a place of spiritual pride and elitism, and as a slight to God's good creation. On the other hand, they affirmed the ordinary life of labor and family as the locus of the highest achievement in the Christian life.[19]

In seventeenth-century Puritan theology of vocation each person is called by God into a life conducive to the good of the whole community. It matters not in what calling one is stationed but in what spirit one carries out one's vocation. The Puritan theologian William Perkins's words bring this view to expression in good Elizabethan English:[20]

> Now the works of every calling, when they are performed in an holy manner, are done in faith and obedience, and serve notably for God's

---

[18]Charles Taylor, *Secular Age*, p. 64. Cannon 21 of the Fourth Lateran Counsel reads in part: "All the faithful of both sexes shall after they have reached the age of discretion faithfully confess all their sins at least once a year to their own (parish) priest and perform to the best of their ability the penance imposed, receiving reverently at least at Easter the sacrament of the Eucharist, unless perchance at the advice of their own priest they may for a good reason abstain for a time from its reception; otherwise they shall be cut off from the Church (excommunicated) during life and deprived of Christian burial in death" ("Medieval Sourcebook: Twelfth Ecumenical Council: Lateran IV 1215," Fordham University, www.fordham .edu/halsall/basis/lateran4.html).

[19]Taylor, *Sources of the Self*, pp. 217-18.

[20]Charles H. George and Katherine George, *The Protestant Mind of the English Reformation, 1570-1640* (Princeton, NJ: Princeton University Press, 1961), p. 138.

glory be the calling never so base. . . . The meaneness of the calling, doth not abase the goodnesse of the worke: for God looketh not at the excellence of the Work, but at the heart of the worker. And the action of a sheepheard in keeping sheep, performed as I have said, in his kind, is as good a worke before God, as is the action of a Judge, in giving sentence or a Magistrate in ruling, or a Minister in preaching.

It is not difficult to see how the grandchildren of these Puritans might retain their enthusiasm for ordinary life well after leaving their piety behind. One might come to believe that giving oneself to family and work is the whole of one's duty to God. Or one might forget God altogether and immerse oneself in the search for worldly success. John Locke and his heirs actually took this step.

John Locke and his friends. John Locke combined Protestant affirmation of ordinary life with the ideal of rational self-control.[21] For Locke the law of nature is revealed in the innate human desire for self-preservation. When we follow this law as interpreted by reason we can be sure that we are also doing God's will:

> For the desire, strong desire of Preserving his Life and Being having been implanted in him, as a Principle of Action by God himself, Reason, which was the voice of God in him, could not but teach him and assure him, that pursuing that natural inclination he had to preserve his Being, he followed the Will of his Maker.[22]

Still, human nature does not possess an inherent bent toward the *good*. Rather, God motivates us to do right by promising rewards and threatening punishments, thereby using our self-love as a foundation for civil life.[23] We are not made for the dizzy heights of "self-abnegating altruism" but for the ordinary life of seeking pleasure and avoiding pain.[24]

---

[21]Taylor, *Sources of the Self*, p. 234.

[22]John Locke, *Locke's Two Treatises of Government*, ed. Peter Laslett (Cambridge: Cambridge University Press, 1967), p. 223, quoted in Taylor, *Secular Age*, pp. 166-67.

[23]Taylor, *Sources of the Self*, p. 241.

[24]Ibid., p. 242. I am leaving out an intermediate step between Locke and the deists. Taylor tells the story of a negative reaction to Locke's hedonist (from the Greek word *hēdon*, or pleasure) theory of morality. The Third Earl of Shaftesbury (1671-1713) developed an understanding of moral sources differing greatly from Locke's. In contrast to Locke, Shaftesbury argues that human nature possesses a natural bent toward social virtue, toward "a love of the whole as good" (*Sources of the Self*, p. 254). Shaftesbury understands virtue as "really something in

The next move toward a completely secular view of human life was accomplished by deism, the intellectual movement that dominated eighteenth-century philosophy. Deism does not reject belief in God and providence; yet it sees God's work limited to promoting human welfare on the purely human plane. Matthew Tindal (1655-1733) argues that God wishes only to promote the "common good, and mutual Happiness of his rational creatures."[25] We can follow God's plan for creation by living according to the natural order, which is designed so that seeking one's own happiness harmonizes with seeking the good of others.[26] "Which means," as Taylor puts it, "fundamentally that we owe [God] essentially the achievement of our own good."[27] Living in harmony with nature does not mean adjusting one's life to the natural order, as it would for Plato; rather, it means balancing the two principles of self-love and reason.[28] Tindal says bluntly:

> Whoever so regulates his natural appetites as will conduce most to the exercise of his reason, the health of his body and the pleasures of his senses taken and considered together (since herein his happiness consists) may be certain he can never offend his Maker; who, as he governs all things according to their natures, can't but expect his rational creatures should act according to their natures.[29]

---

itself and in the nature of things: not arbitrary or factitious . . . constituted from without, or dependent on custom, fancy, or will: not even on the Supreme Will itself, which can no way govern it: but being necessarily good, is governed by it, and ever uniform with it" (*Characteristics of Men, Manners, Opinions, Times* [Cambridge: Cambridge University Press, 2000], p. 267). Following in the wake of Shaftesbury is Francis Hutcheson (1694-1746). He too attacks Locke for his extrinsic morality of self-love and argues for a moral sense that presents the mind with self-evident and irreducible moral ideas (ibid., pp. 259-60). According to Taylor, in both Shaftesbury and Hutcheson "our bent toward the good (1) is thoroughly internalized in *sentiment* and (2) takes the form above all of universal *benevolence*" (ibid., p. 264). Note here that in their rejection of Locke, Shaftesbury and Hutcheson did not return to the traditional understanding of the self as exemplified in Aristotle but continued the trajectory of internalization. However, now the inward-turned self expresses itself not through reason but through sentiment or feeling.

[25]Matthew Tindal, *Christianity as Old as Creation* (London, 1730), p. 14, quoted in Taylor, *Sources of the Self,* p. 271.

[26]Taylor, *Sources of the Self,* p. 275.

[27]Taylor, *Secular Age,* p. 222.

[28]Taylor, *Sources of the Self,* pp. 279-80.

[29]Tindal, *Christianity as Old as Creation,* quoted in James C. Livingstone, *Modern Christian Thought,* 2nd ed. (Upper Saddle River, NJ: Prentice Hall, 1997), 1:23-24.

Tindal's conclusion that creatures should "act according to their natures" involves something more nuanced than Locke's view of living according to nature—simply seeking pleasure and avoiding pain; Tindal means we need to become aware of our inner "inclinations, desires, sentiments" and view them as guiding norms.[30] Taylor explains the significance of this difference:

> Sentiment is now important, because it is in a certain way the touchstone of the morally good. . . . [U]ndistorted, normal feeling is my way of access into the design of things, which is the real constitutive good, determining good and bad. . . .
>
> The new place of sentiment completes the revolution which has yielded a modern view of nature as normative, so utterly different from the ancient view. . . . [I]t is ready to become the voice within, which Rousseau will make it, and to be transposed by the Romantics into a richer and deeper inwardness.[31]

The history of the affirmation of ordinary life, which began as affirmation of God's creation and the dignity of whatever vocation God gives us, thus ends as the sanctification of our inner nature as revealed in our "inclinations, desires and sentiments." Once this sanctification occurred it would not take long for some thinkers to begin to view any effort to discipline this inner inclination in view of moral law or divine commands as oppression and any form of its expression as legitimate.

The moral space of the affirmation of ordinary life. Where does this history place us in the moral space determined by the three axes: respect, fullness and dignity? *Respect* for others must be grounded in the inherent properties of the individual rather than in any external relation or order; specifically, it is grounded in the inner desires of the individual, which presumably reveal the design of the Creator. *Fullness* can be found only in living according to nature as it is revealed in one's affections. A full life can be enjoyed not only by moral elites or heroes who attain it with great self-sacrifice or bold action; it is available to the vast majority of people in the ordinary course of life: marriage, children, work and play. A sense of one's *dignity* can be experienced in feeling the moral law come to light in one's feelings and inclinations. The imperatives

---

[30]Taylor, *Sources of the Self*, p. 282. According to Taylor, Tindal is influenced to adopt a more nuanced view of nature by Hutcheson's theory of moral sentiment.

[31]Taylor, *Sources of the Self*, p. 284.

of morality come from within and cannot be imposed by an external authority. Though at this stage the moral law is still understood to derive from God's creation, all attempts to impose law from without now seem incommensurate with affirmation of human dignity. The stage is now set for declaring God completely unnecessary for living a flourishing human life.

The inner voice of nature. Deism prepared the soil for modern atheism. It had already internalized all moral sources, declared that human welfare in this life should be our major concern and relegated God to a mere presupposition of the order of nature. The final step of declaring God a needless hypothesis was taken by the "radical Enlighteners" Denis Diderot (1713-1784), Baron d'Holbach (1723-1789), Jeremy Bentham (1748-1832) and Julien Offray de La Mettrie (1709-1751).[32] These thinkers do not consider nature an embodiment of divine law but a neutral field for the play of reason in maximizing pleasure and minimizing pain. They developed a utilitarian ethical theory in which reason calculates which behaviors will lead to the best consequences in keeping with the goal of maximizing pleasure. As self-contradictory as it may seem, however, most late-eighteenth-century atheist thinkers passionately defended the same order of goods deism had defended: "self-responsible reason, affirmation of ordinary life and benevolence."[33] They differed from deism in their contention that atheism is superior to belief in God in defending these goods. The radical enlightenment looked to nature alone, uncreated and unguided, for human well-being and happiness. Baron d'Holbach speaks in the voice of nature to humans mired in religion:

> "O thou!" cries this nature to man, "who, following the impulse I have given you, during your whole existence, incessantly tend towards happiness, do not strive to resist my sovereign law. Labour to your own felicity; partake without fear of the banquet which is spread before you, and be happy; you will find the means legibly written on your own heart. . . . Dare, then, to affranchise thyself from the trammels of religion, my self-conceited, pragmatic rival, who mistakes my rights; renounce those Gods, who are usurpers of my privileges, and return under the dominion of my

---

[32]Taylor speaks of this movement as the radical Enlightenment and uses the term *radical Aufklärer,* which substitutes the German word for *enlightener* (*Sources of the Self,* p. 321).
[33]Ibid., p. 322.

laws. It is in my empire alone that true liberty reigns. Tyranny is unknown to its soil. . . . Return, then, my child, to thy fostering mother's arms![34]

But not everyone in the late eighteenth century found atheism and utilitarianism appealing. Jean-Jacques Rousseau (1712-1778) began as an admirer but later became a leading critic of the Enlightenment. According to Rousseau, the Enlightenment was too optimistic about the innocence of human nature. As we experience it, human nature possesses a dark side and needs transformation. However, Rousseau did not return to orthodox Christianity's view of the fall, original sin and divine grace. Rather, he blamed civilization for poisoning the original impulses of nature with its artificial overlay. We do not need more science, more knowledge or more scholars. We need to listen to the voice of nature within, depend on ourselves rather than on others and find power within ourselves for our actions.[35] The first line in his novel *Emile, or On Education*, Rousseau declares, "Everything is good in leaving the hands of the Creator of things; everything degenerates in the hands of man."[36] Later he says, "Let us lay it down as an incontrovertible rule that the first impulses of nature are always right; there is no original sin in the human heart."[37] He continues almost to the point of deifying the inner voice:

> Conscience! Conscience! Divine instinct, immortal voice from heaven; sure guide for a creature ignorant and finite indeed, yet intelligent and free; infallible judge of good and evil, making man like to God! In thee consists the excellence of man's nature and the morality of his actions; apart from thee, I find nothing in myself to raise me above the beasts—nothing but the sad privilege of wandering from one error to another, by the help of an unbridled understanding and a reason which knows no principle.[38]

---

[34]Baron D'Holbach, *The System of Nature* (Kitchener, Ont.: Batoche, 1868), 2:161-62.

[35]Taylor, *Sources of the Self*, p. 361.

[36]Jean-Jacques Rousseau, *Emile, or On Education* 1.10, Institute for Learning Technologies, www.ilt.columbia.edu/pedagogies/rousseau/em_eng_bk1.html.

[37]Jean-Jacques Rousseau, quoted in Taylor, *Sources of the Self*, p. 357.

[38]Ibid., p. 358. For the sake of the reader for whom this history is all new, I will relegate the place of Immanuel Kant (1724-1804) in this story to this footnote. Kant instituted another line of criticism of the Enlightenment. Kant also rejects the hedonism and utilitarianism of the Enlightenment and like Rousseau finds guidance in an inner voice. However, Kant's inner voice did not speak in the language of feelings or sentiments but through the demands of our rational will or practical reason. We act morally when we act consistently with our rational nature, which is our essential being. And since freedom is the power to act according to one's being, in acting morally we also act freely. In Kant, moral sources have been

Certain thinkers in the late eighteenth and early nineteenth century continued the course pioneered by Rousseau, pursuing the idea that the inner voice of nature seeks expression in our words and feelings.[39] In some writers the voice of nature is considered part of a great current of feeling flowing through all things and given voice in individuals. That great current can be interpreted as a divine power or as the prompting of my unique individual nature, which determines my way to freedom and joy.[40] Hence, articulating my unique nature becomes crucially important to authentic living, to a life that arises out of my genuine individuality. Philosopher of language Johann Gottfried Herder (1744-1803), sounding almost like a contemporary celebrity offering advice as unsolicited as it is half-baked, gave classic expression to this now familiar philosophy: "Each human being has his own measure, as it were an accord peculiar to him of all his feelings to each other."[41] Experiencing my true self fully requires that I put my inner nature into an external medium: words, visual art, dance, song or other acts. In expressing myself I do not simply make an outer copy of something already complete inside; rather, I complete and further define myself.[42] Expressive individualism provides no guarantees that our inner voice will impel us toward virtuous behaviors or conventional goods.[43] Self-expression and the feeling of joy or sense of freedom it engenders are not valued for the sake of higher goods or right actions; they are ends in themselves. Such expressive individualism "has become one of the cornerstones of modern culture."[44]

---

completely internalized and made normative. Acting morally requires no reference to external orders or commands or ends. Even as he criticized Enlightenment rationalism and utilitarianism, Kant brought its ideal of self-responsible reason to its logical end in his concept of autonomy, which is another kind of near deification of the inner voice.

[39]Taylor points out that this view of nature as a moral source, though characteristic of Romanticism, was not limited to that movement (ibid., p. 368).

[40]Ibid., p. 371.

[41]Johann Gottfried Herder, quoted in ibid., p. 375.

[42]Taylor points out that the mimetic (imitation) view of art and poetry came under fire earlier in the eighteenth century and was replaced by an expressive understanding. In the late eighteenth century "the expressive theory of art is given a crucially human and even cosmic significance, in being taken up into the expressivist conception of mankind and nature" (*Sources of the Self*, p. 377).

[43]Ibid., pp. 372-73.

[44]Ibid., p. 376. According to Taylor, the expressive idea of the self provides "the grounds for construing this inner domain as having depth, that is, a domain which reaches farther than we can ever articulate, which still stretches beyond our furthest point of clear expression" (ibid., p. 389).

The moral space of the expressive view of nature. Where does this history place us in the moral space determined by the three axes: respect, fullness and dignity? *Respect* for others is grounded in the uniqueness of their individual and private inner natures, which must be given space to find expression. To judge them as unworthy examples of humanity or dictate how they should express their uniqueness would violate their essential personhood. *Fullness* can be found only in the freedom and joy engendered by bringing to external expression one's inner nature. It cannot be found by conforming to an external code or submitting to an alien authority or seeking a transcendent good. A sense of one's own *dignity* is rooted in one's uniqueness and in the power of self-creation and self-definition by means of self-expression. The modern self asserts, "I am irreplaceable, and none can tell me how to realize my own uniqueness or judge my choice of ways of self-expression. I have every right to celebrate my own utterly unique being in ways that I experience as fulfilling."

Realistic expectations. Taylor's analysis confirms what I have experienced in interactions with my contemporaries: The modern self is me-centered. Most people are not self-centered in the crass sense of being selfish or narcissistic; nevertheless they locate all values and sources of fulfillment within the self, in its feelings, preferences, thoughts, opinions and wishes. Even when they cannot articulate it this way, they ground the *respect* they feel for others in such inward qualities as autonomy, inner desires and a unique inner depth that requires expression. It would seem odd to ground respect for others in something extrinsic, such as divine creation or divine love or a divine command. Withholding respect from others because of their choices or desires or ways of self-expression strikes our contemporaries as irrational and hateful. We can expect that most people we meet are seeking *fullness* by realizing the potential within by way of rational self-mastery or through self-expression of an inner depth. They reject the notion that fullness is reserved for an elite group, that it is received by grace or that it must wait until an afterlife. We need not be surprised that most people will understand their *dignity* as rooted in qualities intrinsic to their persons, in their autonomy or feelings of worth or unique individuality. They cannot conceive of their dignity as rooted in something extrinsic, a relationship to God, for example.

THE SELF IN A CULTURE SET ADRIFT

In his trilogy, *After Virtue* (1981), *Whose Justice? Which Rationality?* (1988), and *Three Rival Versions of Moral Enquiry* (1990), moral philosopher Alasdair MacIntyre sets out his understanding of the contemporary moral situation, gives a historical account of how this state of affairs developed and defends an alternative moral understanding. As MacIntyre sees it, from the halls of the university to the street corner contemporary society has lost its ability to carry on rational discussion of moral issues. In the background of all moral discussions today lurks the assumption that moral judgments do not make judgments of fact or truth. Instead they express feelings of approval or disapproval, of pleasure or distress at some situation, a theory MacIntyre identifies as emotivism.[45] Even arguments that seem to appeal to facts or truths quickly reveal themselves as efforts to express feelings and create those feelings in others. "We might conclude," says MacIntyre, "that there is nothing to such contemporary disagreements but a clash of antagonistic wills, each will determined by some set of arbitrary choices of its own."[46] It is as if some great catastrophe had taken place in which all memory of how to reason morally was erased, leaving only scattered fragments of moral ideas lying about a ruin. What passes for moral arguments are really strings of incoherent assertions uprooted from their original settings. But why, then, do people still assert their preferences in the form of rational arguments? Perhaps a residual suspicion remains that moral claims need justifying with reference to fact or truth after all, and this suspicion makes the rhetorical ploy necessary and effective.

The emotivist self. In premodern societies, a person was identified by membership in a tribe, village or family. One is a daughter, a cousin, a grandson, a farmer or a cobbler. These are not accidental characteristics or roles I can disengage my real self from. They are my substance, my very self. An individual self is not merely an extensionless point but a set of relationships extended in space and in movement toward an end fitted to its nature.[47] In contrast, the self presupposed by emotivism possesses no "necessary

---

[45]For MacIntyre's account of the rise of emotivism in the early twentieth century, see MacIntyre, *After Virtue*, pp. 12-22.
[46]Ibid., p. 9.
[47]Ibid., p. 34.

social identity" or moral nature or irrevocable commitments. It "can assume any role or take any point of view, because it is in and for itself nothing. . . . [It is] a set of perpetually open possibilities."[48] It is pure will open to any possibility. MacIntyre explores three activities characteristic of this modern self: the arbitrary claim to possess rights, the inclination to protest and the strategy of unmasking. This self asserts certain rights against other people, but can offer no rational justification for these claims.[49] Hence, when the self feels that its rights are being violated, the façade of rational argument quickly falls away leaving nothing but protest and indignation. Protest, according to MacIntyre, is a "distinctive feature of the modern age."[50] Unmasking too is distinctively modern. When you know that rational arguments are but rhetorical stratagems masking self-interest and arbitrary will, unmasking becomes the appropriate counter-strategy. But how was the emotivist self formed?

The end of ends and the Enlightenment quest. According to MacIntyre, the fourteenth through seventeenth centuries saw the gradual breakdown of the ancient moral tradition, the central core of which was Aristotle's *Nicomachean Ethics*.[51] This tradition understood human beings as possessing an "essential nature and an essential purpose or function."[52] The human essence and end are given prior to choice and are unchangeable. Within this framework moral judgments make sense as judgments of fact. To call x—a person, an action or anything—"good" is to say that "it is the kind of thing which someone would choose who wanted an x for the purpose for which x's are characteristically wanted."[53] A watch is good insofar as it keeps time accurately. A right or a just action is what "a good man would do in such a situation; hence this type of statement too is factual."[54] Virtues are characteristics that enable an individual to attain the end implicit within the human essence. The human end cannot be attained apart from those virtues because becoming a good human being is an essential

---

[48]Ibid., p. 32.
[49]Ibid., pp. 68-70.
[50]Ibid., p. 71.
[51]Ibid., p. 117.
[52]Ibid., p. 58.
[53]Ibid., p. 59.
[54]Ibid.

aspect of that achievement. But when a culture denies that human beings possess essential natures and ends, the notion that moral judgments are statements of fact also drops away; it then becomes necessary to find other justifications for desired actions.

MacIntyre tells the story of the Enlightenment's futile search for a replacement for the teleological understanding of human nature. He begins at the end, at the point where it becomes clear that the quest has failed, and works backward. Søren Kierkegaard (1813-1855) wrote *Either/Or* as a epitaph for Immanuel Kant's project of grounding morality in reason. Kierkegaard presents the reader with two completely incommensurable ways of life, the esthetic (A) and the ethical (B). The esthete (A) is immersed in the pursuit of pleasure without regard to the distinction between good and evil. It is not as if the esthete chooses evil over good; rather, for the esthete the ethical framework that makes the choice necessary simply does not exist. All that matters is the feeling of pleasure. The ethical (B) person lives life structured by the distinction between good and evil, typified by the traditional morality of marriage, truth telling and promise keeping. In *Either/Or*, "the choice between the ethical and the aesthetic is not the choice between good and evil, it is the choice whether or not to choose in terms of good and evil."[55] According to MacIntyre, Kierkegaard assumes the failure of all previous attempts to justify living a moral life and presents it as something to be chosen without the possibility of giving rational grounds.[56]

Kierkegaard was responding primarily to Immanuel Kant's (1724-1804) effort to ground morality in reason. Kant denied that morality could be justified with reference to human desires, sentiments or feelings, or with reference to divine commands. He rejected utility and the tendency to produce individual happiness as moral criteria. The moral life can be secured only by reason; for the moral character of rules can be maintained only if they are universally recognizable and binding on everyone under all conditions. As Kant sees it, the task of moral philosophy is to discriminate between moral rules or maxims that are universal in scope and those that cannot be universalized. Kant proposed the following test of a maxim's universal scope: "Never act except in such a way that one could also will that

---

[55]Ibid., p. 40.
[56]Ibid., pp. 39-43.

the maxim should become a universal law."[57] Kant argues that the basic rules of traditional morality, such as "always tell the truth," "always keep your promises" and "don't commit suicide," pass the rational test. However, according to MacIntyre, Kant uses "notoriously bad arguments" to sustain his case. For example, in the case of suicide, Kant argues that such an action contradicts the innate impulse to preserve our lives. His appeal to "innate impulse" seems to reintroduce desires or feelings into the project of justifying morality after Kant had earlier rejected such justifications. Additionally, Kant's test allows many obviously immoral or nonmoral maxims to slip through. Such maxims as "Keep all your promises throughout your life except one," "Persecute all those who hold false religious beliefs" and "Always eat mussels on Mondays in March" pass the test handily. Hence, as Kierkegaard saw clearly, Kant's project failed.

Kant was responding to Denis Diderot, David Hume (1711-1776) and others who attempted to justify the moral life with reference to innate passions, desires or sentiments. In Diderot's dialogue *Rameau's Nephew*,[58] the narrator ("Me") defends traditional morality against Rameau's objections. The narrator argues that the rules of conservative morality lead to the most fulfilling realization of the passions and desires of human nature over the long haul. Rameau, whom the narrator describes as "one of the most bizarre people in this country," objects that (1) immediate gratification of desire sometimes warrants breaking the moral code, (2) that even a long-term view justifies obeying the rules only insofar as they serve our desires and (3) that the world does not really work the way the moralist envisions. According to MacIntyre, Rameau's objections cannot be answered within Diderot's framework:

> For what divides them is the question of precisely which of our desires are to be acknowledged as legitimate guides to action, and which on the other hand are to be inhibited, frustrated or re-educated; and clearly this question cannot be answered by trying to use our desires themselves as some sort of criterion.[59]

---

[57]Immanuel Kant, *Groundwork of the Metaphysics of Morals*, trans. Mary Gregor (New York: Cambridge University, 1998), p. 15; MacIntyre paraphrases Kant this way: "can we or can we not consistently will that everyone should always act on it" (*After Virtue*, p. 45).

[58]For an online text see Denis Diderot, *Ramaeu's Nephew*, Marxists Internet Archive, http://marxists.org/reference/archive/diderot/1769/rameaus-nephew.htm.

[59]MacIntyre, *After Virtue*, p. 48.

David Hume assumes that morality must be explained and justified either by reason or by the passions. Since he does not think reason can do the work, Hume develops a moral theory based on innate desires and passions. Hume explains:

> Since morals, therefore, have an influence on the actions and affections, it follows, that they cannot be deriv'd from reason; and that because reason alone, as we have already prov'd, can never have any such influence. Morals excite passions, and produce or prevent actions. Reason of itself is utterly impotent in this particular. The rules of morality, therefore, are not conclusions of our reason.[60]

In his *Treatise of Human Nature* (1739-1740), Hume faces the same challenge Diderot confronted: if we are clear that abiding by a moral rule does not serve our long-term interest, why not abandon it? According to MacIntyre, this question is no more answerable by Hume's theory than within Diderot's framework. In his later work *Enquiry Concerning the Principles of Morals* (1751), Hume invokes natural "sympathy" or altruism to bridge the gap between the "general and unconditional rules" that morality demands and "our particular fluctuating, circumstance-governed desires, emotions, and interests."[61] But why should "sympathy" be given such a privileged position among human motives? In MacIntyre's opinion, it is simply a "philosophical fiction" invented to keep Hume's system from collapsing.[62]

According to MacIntyre, the Enlightenment project of justifying morality without reference to human nature and its end had to fail. Diderot, Kant and Kierkegaard all agree in rejecting the ancient teleological understanding of human nature, which assumed that human beings possess an essence that can be actualized only by achieving its appropriate end.[63] To reject this teleological understanding is to drive a wedge between descriptions of fact and assertions of moral obligation. Within the teleological framework no such separation exists. To say that so-and-so is a good person is a description of fact; it is a description of the relationship between this

---

[60]David Hume, *Treatise of Human Nature* 3.1.1, ed. L. A. Selhy-Bigge, 2nd ed. (Oxford: Oxford University Press, 1978), p. 457.
[61]MacIntyre, *After Virtue*, p. 49.
[62]Ibid., p. 49.
[63]Ibid., p. 54.

person's actions, affections and virtues and their essence and end. But within the Enlightenment framework no description of innate desires or reason, however subtle, can found and justify universal and binding moral obligations. And this failure has led modern culture into a night of moral confusion and strife where all parties assert rights arbitrarily, indignantly protest and engage in endless unmasking of their opponents.

SPEAKING OF CHRISTIANITY IN A POST-CHRISTIAN CULTURE

In light of Taylor's analysis of the self-understanding of contemporary Western society, we can see the difficulties facing anyone wanting to communicate the Christian view of God, human freedom or dignity to the modern self. While our contemporaries look within themselves for moral sources and authority to guide them toward fullness, Christianity points to the transcendent God, who is Lord and Judge. Hence, God may appear to them as a threat to their dignity, which they identify with autonomy. Even though Christianity affirms the ordinary life of work, marriage and children, it calls us to higher levels of holiness, devotion, love and faithfulness within this sphere. Whereas our contemporaries trust the innocence of their inner depths and seek expression in ways that transgress the bounds of traditional morality, Christianity denies the unambiguous goodness of nature's first impulses. It warns against unruly passions, urges a self-discipline guided by divine law and urges us to love God above all other things. Christianity locates genuine human identity at a point in the space determined by the three axes of respect, fullness and dignity very different from that of contemporary society; indeed, it is so different that, from the perspective of the modern self, it can appear as disrespect, unhappiness and debasement instead of respect, fullness and dignity.[64]

Alasdair MacIntyre's analysis, no less than Charles Taylor's, shows how

---

[64]According to David Kinnaman, the younger generation (under thirty years old) thinks Christianity is hypocritical, antihomosexual, sheltered, too political and judgmental. Interestingly these negative perceptions are all moral. The only one that seems to involve rationality is the one about being sheltered. Each of these attitudes reflects the trends in Western culture spoken of in Taylor: inwardness, affirmation of ordinary life and expressivism (David Kinnaman, *unChristian: What a New Generation Really Thinks About Christianity . . . And Why It Matters* [Grand Rapids: Baker, 2007]). Dan Kimball, another observer of the "emerging generations," offers an equally disturbing assessment of the coming generation. See Dan Kimball, *They Like Jesus but Not the Church* (Grand Rapids: Zondervan, 2007).

difficult it will be to explain the Christian understanding of God's relationship to human freedom and dignity to our contemporaries. The current moral culture was founded on rejection of the traditional claim that human beings are given their essence and end by God. Even if it now also rejects all other foundations for morality—in reason or innate desires—it is not therefore more open to returning to tradition. Many of our contemporaries exhibit a viscerally negative reaction to assertions of authority, pretense of objectivity or arguments to truth in the moral sphere. They instinctively suspect all such claims as masking desire for power, and making those claims sets in motion the process of unmasking. To many people Christian calls for obedience to the divine law, for repentance and moral transformation sound like recipes for oppression. Promises of ultimate happiness and eternal life can be interpreted as attempts to rob people of the fullness possible in this life. And such worn Christian slogans as "true freedom is found in slavery to God" or "we find our real dignity on our knees" will sound as false as they do ridiculous.

Both Taylor and MacIntyre teach lessons we would be wise to take seriously if we care about explaining Christianity to our wary and wounded contemporaries. If Taylor is correct we must take seriously the three "strongly valued goods" of contemporary culture: respect, fullness and dignity. No one who appears to reject them can gain a hearing. Christians can affirm these values but not in the way the modern self understands them. Our first challenge, then, will be to show how the modern self's aspirations fall short of our highest hopes for respect, fullness and dignity. Next, we need to explain how the Christian view of these values fulfills them in a way that secular thought does not. MacIntyre's work teaches us to avoid the rhetoric of exclusive claims, protestations to objectivity and infallible proofs. Our contemporaries interpret these strategies as masking the "will to power" and dismiss them for that reason alone. Approaching people with the least hint of judgment or arrogance or love of argument will fail to produce the desired engagement. In my experience, patient listening, sincere probing and autobiographical confession is the only way to engage with our contemporaries in meaningful conversations about important matters.

LOOKING AHEAD

The next three chapters explore three distinct attitudes toward God, each of which arises out of contemporary moral space. Understanding their humanity in terms of the values of respect, fullness and dignity, as these are understood by the dominant culture, determines the way modern people view God. The majority of our contemporaries reflexively defend the modern understanding of these values as self-evident and nonnegotiable. Since they hold these ideals as foundational they tend to view God as threatening or irrelevant to them.[65] Those who suspect that modern values are threatened by the idea of God will adopt an attitude of *defiance* or *subservience* toward God. Others attempt to live in *indifference* or forgetfulness of God. Each of these three attitudinal stances projects a certain image of God, which proves to be at variance with the image of God portrayed in the Christian faith.

---

[65]I will explore the third possibility in part two, "The God-Centered Self." Instead of viewing God as a threat or indifferent to our freedom and dignity, we can come to see God as their deepest ground. We can begin to love God in the freedom given by God's love for us enacted in Jesus Christ and in this way discover our true worth.

2

DEFIANCE

*The Promethean Dimension
of the Modern Self*

We view some things as means to happiness and others as barriers. Friends, a good job and a winning lottery ticket beckon as ways to happiness. Illness, lack of money and enemies stand as obstacles in our path. But most of the time the same thing works as both means and barrier. Friends can betray, family can restrict and money can corrupt. It seems that nothing is so conducive to our happiness that it does not limit us in some way. Does this pattern apply to our relationship with God as well? Along with the advantages the existence of God brings, might there also follow disadvantages? Indeed, some people view God in a largely negative light. Many wish to put the thought of God out of their minds and immerse themselves in the search for pleasure, wealth or power. Others may be tempted to doubt or deny God's existence. A few even hate the thought of God. They view God as the ultimate enemy and guard their freedom and dignity against encroachment with flinty defiance.

PROMETHEUS: THE MYTH

The Greek god Prometheus descended from the race of the Titans, the gods that ruled the world before the reign of the Olympians, who were headed by the ruthless Zeus. The playwright Aeschylus portrays Prometheus as a friend and protector of humanity against the enmity and tyranny of Zeus. Zeus wanted human beings to remain in their primitive and powerless condition, lest they eventually overthrow Zeus, just as Zeus subjugated the Titans. But Prometheus defied the will of Zeus by bringing fire and civilization to human beings. For his "crime," Zeus had Prometheus fastened to the face of a granite mountain and sent a giant eagle to tear at his insides. His executioners Hephaestus and Kratos debated the justice of his punishment, but both gods agreed that the will of Zeus was inescapable and that

> All things are a burden, save to rule
> Over the Gods; for none is free but Zeus.[1]

Prometheus views the situation differently. He admits that he provoked punishment with his actions but denies that his punishment is just. Prometheus rejects advice from friends to moderate his accusations and admit wrongdoing, telling them,

> Go thou and worship; fold thy hands in prayer,
> And be the dog that licks the foot of power!

Instead of submitting to Zeus, Prometheus proclaims his hatred of Zeus and "all gods" all the louder. He knows he is doomed but remains defiant. He will not give Zeus the final victory of breaking his spirit. He cannot resist omnipotence, but he will never admit that omnipotence can be free from the demands of justice. Zeus rules sky and earth, land and sea, gods and men and beasts, but he cannot force Prometheus to believe that Zeus is right. The will that defies unjust rule is the last preserve of dignity.

The figure of Aeschylus's Prometheus excites our sympathy and admiration. Whatever the playwright intended to communicate to his contemporaries, it is almost impossible to resist seeing humanity—and consequently ourselves—symbolized in Prometheus. The play constructs a world in which God and humanity are defined as competitors ("For none is free but Zeus!"). Humanity could realize its great potential if only it were released from the tyranny that keeps it in check. Even if humanity is crushed by ruthless omnipotence, it can maintain its heroic dignity and inner freedom by refusing to acquiesce to the order that demands subservience.

---

[1] Aeschylus, *Prometheus Bound*, Internet Classics Archives, http://classics.mit.edu/Aeschylus /prometheus.html.

Hence, Prometheus has become the patron saint of those who dare defy God (or fate or chance) in the name of human freedom and dignity.

PROMETHEUS: THE METAPHOR

Prometheus and his character type appear over and over in Western dramatic and epic literature. In *Paradise Lost,* for example, Milton develops the character of Satan on the Promethean model. Defeated by God, Satan finds himself in hell surrounded by his fellow conspirators. Surveying his new realm, he begins to rally his troops with infinite defiance against God's "tyranny":

> What though the field be lost?
> All is not lost; the unconquerable Will,
> And study of revenge, immortal hate,
> And courage never to submit or yield:
> And what is else not to be overcome?
> That Glory never shall his wrath or might
> Extort from me. To bow and sue for grace
> With suppliant knee, and deify his power.[2]

Knowing that he cannot overcome God by force, Satan determines to work by deceit. He resolves to rid himself of any remnants of goodness. From now on he will study only evil and war against all goodness in hopes of overthrowing divine providence. Satan thus proclaims the infinite creativity of his iron will:

> Hail, horrors, hail
> Infernal world, and thou, profoundest Hell,
> Receive thy new possessor: One who brings
> A mind not to be chang'd by Place or Time.
> The mind is its own place, and in itself
> Can make a Heav'n of Hell, a Hell of Heav'n.
> . . . .
> Here at least
> We shall be free; th' Almighty hath not built
> Here for his envy, will not drive us hence:
> Here we may reign secure, and, in my choice,

---

[2]John Milton, *Paradise Lost,* 1.105-12 (London, 1667). I have modernized the spelling.

To reign is worth ambition though in Hell:
Better to reign in Hell than serve in Heav'n.[3]

Having lost heaven's "happy fields," Satan rejoices in what he retains. He preserves a space inside his mind unconquered and unconquerable even by the Almighty. In that retreat he can will, imagine, hate and plot without limit. In hell, where God dare not enter, Satan finds true freedom. Cast from the heights, Satan discovers a new kind of dignity in an inner sanctuary where he refuses to "bow and sue for grace."

Satan's theology bears a striking resemblance to that of Prometheus. For Satan, the Almighty is just another will that desires to dominate all things; the only difference is that God has unlimited power to enforce *his* will. In other words, Satan believes that God is like him at heart and would be nothing without subjects and power to dominate. Even if Satan now has to admit that he is not God's equal in power, he will not admit that he is God's inferior in will. He thinks of God's power and goodness as accidental features of God's being. God's essential being and core identity is pure will no different from Satan's essential being. That God is almighty rather than Satan is the result of mere chance. In refusing to bow the knee, Satan thinks he can impose some limit on God's sovereignty: "Here at least we shall be free."

Of course, Milton does not want us to admire Satan, but despite our efforts to resist we find ourselves admiring the arch rebel, vanquished but still defiant. We are stirred by his determination, by his refusal to accept defeat and especially by his assertion of inviolable dignity and inner freedom in the face of a greater force. Satan pictures God as an almighty tyrant and contrasts himself as a tragic, heroic figure. Milton knows very well that Satan's picture of God is false and hence that his heroic self-understanding is also false. The poet reminds the reader of this during Satan's speech by explaining, "So spake th' Apostate Angel, though in pain, / Vaunting aloud, but rackt with deep despair."[4] But Milton also knows that deep in the human heart lies suspicion that God really is a tyrant, that rebellion is heroic and that subservience to such a power-being is demeaning. By putting these eloquent lies on *Satan's* lips, perhaps Milton hopes that we will recognize

---

[3]Ibid., 1.250-63.
[4]Ibid., 1.125-26.

the source of these thoughts when they arise in our hearts. By allowing us to feel the lure of Satan's heroic rhetoric and then see what comes of it, we will be armed against the devil's wiles.[5]

Near the end of the eighteenth century, at the height of the Romantic movement, some readers of Milton began to find his picture of Satan enduringly attractive despite Milton's later subversion of that initial impression.[6] It was no coincidence that at the same time Prometheus became the patron saint of Romanticism, especially of its atheist wing. The young Johann Wolfgang von Goethe wrote a poem titled "Prometheus" (1773), in which Prometheus obviously symbolizes himself and humanity come of age, and Zeus symbolizes the idea of God. Goethe taunts the gods for their rage, envy and poverty, and expresses admiration for Prometheus's spirit of defiance. In the following lines Goethe's Prometheus ridicules Zeus for thinking himself worthy of worship, for Zeus cannot escape "almighty time and eternal fate" any more than lesser beings. Prometheus then predicts a future Promethean age, no doubt Goethe's own, in which mature humanity will put the childish thought of God behind it:

> And I should reverence thee?
> Wherefore? Hast thou ever
> Lighten'd the sorrows of the heavy-laden?
> *Thou* ever stretched thy hand, to still the tears
> Of the perplexed in spirit?
> Was it not
> Almighty Time and ever-during Fate,
> My lords and thine—that shaped and fashion'd me
> Into the man I am?
>
> . . . .
>
> Here do I sit, and mould
> Men after mine own image—

---

[5]According to Stanley Fish, "Milton's method is to re-create in the mind of the reader . . . the drama of the Fall, to make him fall again exactly as Adam did and with Adam's troubled clarity, that is to say, 'not deceived' " (see Stanley Eugene Fish, *Surprised by Sin: The Reader in Paradise Lost* [Berkeley: University of California Press, 1971]).

[6]C. S. Lewis refers to Percy Shelley and William Blake as admirers of Milton's "hero" Satan. See C. S. Lewis, *A Preface to Paradise Lost* (London: Oxford University Press, 1942), p. 92. For another study of Satan in *Paradise Lost*, see G. Rostrevor Hamilton, *Hero or Fool? A Study of Milton's Satan* (New York: Haskell House, 1969).

A race that may be like unto myself,
To suffer, weep; to enjoy, and to rejoice;
And, like myself, unheeding all of thee![7]

Lord Byron, the English Romantic, also wrote a poem titled "Prometheus" (1816). He sees in the defiant god a symbol of humanity's spirit, which even in death can gain victory over its foes, divine and human, by remaining resolute:

In the endurance, and repulse
Of thine impenetrable Spirit,
Which Earth and Heaven could not convulse,
A mighty lesson we inherit:
Thou art a symbol and a sign
To Mortals of their fate and force;
Like thee, Man is in part divine,
A troubled stream from a pure source;
And Man in portions can foresee
His own funereal destiny;
His wretchedness, and his resistance,
And his sad unallied existence:
To which his Spirit may oppose
Itself—and equal to all woes,
And a firm will, and a deep sense,
Which even in torture can decry
Its own concenter'd recompense,
Triumphant where it dares defy,
And making Death a Victory.[8]

Karl Marx, author of the *Communist Manifesto*, admired Prometheus's rebellion against the inflexible powers that enslave people and keep them down. He praised Prometheus in the foreword to the published edition of his dissertation (1841):

Philosophy makes no secret of it. The confession of Prometheus: In simple words, "I hate the pack of gods" is its own confession, its own

---

[7]Johann Wolfgang Goethe, *The Poems and Ballads of Johann Wolfgang Goethe*, ed. W. Edmondstoune Aytoun and Theodore Martin (New York: William Gowans, 1863), pp. 112-13.
[8]Lord Byron, *Poetry*, vol. 4, *The Works of Lord Byron* (New York: Charles Scribner's, 1901), pp. 48-51, italics added.

aphorism against all heavenly and earthly gods who do not acknowledge human self-consciousness as the highest divinity. It will
have none other beside. But to those poor March hares who rejoice
over the apparently worsened civil position of philosophy, it responds
again, as Prometheus replied to the servant of the gods, Hermes: "Be
sure of this, I would not change my state of evil fortune for your ser-
vitude. Better to be the servant of this rock than to be faithful boy to
Father Zeus." Prometheus is the most eminent saint and martyr in the
philosophical calendar.[9]

The list of modern authors who idealize Prometheus is extensive and
includes William Blake (1757-1827), Richard Wagner (1813-1883) and
Friedrich Nietzsche (1844-1900). But I have made the point: some modern
people self-consciously and explicitly define God as the chief competitor of
human dignity and freedom; others admire the defiant attitude even if they
dare not imitate it. The words of Charles Taylor well summarize this new
situation: "The dignity of free, rational control came to seem genuine only
free of submission to God; the goodness of nature and/or our unreserved
immersion in it, seemed to require its independence, and a negation of a
divine vocation."[10] Speaking of American Victorian intellectuals, James
Turner concludes that for many of them "the autonomy of the inner self was
so precious—and so precarious—that submission to any external authority,
even God, potentially endangered the moral integrity of the person."[11]

I will close this chapter by quoting William Ernest Henley's (1849-1903)
poem "Invictus" (1875). It contains some very familiar lines, which,
without knowing their source, may have stirred us to feel something of
the Promethean spirit:

> Out of the night that covers me,
> Black as the Pit from pole to pole,
> I thank whatever gods may be
> For my unconquerable soul.

---

[9]Karl Marx, *The Difference Between the Democritean and Epicurean Philosophy of Nature*,
March 6, 2007, www.marxists.org/archive/marx/works/1841/dr-theses/index.htm.
[10]Charles Taylor, *Sources of the Self: The Making of Modern Identity* (Cambridge, MA: Harvard University Press, 1989), p. 315.
[11]James Turner, *Without God, Without Creed: The Origins of Unbelief in America* (Baltimore:
Johns Hopkins University Press, 1985), p. 211.

In the fell clutch of circumstance
I have not winced nor cried aloud.
Under the bludgeonings of chance
My head is bloody, but unbowed.

Beyond this place of wrath and tears
Looms but the Horror of the shade,
And yet the menace of the years
Finds, and shall find, me unafraid.

It matters not how strait the gate,
How charged with punishments the scroll,
I am the master of my fate:
I am the captain of my soul.[12]

---

[12]William Ernest Henley, "Invictus," in *Modern British Poetry*, ed. Louis Untermeyer (New York: Harcourt, Brace, 1950), p. 53.

3

SUBSERVIENCE

The Religion of Idols,
Hypocrites and Hirelings

As we saw in Aeschylus's play, an image of God that stirs up defiance in one person may inspire terror in others. Both defiance and subservience may view God as pure power to whom they merely adopt opposite attitudes. Prometheus rebelled while Hephaestus and Kratos cowered, but both sides understood Zeus alike. Hence striking a pose of submission is not an infallible sign that we harbor no distorted images of God. Thinking of God primarily as the Almighty may inspire a fear-based or reward-focused religion, which Jesus labeled disparagingly "pagan" (Mt 6:32) because of its lack of inner devotion.[1] Subservience falls far short of sincere love for God.[2]

---

[1]In Mt 6:32, Jesus instructs his disciples not adopt the piety of the *ethnē* ("nations" or "heathen" or "pagans"). Søren Kierkegaard criticized his fellow Danish Christians for thinking like pagans rather than Christians (*Christian Discourses*, trans. Howard and Edna Hong [Princeton, NJ: Princeton University Press, 1997], p. 12). Kierkegaard defines paganism in this way: "All paganism consists in this, that God is related directly to a human being, as the remarkably striking to the amazed" (*Concluding Unscientific Postscript*, trans. Howard and Edna Hong [Princeton, NJ: Princeton University Press, 1992], p. 245).

[2]Subservience must be distinguished from submission. In the act of submission Christians conform their will to God's will even though the goodness and excellence of what is willed by God cannot be perceived at the moment due to ignorance or indwelling sin. Under these conditions the believer submits to the specific will of God because of a basic trust in the goodness of God even though God's goodness is hidden for the present. But *love* of God is the higher attitude. The believer's act of love is a response to the clear revelation of God's love; it is not eclipsed by ignorance or sin. Submission will be surpassed by love and love will last forever.

DEFAULT RELIGION

Human beings are by nature religious. In the ancient world people found themselves surrounded by natural forces that sustained life and threatened it, provided good and visited evil, gave and took. People were unmistakably aware of their dependence on the powers of birth and death, sun and storm, earth and seas, moon and stars, and all the rest. If forests and fields and rivers and seas do not give up their produce, human beings die. Flood or earthquake or fire can destroy at will with none to hinder. These awe-inspiring forces were clearly higher on the scale of existence than humanity, for they possessed more power, longer life and more glory than human beings. This scale of being and relationship of dependence define the distinction between humanity and divinity. Every being higher than humanity on the scale of existence is by definition divine. As Robert Sokolowski has observed about pagan religion, "the gods represent necessities that must be accepted and against which a man can pretend to act only at his peril."[3]

One has no choice but to respect and deal with divine necessities. In relating to higher powers the ancients did not treat them as impersonal manifestations of chance and necessity but as quasi persons who possessed knowledge, will and power. Unlike mechanical processes, gods may be influenced and moved by sacrifice, prayer and other religious actions. This distinction marks the difference between religion and mere worldly shrewdness. Religion centered on giving the gods their due in hopes of avoiding their wrath and securing their favor. The religion natural to humanity relates to the divine as a means of attaining goods that sustain and enhance life and avoiding the evils that disrupt life and diminish its joy. At the end of the day, this type of religion is not all that different from worldly shrewdness. No practitioner of natural religion thought of relating to the divine with love and adoration, anymore that we think of relating to the laws of nature in this way.

The pagan understanding of God and religion is no relic of the ancient past. It arises perennially in the human heart, and this is why I designate it "default" religion. We tend naturally to view God as the possessor and dispenser of the goods we need and the privileges we want. Even if we believe

---

[3]Robert Sokolowski, *The God of Faith and Reason: Foundations of Christian Theology* (Washington, DC: Catholic University of America Press, 1994), p. 13.

our religious relation to God secures for us the things we need, this view of God tends to evoke envy and resentment. For default religion does not understand *God* as the good we need; rather it sees God as *enjoying* these goods in an unlimited way and only grudgingly sharing them with us. We have to beg. I will illustrate this innate tendency with the three examples to follow.

The wish reveals the heart. My parents took me to church twice every Sunday and on Wednesday evenings. My father sang hymns as he worked on our farm, and many evenings I noticed him reading his Bible in his favorite easy chair. The gentle Jesus was my friend, and I wanted to be a "good boy." And yet, when I was about six years old, perhaps annoyed with the limits placed on me by my parents, society and the world, I found a thought entering my mind: *Why wasn't I born God? Why does God get to live as "God" and not me?* The moment I realized what I was thinking, I grew frightened and pushed it out of my mind. I was sure God would not be pleased with such envious musings.

Was this envious thought something that just happened to me, like being hit by a falling acorn? Or does it reveal something deeper—a vague urge to be all and possess all and fear that we will be used, controlled or absorbed by an alien power? We are born into this world unaware that we are limited, weak and mortal. It seems that our first lesson in life is to distinguish ourselves from our surroundings. Although we cannot articulate the lesson, we have to learn the painful truth: I am not all. There is something other than me. Simultaneously, we discover a second hard truth: the external world will not accommodate my every wish. There are boundaries, dangers and rules everywhere. The world offers pleasure, safety and freedom, but also presents pain, danger and limits. A child must learn to achieve the first and avoid, escape or break through the others.

However sophisticated we become, we never seem to give up our desire to return to the primitive feeling *I am all and I control all*. But roadblocks and competitors of different kinds block our way. Impersonal objects may be approached with a controlling attitude. Mountains, forests and laws of nature present themselves as limits we want to conquer, circumvent or turn to our advantage. Even if they are huge and unchangeable, such things are still passive, and we can find ways to control them to some extent. People present a different kind of barrier. Other people are active and also desire to become all and control all. But only one can be all. And for another person to become all, we would have to become nothing, absorbed into his being or made subservient to her will. People are more than barriers; they can become competitors and potential enemies. For this reason I do not think my childhood envy of God was merely a passing fancy. If other limited human beings entered my consciousness as competitors and potential enemies or allies, how much more would almighty God!

Adults seem almost omniscient and omnipresent when you are a small child, but soon you learn to hide inside your mind, if you cannot hide physically. You learn that deceit and lying sometimes work. We are told, however, that God does not suffer such limits and weaknesses. God is everywhere and knows everything. Even your thoughts are open to God. It may be comforting to know that God is qualified to take care of us, but it would be easy to resent the all-knowing One for not respecting the boundary between us and everything else. A little privacy, please! Even if we cannot extend ourselves to infinity, surely we deserve an inner closet where not even God is free to enter without knocking. On top of this, we are told that God is all-powerful and immortal. God's will must be done! Oh, I see: God has it all! You can see why we are tempted to envy God.

The original sin. Our ambivalence toward God and our tendency to envy him is well illustrated in the story of the fall, in Genesis 3. In the previous chapter, the Lord gave Adam liberty to eat from every tree in the garden except the tree of the knowledge of good and evil. But the crafty serpent said to Eve, "Did God really say, 'You must not eat from any tree in the garden?'" The tempter begins not with open contradiction of God's command but with a question of interpretation. Dietrich Bonhoeffer sees this as "the first religious question in the world," which initiates a "conversation about God" designed to replace Eve's previous conversation with God.[4] With counterfeit piety the serpent says, "God could not possibly have meant it in this way. God, the good creator, would not impose such a thing upon his creature; this would be a limitation of his love."[5] But the issue of

---

[4]Dietrich Bonhoeffer, *Creation and Fall, Temptation: Two Biblical Studies*, trans. John C. Fletcher (New York: Macmillan, 1959), pp. 67, 69. For Bonhoeffer, insofar as it is a conversation about God, theology is a sign of the fall.

[5]Ibid., p. 67. Bonhoeffer follows Karl Barth in critiquing "religion" insofar as it embodies human effort to co-opt God for human ends. Religion in this sense is a sign of the fall. Religion can be

interpretation hides the true intent of the question. For the serpent's expansion of God's prohibition from one to all the trees is designed to cast doubt on God's goodness and fairness in forbidding even the one. Eve quickly corrects the serpent's "paraphrase" of the divine command. We can eat from every tree in the garden, she explains, except the one in the middle. We are not even allowed to touch it.[6] But the snake has made his point: even if God denies you only one good thing, you possess other good things only at his pleasure. Think about what you are doing. You are trusting God to make your decisions about what is good and bad for you. Aren't you able to do this for yourself? Don't you know best what you need? Eve replies that God had warned that eating fruit from the forbidden tree would bring death. In effect, she says that God is not (or says he is not) withholding good from us but protecting us from evil.

But the tempter advances an alternative explanation: "You will not surely die. For God knows that when you eat of it your eyes will be opened, and you will be like God, knowing good and evil." Although Eve corrected the snake's first misrepresentation, which she knew to be false, she does not try to correct this one. He has touched a nerve and planted a doubt, not about what God said but about why he said it. Why does God want to keep this knowledge to himself? Why not share it with us? The tempter addresses the universal human desire to live without limits and portrays God as the ultimate limit. Just as I as a child envied God's freedom and power, Eve begins to resent God for being God. The lying snake has succeeded in defining God as a potential competitor: God has his own interests and cannot be trusted to work for our good in all circumstances. Perhaps God withholds things from us not for our good but (like Zeus) to preserve a monopoly on them and to keep us down. For the first time, Eve begins to think, *Who can judge my interests better than I can?* Now she looks at the fruit with her own eyes. It looks good to eat and it is beautiful. Just imagine the power godlike wisdom will impart! So she ate. Adam ate. And we eat.

"true" only insofar as it is a result of the grace of God. Their views of religion correspond to Bernard's second stage of love—in which we love God for ourselves' sakes—to be discussed later. See Karl Barth, *Church Dogmatics*, vol. 1. pt. 2, ed. G. W. Bromiley and T. F. Torrance, trans. G. T. Thomson and Harold Knight (Edinburgh: T & T Clark, 1978), pp. 297-361.

[6]Bruce Vawter detects a "touch of resentment" already lurking in Eve's addition of the prohibition against touching the tree (*On Genesis: A New Reading* [Garden City, NY: Doubleday, 1977], p. 78).

The unoriginal sin. In his spiritual autobiography, *Confessions*, Augustine relates a story that epitomizes his own fall and connects his story to the original fall and hence to us. He and other boys sneaked into a neighbor's orchard late at night and stole armloads of pears. The stolen pears were not very good, and the boys ate only a few. The rest they threw at nearby pigs. Most people would consider this theft just a stupid boyhood prank, but Augustine cannot dismiss it so lightly. He discerns something more sinister at work, so that he can choose this incident as an archetypical example of human sin. He does not select an act of Promethean defiance, murder or adultery. A Promethean example might excite admiration, and a case of adultery, murder or treason could be explained, if not excused, as a means to some end not altogether unworthy. For Augustine, the deed's stupidity makes it an even better example. This act was done for no reason other than to experience being a thief and feel the thrill of doing something forbidden. As Augustine puts it, "My feasting was only on the wickedness which I took pleasure in enjoying."[7]

Perhaps other sins disturb creation and damage society more than his petty theft. But Augustine discerns profound wickedness in his juvenile stunt. In his deception and theft he achieves a momentary illusion that he is divine and free from all limits. The thrill of the act was derived from this fantasy, which he calls a "nothing." As he probes further into the nature of his offense he concludes that *every* sin imitates God out of envy:

> Pride imitates what is lofty; but you alone are God most high above all things. What does ambition seek but honor and glory? Yet you alone are worthy of honor and are glorious for eternity. The cruelty of powerful people aims to arouse fear. What is to be feared but God alone? . . . Avarice wishes to have large possessions; you possess everything. Envy contends about excellence; but what is more excellent than you? Anger seeks revenge; who avenges with greater justice than you?[8]

At the end of his analysis Augustine concludes: "In their perverted ways all humanity imitates you."[9] Augustine understands that the root sin of all

---

[7]Augustine, *The Confessions of Saint Augustine* 2.6, trans. Henry Chadwick (New York: Oxford University Press, 1991), p. 31.
[8]Ibid., p. 31.
[9]Ibid., p. 32.

sins, great and small, is the willing embrace of the illusion of limitlessness, the fantasy that only our lack of courage stands between us and our unlimited freedom. We resent the apparently arbitrary limits imposed on the infinite human essence by external reality. In our "perverted" understanding, we envy God's unlimited freedom, chafe at the limits he imposes and imagine that we can attain the infinite by bursting through the boundaries God has set. The pleasure we experience in sinful acts derives not so much from gaining the "good" that we grab but from the illusion that we are acting as God. Even our little sins reveal envy of God's divine status.

The innate human ambivalence toward God and envy at his status revealed in my experience at the age of six, in the story of the fall and in Augustine's analysis of sin can come to expression not only in outright defiance. They have religious expressions too. They can appear in attitudes that seem submissive and pious but really care only for the blessings God can bestow or the advantages the appearance of piety can confer; that is, they treat God merely as a means to their ends. Kierkegaard perceives that an ironic relationship exists between religious admiration and envy. Admiration for God certainly has the appearance of piety, but it easily transforms into envy when I begin to wish "for my part to be the object of my admiration."[10] This religious attitude manifests itself in different forms: idolatry, externality or a lack of authenticity, political or ethnic religion and self-righteousness.

CRITICS OF DEFAULT RELIGION

The Bible. Undoubtedly, the Bible is the first and the most radical critic of the religious impulse natural to human beings. The prophets of Israel are incessant in their criticism of idolatry outside and within ancient Israel. An idol is a physical object that provides a place for a god to become present and active for the worshiper.[11] In theory each god exists as a particular force within nature, as wind, sun or fertility; they are not merely identical to the idol. In popular religion, however, the idol is treated as the god itself. Regardless of whether the pagan possesses a primitive animistic or a more

---

[10]Søren Kierkegaard, *Training in Christianity*, trans. Walter Lowrie, ed. John F. Thornton and Susan B. Varenne (New York: Vintage Books, 2004), p. 219.
[11]Edward M. Curtis, "Idol, Idolatry," in *Anchor Bible Dictionary*, ed. David Noel Freedman (New York: Doubleday, 1992), 3:376-81.

sophisticated symbolic understanding of idols, the central point of biblical critique remains the same: we should not expect something in the created world to give us what only the Creator can provide.[12]

The first of the Ten Commandments demands that the Israelites give their devotion exclusively to the Lord who saved them from Egypt. The second forbids making an image for religious use: "You shall not bow down to them or worship them" (Ex 20:5). These early strictures could be interpreted merely as limiting Israelite worship to one particular god, the Lord of Israel, with implicit acknowledgment of existence of other gods. In later parts of the Old Testament, however, the critique of idols gains sharpness and precision. Jeremiah urges his hearers not to "learn the ways of the nations or be terrified by signs in the sky. . . . For the customs of the peoples are worthless" (Jer 10:2-3 NIV 1984). Jeremiah describes with irony and sarcasm the procedure for making an idol. A craftsman cuts down a tree, carves it into the shape he desires and adorns it with gold and jewels. He then fastens it to its pedestal so it will not fall over. The image cannot speak or walk or do anything else. Idols are fraudulent and worthless, concludes the prophet. Jeremiah then contrasts these pieces of dead wood with the true and living God who made heaven and earth (Jer 10:10-13). The prophet Isaiah contrasts the idols of Babylon, made of silver and gold, with the God who controls every force of nature.

> I am God, and there is no other;
> I am God, and there is none like me. . . .
> My purpose will stand,
> and I will do all that I please. (Is 46:9-10)

The New Testament continues the biblical critique of idolatry but extends and interprets the concept to include relating to any finite thing as if it were the ultimate source of good. Paul warns against greed because it involves idolatry (Col 3:5). In greed we seek our ultimate good in wealth when our ultimate good can be found in God alone. This principle can be applied across the board. We become idolaters whenever we treat a finite thing with ultimate, or even inordinate, significance.

---

[12]John Gray, "Idolatry," *Interpreter's Dictionary of the Bible*, ed. George A. Buttrick (Nashville: Abingdon, 1962), 2:675-78.

Implicit in the conceptual structure of idolatry is a religion that treats the divine as a means to a worldly end. The idols and the gods they represent are symbols of the finite goods human beings naturally seek and the evils they fear. It is inconceivable that one would approach the storm god or the goddess of fertility for any reason other than that one wants abundant rain for the fields or prodigious reproduction for the flocks. The essence of the storm god *is* rain and the essence of the fertility goddess *is* reproduction. And so it is for all the gods. The Bible criticizes idolatrous religion because it never really rises to the level of genuine religion, that is, love and devotion to God as the sole source of good things and the only object worthy of worship. Idolatry is a kind of religious worldliness that seeks by religious means a life of health and prosperity in this world. Idolatry does not challenge our innate self-centeredness; rather its main goal is to extend our control over our lives by a kind of religious management of the divine.

The Bible also critiques a second manifestation of the natural religious impulse. It goes by many names: hypocrisy, externality or ritualism. This attitude arises when one lacking in inner devotion, love and determination in relation to God nevertheless maintains the external appearance of such devotion. The hypocrite wants to appear as a good person to gain the social and economic advantages of this status without having to make the sacrifice required to become such a person. Hypocrites think they can secure God's worldly blessings through religious rituals apart from loving their neighbors and doing justice. The prophet Amos berated Israel for bringing offerings and sacrifices to the Lord, celebrating religious feasts and singing religious songs while at the same time living immoral and unjust lives. According to Amos, God despises religion bereft of genuine devotion and justice. Instead of engaging in empty rituals, the genuinely religious person will "let justice roll on like a river, righteousness like a never-failing stream!" (Amos 5:24). Jeremiah too warns the people of Judah that God requires more than just maintaining the temple and making the required sacrifices. He declares:

> Hear the word of the LORD, all you people of Judah who come through these gates to worship the LORD. This is what the LORD Almighty, the God of Israel, says: Reform your ways and your actions, and I will let you live in this place. Do not trust in deceptive words and say, "This is the

temple of the Lord, the temple of the Lord, the temple of the Lord!" If you really change your ways and your actions and deal with each other justly, if you do not oppress the foreigner, the fatherless or the widow and do not shed innocent blood in this place, and if you do not follow other gods to your own harm, then I will let you live in this place, in the land I gave your ancestors for ever and ever. (Jer 7:2-7)

Jesus criticized the hypocrisy of the religious leaders of his day the way Amos, Jeremiah and the other prophets criticized the ancient temple authorities. Like the prophets, Jesus condemned the habit of combining external worship with immoral and unjust behavior. But he also turned his searchlight on another form of hypocrisy. Jesus urged that practicing true religion includes not only performing the required ceremonies and living justly and morally, but must also encompass the inner affections and motives of the heart. The Sermon on the Mount (Mt 5–7) can be read as an intensification and internalization of religious and moral law. Every external action, religious or moral, must arise from a pure heart, a heart devoted wholly to God. Our actions cannot be counted genuinely meritorious if performed for the wrong reasons: from fear of punishment, to appear righteous, to gain favor, from habit, because of ethnic identity or from natural compassion. In his teaching, Jesus draws our moral obligations into an intimate relationship with religion, a religion centered on the heart. A hypocrite is no longer understood primarily as someone who lives in contradictory ways in different aspects of external life. Jesus traces external hypocrisy to the contradiction of divided loyalties within the heart. The internal contradiction is primary and accounts for all the external ones.

Paul's critique of religion differs from Jesus' critique in form and tone, but not in substance. Paul speaks consistently with the Sermon on the Mount when he says:

If I speak in the tongues of men or of angels, but do not have love, I am only a resounding gong or a clanging cymbal. If I have the gift of prophecy and can fathom all mysteries and all knowledge, and if I have a faith that can move mountains, but do not have love, I am nothing. If I give all I possess to the poor and give over my body to hardship that I may boast, but do not have love, I gain nothing. (1 Cor 13:1-3)

No religious activity by itself—even martyrdom—is beyond the possibility of motivational ambiguity and hypocrisy. Each could arise from a wrong motive and result in pride. Religion without love is vain.[13] In the book of Romans Paul denies that the definitive test of our status before God is conformity between the words of the law and our external behaviors. A religious attitude that understands righteousness to be such conformity will issue forth in blind self-righteousness and ugly judgmentalism (Rom 2). But how does one achieve the purity of heart that leads to the religious and moral uprightness God requires? For Paul, such a state cannot be achieved by one's own efforts. Try as it may, the impure heart cannot purify itself (Rom 7). Our wills can never become the originating source and substance of our own goodness. We can become righteousness only by being caught up in God's own righteousness made available in Jesus Christ and made actual in us by the Holy Spirit (Rom 3–8). In Paul's teaching, Christ and the Spirit liberate, enlighten and empower us to live a new life. In this way God's righteous acts become ours.

Hypocrisy like idolatry treats God as a means to an end and so arises from the natural religious impulse I have called "default religion." Hypocrisy becomes observable as the contradiction between two sets of behaviors, for example, between one's words and one's actions. Hypocrites want the pleasure of the good opinion of others who judge them only by their words and the pleasure of doing what contradicts their words. The visible contradiction springs from inner contradiction, from a heart that wills two things, attempts to serve two masters (Mt 6:24) and is of two minds (Jas 1:8; 4:8). But with reference to God one cannot will two things. One cannot will God's will and something that contradicts God's will. One can only wish to appear devoted to God's will while actually pursuing one's own will. But in this case God is willed merely as a means to the good opinion of others, which is just another way to pursue one's own will.[14]

---

[13]What is love, and how does it come to fill our hearts and motivate us? Paul does not answer this question in 1 Corinthians. In Romans 5:5 love is put into our hearts by the Holy Spirit. John observes that "We love because he first loved us" (1 Jn 4:19). Our love for others is spontaneous self-giving that resonates with the self-giving of God.

[14]For a piercing analysis of the idea of purity of heart and double-mindedness, see Søren Kierkegaard, *Purity of Heart Is to Will One Thing* (Radford, VA: Wilder Publications, 2008).

Modern critics. As one of the most perceptive insider critics of religion in the nineteenth century, Søren Kierkegaard complains that the reflective and theoretical attitudes of modern science and philosophy have captured ethics and religion.[15] Hence on the important matters dealt with in ethics and religion his contemporaries lack the passion that arises from personal conviction and are trapped in endless reflection, which prevents them from acting decisively. Scholarship degenerates into a pleasurable game, and seeking to comprehend becomes an excuse for not doing what we understand. Kierkegaard unmasks this secret hypocrisy with surgical skill:

> That is why human beings, sly as always with regard to God and divine truth, have directed all our attention to understanding, to knowing. We make out as if the difficulty were there and as if it would follow naturally that if we only understand the right it follows automatically that we would do it. What a grievous misunderstanding or what a sly fabrication! . . . [No] All my work orientated to knowing does not touch my life at all, its desires, its passions, its selfishness and leaves me completely unchanged—my *action* changes my life.[16]

Kierkegaard accuses biblical scholars and pastors of obfuscating "the existentially strenuous passages of the New Testament. We hush them up— and then we arrange things on easier and cheaper terms. We probably think that since we do not mention these passages God does not know they are in the New Testament."[17] People confound a discussion of what Jesus meant in

---

[15]I include in this section only insider critics of religion because I am focusing here on the defects of "default religion," not the idea of religion as such. Of course there is no shortage of external critics. Sam Harris, in *The End of Faith: Religion, Terror and the Future of Religion* (New York: W. W. Norton, 2004), blasts religion as irrational, anti-human and prone to violence. Richard Dawkins, in *The God Delusion* (Boston: Houghton Mifflin, 2006), asserts that belief in God has no basis in reason. To the contrary, natural science has now shown God to be unnecessary for explaining the physical world or providing a basis for morality. And Christopher Hitchens, in *God Is Not Great: How Religion Poisons Everything* (New York: Twelve, 2007), rehearses many of the bad arguments for the existence of God and refutes them with equally bad arguments against God's existence. He gives his chapters such ironic titles as "Religion Kills" and "Religion as an Original Sin," and peppers the book with his trademark sarcastic barbs.

[16]Søren Kierkegaard, *For Self-Examination, Judge for Yourself*, ed. and trans. Howard V. Hong and Edna H. Hong (Princeton, NJ: Princeton University Press, 1990), pp. 115-16, italics added.

[17]Søren Kierkegaard, *Søren Kierkegaard's Journals and Papers*, vol. 3, 2881, trans. Howard V. Hong and Edna H. Hong (Bloomington: Indiana University Press, 1975), p. 277. For a study of this theme in Kierkegaard, see John W. Elrod, *Kierkegaard and Christendom* (Princeton, NJ: Princeton University Press, 1981).

his teaching with actually becoming a follower of Jesus, substituting admiration for discipleship.[18] They confuse a bishop who sermonizes endlessly on Sundays but lives every other day as "shrewdly" as any man of the world with what the New Testament calls a "witness." An authentic witness is one who suffers for his profession of Christianity, not one who enjoys "worldly goods, advantages, luxurious enjoyment of the most exquisite refinements" for preaching "in the quite hours on Sundays."[19] The established form of "Christianity" has become a sort of anesthetic that dulls people's consciences to the demands of Jesus' teaching; it is a side show, a diversion that distracts them from awareness of God. Its function is to allow them to pursue their worldly self-interest in the name of being good Christians. "Christendom," Kierkegaard charges, "has done away with Christianity, without being quite aware of it. The consequence is that, if anything is to be done, one must try again to introduce Christianity into Christendom."[20]

One of the harshest critics of default religion in the twentieth century is also one of the century's greatest theologians. Karl Barth (1886-1968) considered human religiosity as it arises spontaneously from the human heart one of the greatest enemies of genuine Christian faith. Barth can speak of God's living and dynamic revelation in Jesus Christ as "the abolition of religion."[21] From the perspective of this revelation, religion as a purely human activity, whether crude or sublime, is unmasked as "unbelief."[22] Barth understands religion as any human effort to deal with the divine on our own terms and from our own resources. When we attempt this feat we replace God's revelation with "a concept of God arbitrarily and willfully evolved by man . . . by his own means, by his own human insight and constructiveness and energy."[23] God is imaged as a being that corresponds to human needs and wishes as they are conceived within our own self-understanding.

---

[18]Kierkegaard, *Training in Christianity*, p. 218: "What, then, is the distinction between 'an admirer' and 'a follower'? A follower is or strives to be what he admires; an admirer holds himself personally aloof, consciously or unconsciously, he does not discern that the object of his admiration makes a claim upon him to be or strive to be the thing he admires."

[19]Søren Kierkegaard, *Attack on Christendom*, trans. Walter Lowrie (Princeton, NJ: Princeton University Press, 1968), pp. 8-9.

[20]Kierkegaard, *Training in Christianity*, p. 31.

[21]Karl Barth, *Church Dogmatics* 1.2, ed. G. W. Bromiley and T. F. Torrance, trans. G. T. Thomson and Harold Knight (Edinburgh: T & T Clark, 1978), p. 297.

[22]Ibid., p. 299.

[23]Ibid., p. 302.

Once we imagine God in this way, we can begin to placate, flatter or bribe God to fulfill our needs and wishes. Barth sees this religious activity as the effort to secure and provide for oneself, to justify and sanctify oneself: "Unbelief is always man's faith in himself. And this faith invariably consists in the fact that man makes the mystery of his responsibility his own mystery, instead of accepting it as the mystery of God. It is this faith which is religion."[24] According to Barth, true religion exists only in response to God's word as empowered by the Holy Spirit. It never exists as a psychological or sociological fact that can be grasped in human terms. It takes shape as genuine faith, love and praise toward the Father, Son and Holy Spirit.[25] In contrast, the religion that arises from humanity, despite its show of piety toward its image of God, places faith in only itself, loves only itself and praises only itself.

A medieval critic. Bernard of Clairvaux (1090-1153), a French monk and head of his monastery, became well known for his sermons on the love of God. Late in his life Bernard received a request from Cardinal Haimeric of Rome to write an essay on why and how much we should love God. In response, he began his little composition *On Loving God* in this way: "You want me to tell you why God is to be loved and how much. I answer, the reason for loving God is God Himself; and the measure of love due to Him is immeasurable love."[26] Bernard conceives of our relationship with God as taking shape in four ascending stages or degrees: (1) we love ourselves for ourselves' sake; (2) we love God for ourselves' sake; (3) we love God for God's sake; and (4) we love ourselves for God's sake. Bernard's four stages of devotion are ideally suited to highlight the attitude I want to focus on in this chapter.

According to Bernard, "nature is so frail and weak that necessity compels her to love herself first; and this is carnal love, wherewith man loves himself first and selfishly. . . . This is not as the precept ordains but as nature directs."[27] At this stage we love only ourselves. I am both the object of my love and the goal for my love. In other words, I focus on myself to enjoy myself. I treat the outside world as an extension of myself, unworthy of my attention for

---

[24]Ibid., p. 314.

[25]Ibid., pp. 371-454.

[26]Bernard of Clairvaux, *On Loving God*, chap. 1, Christian Classics Ethereal Library, www
.ccel.org/ccel/bernard/loving_god.titlepage.html.

[27]Ibid., chap. 8.

its own sake. My only desire is to feel myself and expand myself.[28] But God will not allow us to remain self-enclosed and unaware of God's benefits. As Bernard observes,

> That we might not be ignorant of this, or vainly attribute to ourselves the beneficence of our Creator, God has determined in the depths of His wise counsel that we should be subject to tribulations. So when man's strength fails and God comes to his aid, it is meet and right that man, rescued by God's hand, should glorify him . . . in such wise man, animal and carnal by nature, and loving only himself, begins to love God by reason of that very self-love; since he learns that in God he can accomplish all things that are good, and that without God he can do nothing.[29]

Creation, says Bernard, contradicts experience too blatantly for us to remain deluded that we are the only reality. Through suffering, pain, failure, disappointment and guilt, we begin to realize that we are not alone. We are weak, vulnerable and needy. Illness and death await us. We cannot hope to compete with God. At this point we give up struggling against God and do what Satan would not do: "bow and sue for grace with suppliant knee."

At the second degree we begin to think about God and even to love him in a way, but it is still primarily for our own advantage. Though this type of interaction with God can be called "religious," it does not fully escape the self-centeredness of the first stage. We rise no higher than the natural religious impulse can take us. We begin attending church, praying and reading the Scriptures. We may even witness to others about our conversion and moral transformation. Knowing now that God is the source of everything needed, we seek God's blessings. But we do not yet enjoy God for God's sake. We merely acknowledge that we need God to supply things that stimulate enjoyment of ourselves. If we could escape suffering and secure what we want without dealing with God, we might take that route. That is, we have ourselves and our interests in mind when we obey, worship and pray to God. We have come to terms with the fact that God can reward and punish and none can escape his judgment. We are not stupid! We want God on our side, so we cut a deal and aim to please God.

---

[28]I will return to this attitude in my discussion of the esthetic outlook in chap. 4 on indifference.
[29]Bernard, *On Loving God*, chaps. 8 and 9.

Perhaps you become a great defender of orthodoxy, or religious freedom may be your passion. Maybe you are gifted at planning beautiful worship services, or you have a talent for building megachurches. Or suppose you spark a renaissance of Christian spirituality or ignite a social movement to elevate the poor and marginalized. Does devoting yourself to these good works guarantee that you have ceased to treat God as an object of envy? I think not. Without the love of God, orthodoxies and idealisms degenerate into ideologies that differ little from other private causes. Great religious projects and empires and movements turn out to be exercises in vanity. Unless we love God for God's sake, writing volumes of theology, preaching eloquent sermons and writing Christian music are just ways of drawing attention to ourselves.

Once we see the hypocrisy of this attitude it becomes apparent that stage-two religion still treats God merely as a means. We do not behave as Prometheus or Milton's Satan. We surrender, pledge to give God whatever God asks, but earnestly pray that God does not ask for too much. We want what God wants for us only when we want it anyway; we submit our wills to God in areas where we would prefer something else only because we must. For most of us, our stage-two religion does not manifest itself so obviously. We do not spend time considering how to get the most from God for the least coin. Rather, it manifests itself in our lack of passion for God, in our inability to love God with our whole heart. We do not consciously think of God as a threat, but neither do we see God as our soul's passion, the one thing for whom giving everything up is worth doing. We do not rise to the level of loving God for God's sake.

4

INDIFFERENCE

A Study in Thoughtlessness

In his June 1749 letter to Voltaire, the French atheist Denis Diderot fa-
mously ruled that it is "very important not to mistake hemlock for parsley;
but to believe or not believe in God, is not important at all. . . . [God has
taken his place among] *ces très sublimes et très inutiles vérités*" (those very
sublime and very useless truths).[1] But one does not have to become an
atheist to lose a feel for God's importance. Many people simply immerse
themselves in the practical affairs of life, in pleasure seeking or in maintaining an illusory identity. They do not defy God or attempt to use God as
a means; they just do not think about God or examine themselves before
God.[2] And the thoughts they have of God make no practical difference.
Such people may believe in God or not; they may even acknowledge the
truth of Christianity. Religious ideas can easily become just one more aspect
of the environment where one lives, to which one adjusts and then forgets.
In this chapter we will examine some ways of being indifferent and attempt
to bring to light the image of God embedded in the attitude of indifference.

---

[1]Denis Diderot, "Letter from Diderot to Voltaire, June 11, 1749," ed. Arthur M. Wilson,
Revue d'Histoire Littéraire de la France 51, no. 3 (July-September 1951): 258-60, quoted in
Michael Buckley, *At the Origins of Modern Atheism* (New Haven, CT: Yale University Press,
1987), p. 225.
[2]Indifference as an attitude toward God does not imply indifference toward everything. I am
not speaking of Stoic negation of all passion.

THE IDEA AND PRACTICE OF INDIFFERENCE

The indifferent do not adopt indifference as a conscious attitude. To decide to be indifferent to someone would not be genuine indifference but a kind of hostility, an intentional callousness designed to wound. The indifference toward God of which I am speaking is a byproduct of getting absorbed in something else. This indifference is as unaware of itself as it is of God. When you are threading a needle or driving a nail, you become so focused on the task at hand that you lose awareness of all else. To enjoy dark chocolate or a piece of great music fully you close your eyes. And nothing is so annoying as you stand in the presence of a great work of art or a sublime nature scene as chatter from the uncomprehending. When one sense becomes the avenue of pleasure you try to minimize the "noise" from the others.

The need to maintain focal awareness when working or experiencing pleasure is the common experience of humankind. But when these activities come to occupy every waking moment we slip into indifference toward God and others and become forgetful of ourselves. In indifference one focuses exclusively on the activities of work or play or pleasure. One never stops to raise one's eyes to heaven or look in the mirror to ask: What am I doing? Who am I? Why am I here? What does God think of me? Indifference toward God is a kind of existential secularity or practical atheism.

Ways of being indifferent. The esthetic. The first way of being indifferent to God is to immerse oneself so thoroughly in esthetic experience—which is the immediate impressions of the senses on consciousness—that one loses all awareness of God.[3] Søren Kierkegaard describes and analyzes extensively the myriad expressions of the esthetic form of existence. In the first part of *Either/Or*, Kierkegaard identifies the basic characteristic of the esthetic as immediacy, that is, immersion in feeling without the interruption of thought. For Kierkegaard, the epitome of the esthetic is the erotic, and the essence of the erotic is embodied in the figure of Don Juan, who is said to have seduced 1,003 women. The immediacy of the erotic cannot be expressed in words but only in music. And Mozart's opera *Don Juan* is the definitive and unsurpassable expression of this mood. But esthetic immediacy takes many forms,

[3]In an alternate but similar classification Alasdair MacIntyre thinks three characters typify our age: the rich esthete, the manager and the therapist (*After Virtue: A Study in Moral Theory*, 2nd ed. [Notre Dame, IN: University of Notre Dame Press, 1984], p. 30).

the erotic being only one. *Either/Or* contains several anonymous addresses given before meetings of the Fellowship of the Dead in which various esthetic themes are pursued.[4] The last speech, "The Rotation Method," addresses the problem of boredom. The author gives all sorts of absurd advice about how to avoid boredom, the chief of which is to avoid commitments— such as friendship and marriage—to cultivate novelty and learn the art of arbitrariness. He gives the following example:

> There was a man whose chatter I was obligated to listen to because of the circumstances. On every occasion, he was ready with a little philosophical lecture that was extremely boring. On the verge of despair, I suddenly discovered that the man perspired exceptionally much when he spoke. This perspiration now absorbed my attention. I watched how the pearl of perspiration collected on his forehead, and then united in a rivulet, slid down his nose, and ended in a quivering globule that remained suspended at the end of his nose. From that moment on, everything was changed; I could even have the delight of encouraging him to commence his philosophical instruction just in order to watch the perspiration on his brow and on his nose.[5]

The last and most famous section of *Either/Or (Part One)* is "Diary of the Seducer," which chronicles Johannes's seduction of a young girl, Cordelia, from a chance sighting until he abandons her to misery. Johannes's every glance, word and gesture has only one end, esthetic pleasure. Cordelia is nothing but an occasion for an infinite variety of esthetic experiences. She is a glass of wine that Johannes sniffs, swirls and observes from April to September before he drinks. For Johannes, maximum esthetic pleasure can be had only if taking possession of Cordelia's body is the final outcome of taking possession of her soul. For anyone who knows something of genuine love, entering the mind of this seducer and watching Cordelia fall under his power is soul-wrenching. Such a character seen from the ethical perspective

---

[4]In *Stages on Life's Way*, Kierkegaard continues to pursue the esthetic existence type. Five esthetes meet at a banquet to drink, eat, listen to Mozart's *Don Juan* and to give speeches on erotic love. The speeches differ wildly in their estimation of women and the wisdom of getting involved in erotic relationships; however, they all agree that the esthete must avoid marriage. Getting married places one in the ethical sphere and ends the life of immediacy.
[5]Søren Kierkegaard, *Either/Or*, pt. 1, trans. Howard and Edna Hong (Princeton, NJ: Princeton University Press, 1987), p. 299.

appears as inhuman or even nonhuman. And from a religious perspective he is revealed as demonic, as a devil who in his unhappiness can escape boredom briefly only by engulfing others in his misery.

In these sketches Kierkegaard portrays the esthetic life in its purity unmixed with moral or religious impulses. It is a life without ethical sensitivity, in which others are used merely as means and not cherished as ends. It possesses no awareness of being known by God, of being under God's command and accountable to God's judgment. Thankfully, we rarely encounter such pure esthetes. Yet we know of individuals who work or study because they must but live for sensual stimulation. They drink too much, drive too fast and party too hard. They "raise hell" on the weekends and talk about it during the week. And even the more responsible among us find ourselves engrossed in our own "safe" experiences: in music, cinema, athletic activities and hobbies. Esthetic experience can be integrated into a life that is ethically and religiously aware and thus raised to a higher level.[6] Unfortunately, there are still other ways to dull our awareness of God.

The conformist. While the goal of the esthete is pleasure, the goal of the conformist is success, success as it is defined by the dominant culture. The conformist invests his life energy in achieving and maintaining the appearance of financial security and abundance, respectability and personal well-being. Though the conformist derives pleasure from experiencing the trappings of success, the main driving force is the appearance of success. "Because success is whatever passes for success, it is in the regard of others that I prosper or fail to prosper."[7] Whether the conformist is working or shopping or playing, all is done with a view to what others do. Material gain, academic achievements and professional attainment; the car one drives, the house one lives in, the clothes one wears and the vacations one takes—nothing is done simply for the pleasure derived from the thing itself (the esthetic) or because of a moral imperative (the moral), much less in response to God's command or in view of God's judgment and grace (the religious). It is all done with at least one eye on the reactions of other people.

---

[6]Showing how this is true is the task of the main character of the second half of Kierkegaard's *Either/Or.*

[7]MacIntyre, *After Virtue*, p. 115. MacIntyre's words summarize the view of the sociologist Erving Goffman.

The conformist character type is skewered frequently in the literature of the nineteenth and twentieth centuries where they appear as dull bourgeoisie or soulless bureaucrats. In *Sickness Unto Death*, Kierkegaard describes many ways people live inauthentic lives.[8] *Worldliness* is his designation for what I am calling conformity.[9] The conformist appears to be a real person, an individual deliberately living his own life. But in reality he is "more like a puppet character that very deceptively imitates all the human externalities—would even have children with his wife. At the end of his life, one would have to say that one thing had escaped him: he had not become aware of God."[10] Kierkegaard further describes this mentality thus:

> By seeing the multitude of men about it, by getting engaged in all sorts of worldly affairs, by becoming wise about how things go in this world, such a man forgets himself, forgets what his name is (in the divine understanding of it), does not dare to believe in himself, finds it too venturesome a thing to be himself, far easier to be like others, to become an imitation, a number, a cipher in the crowd . . . spiritually understood, they have no self, no self for whose sake they could venture everything, no self before God—however *self*ish they may be for all that.[11]

Leo Tolstoy tells the story of one such man in *The Death of Iván Ilých*. Iván lived a respectable life as an ambitious but minor government official in late-nineteenth-century Russia. He was "a capable, cheerful, good-natured, and sociable man" who always faithfully discharged his duties. "And he considered his duty to be what was so considered by those in authority."[12] He attended law school, secured a respectable first job and got married. During the next few years Iván received several promotions, but always made a little less money than he "needed." With each advance he secured a

---

[8]Where I use the term *inauthentic* Kierkegaard uses the term *despair*. Despair is the condition of not willing to be oneself or despair of willing to be oneself; that is, either one wants to be a self that one is not and cannot be or one wants to be one's self in truth (that is, as one exists before God) but does not have the power to will it wholly.

[9]*Worldliness* "means precisely attributing infinite value to the indifferent" (*Sickness Unto Death*, ed. and trans. Howard V. and Edna H. Hong [Princeton, NJ: Princeton University Press, 1980], p. 50).

[10]Søren Kierkegaard, *Concluding Unscientific Postscript*, trans. Howard and Edna Hong (Princeton, NJ: Princeton University Press, 1992), pp. 244-45.

[11]Kierkegaard, *Sickness Unto Death*, pp. 51-53.

[12]Leo Tolstoy, *The Death of Iván Ilých and Other Stories*, trans. Louise and Aylmer Maude (London: Oxford University Press, 1971), p. 12.

more spacious house, but it was never quite big enough. At last, he landed a job that paid the 5,000 rubles per year he thought he deserved. He bought a spacious house with plenty of room for entertaining, and he adorned it with "all the things people of a certain class have in order to resemble other people of that class." Iván derived much pleasure from decorating his house and showing it off.[13]

In the process of decorating his new house, Iván fell from a stepladder and bruised his side. He did not think much of it at the time and seemed to recover quickly. But in the following weeks he began to feel a dull pain in his side and an odd taste in his mouth. These symptoms increased and began to spoil his pleasures, sour his disposition and interfere with his work. The doctors dispensed doubtful diagnoses, bad tasting medicine and technical language, all bathed, Iván thought, in indifference. His wife fussed at him continually for not taking his medicine, and his daughter seemed interested only in finding a suitable husband. As his health declined, Iván fought desperately against the thought that his illness would lead to his death. "He had to live thus all alone on the brink of the abyss, with no one who understood or pitied him." What vexed him most was the lie that everyone around him perpetuated: "that he was not dying but was simply ill, and that he only need keep quiet and undergo a treatment and then something very good would result."[14]

As Iván grew closer to death, he began a dialogue within his soul. As he listened, a question arose within him:

"What is it you want?"
"I want to live and not to suffer," his answer came back.
"To live? How?" his soul asked in return.
"Why, to live as I used to—well and pleasantly," Iván responded.
"As you lived before—well and pleasantly"? the voice echoed.

As Iván began to think back over his life, he attempted to recall the most pleasant moments of his life. But "all that had then seemed joys now melted before his sight and turned into something trivial and often nasty."[15] There

---

[13]Ibid., pp. 26, 29. "The pleasures connected with his work were pleasures of ambition; his social pleasures were those of vanity; but Iván Ilých's greatest pleasure was playing bridge."
[14]Ibid., pp. 39, 51.
[15]Ibid., p. 63.

were moments of joy in childhood but the further away from those first memories he got, the worse his life seemed. It came into his mind, "Maybe I did not live as I ought to have done." He tried to suppress this thought, but it came back to him one night about a month later: "What if my whole life has really been wrong?"[16] The next morning as his wife and daughter and doctor came into his room he realized the truth of his suspicion. "In them he saw himself—all that for which he had lived—and saw clearly that it was not real at all, but a terrible and huge deception which had hidden both life and death."[17] Soon after this event Iván began a bout of screaming and crying that lasted three days. He felt himself being thrust by an irresistible force into a dark hole. At the end of the three days, just two hours before he died, Iván realized, "Yes, it was all not the right thing . . . but that's no matter. . . . But what is the right thing?"[18] At that moment his wife and son came into his room. He looked at them and feeling sorry for them attempted to tell them of his compassion. Finally, he had found the "right thing," and his pain no longer tormented him. He searched his soul for the fear of death and did not find it. "There was no fear because there was no death," and in its place he found only "light." He exclaimed aloud, "What joy!"[19] And this joy did not depart in death.

The celebrity. A celebrity is someone who has captured the sustained attention of a public. Possessing an admirable quality or accomplishing something extraordinary does not make you a celebrity. For a celebrity, to exist is to be seen, thought of and talked about. Remaining in the public eye and keeping your name on its lips is the constant work of those who wish to maintain their celebrity status. People do not admire celebrities just for their talents or accomplishments. Fame demands to be admired for its own sake. A fan's devotion far exceeds the celebrity's genuine merit and finds its real object in an imaginary identity in whose power the fan longs to participate. The celebrity's real person is merely an occasion for creating an exaggerated image that exists only within the fan's imagination. What we enjoy about celebrities is the possibilities they give to our fantasy.

---

[16]Ibid., p. 69.
[17]Ibid.
[18]Ibid., p. 72.
[19]Ibid., p. 73.

The longing to be known and to exist in the thoughts of others and have your name on their lips apparently arises from something deep with human nature.[20] Feeling utterly alone, unknown and unloved by others makes life unbearable. We are pleased when others praise us, and we find it nearly impossible to remain undisturbed when others find fault with us. We want to know others and be known by them, to converse with friends and meet new people. But being a celebrity consists in being admired by people who do not know you and whom you do not know. What is desirable about this? There is no doubt that celebrity status bestows a sort of power on us and enhances our ability gain wealth. But does it protect against loneliness or add to our sense of being known and loved? Does it deepen our self-knowledge or help us gain a sense of proportion about our achievements and talents? Even if a friend praises you for a tangible accomplishment, you are wise not to take it too seriously. But when the multitudes press to catch a glimpse of you, you can be sure that it has little to do with the real you. Perhaps the greatest danger a celebrity faces is the temptation to believe the false images projected in the media and held in tenuous being by the imaginations of fickle fans. And the second greatest danger is loss of a sense identity and meaning when the public imagination transfers the illusory image to some other person. Even when we know it is whimsical and ephemeral, the praise of a crowd intoxicates us and fills our heads with fantasies of greatness.

That people desire fame and glory and wish to celebrate famous people is not a recent development. Every culture and every age celebrates its famous men and women: founders of nations, benefactors, generals, warriors, orators and philosophers. In the ancient world it was considered virtuous to aspire to glory and honor.[21] Those who achieved it were celebrated by statues,

---

[20]Augustine spends several pages discussing the temptation to succumb to the love of praise. He begins those thoughts with this warning: "The temptation is to wish to be feared or loved by people for no reason other than joy derived from such power, which is no joy at all. It is a wretched life, and vanity is repulsive" (*Confessions* 10.59, in *The Confessions of Saint Augustine*, trans. Henry Chadwick [New York: Oxford University Press, 1991], p. 213).

[21]For example, Plutarch, in his *Lives of Illustrious Men*, says of Aemilius Paulus that "in his early manhood, which fell at a time when Rome was flourishing with illustrious characters, he was distinguished for not attaching himself to the studies usual with the young men of mark of that age, nor treading the same paths to fame. For he did not practice oratory with a view to pleading causes, nor would he stoop to salute, embrace, and entertain the vulgar, which were the usual insinuating arts by which many grew popular. Not that

monuments and literature. The Roman writer Plutarch (c. A.D. 50-c. 120) wrote biographical sketches in praise of famous Greeks and Romans, most of whom were generals or politicians.[22] Augustine tells of how in his youth he had dedicated a book *On the Beautiful and the Fitting* to a certain Roman orator whom he admired. He had never met the man and had heard only a few lines from his speeches, yet because others had praised him, Augustine too loved him. And why did he love him? "That orator was of the type which I so loved that I wanted to be like him."[23] Augustine observes that had others hated the man, he too would have felt the same. He draws the conclusion: "Certainly the actual facts would have been no different, nor the man himself. The only alteration would have been in the feeling conveyed by the speakers. See how the human soul lies weak and prostrate when it is not yet attached to the solid rock of truth."[24] Augustine touches on the central problem with fame, ancient or modern, which is the disparity between words of praise and flattering images and the truth. A genuine and healthy life must be based on truth, but the flames of celebrity are fueled by falsehood.

Clearly, human nature has not changed since the age of Plutarch and Augustine, but the means of achieving fame and celebrating the famous have dramatically altered. In societies where people communicated orally or in costly manuscripts, most celebrities were local. After the invention of the mechanical printing press (1440), the publication of news pamphlets in Germany as early as 1498 and the advent of such newspapers as the *London Gazette* (1665) and *The Boston News-Letter* (1704), larger volumes of communication could flow at a faster rate over a bigger area.[25] Before the age of photography few ordinary people could have their images immortalized in sculpture or painting. But with the invention of the camera, the motion picture, television, computers, the Internet and mobile communication technology, a world of information and images from around the globe have become available nearly instantaneously. One

he was incapable of either, but he chose to purchase a much more lasting glory by his valor, justice, and integrity, and in these virtues he soon outstripped all his equals" ("Plutarch's Parallel Lives: Aemilius Paulus," About.com, http://ancienthistory.about.com/library/bl /bl_text_plutarch_aemiliuspaulus.htm).

[22]Ibid.

[23]Augustine, *Confessions* 6.23, trans. Chadwick, p. 66.

[24]Ibid.

[25]*Encyclopedia Britannica*, 9th ed., s.v. "newspapers."

can move from obscurity to worldwide notoriety overnight because of a plane crash, a televised beauty pageant, a reality television show or a talent search. And the number of celebrities and moderately famous people increases with advances in communication.

The cult of celebrity so pervades our lives and the means of placing our words and images in front of the world are so available that we are tempted to aspire to something like celebrity status for ourselves.[26] We rent space in the virtual world where we can display our pictures, our curriculum vitae and our contact information. We report to our "friends" what we had for breakfast this morning or what we are thinking this moment. We tell the world about our family vacations and even post our home movies. Or we can create a false identity for ourselves and interact with others as the exciting imaginary person we wish we were rather than the ordinary person we suspect we are. Few of us really think we will become famous because we send and receive 30,000 text messages a month or have 3,000 "friends" we are electronically linked to. But we are seduced by the celebrity view of existence; that is, we do not feel that we exist unless someone is viewing our image, reading our words and thinking about us. Our value is measured by the number of people who know our names, and who we are depends on what people think about us. Just as celebrities devote their best energies to maintaining a hold on the public's attention, we spend hours every day keeping our little publics aware of us. Our concern is with the image of us that exists in other people's minds rather than with who we really are, that is, who we are in relation to God.

In the same way that the esthete seeks only pleasure and the conformist seeks only success, the celebrity seeks only attention. As ideal types these three are distinct. In real life they are often combined. But whether we focus exclusively on one or combine them in various proportions, our attention, passion and energy are focused on the world and not on God. We possess little or no consciousness of God, no sense of God's relationship to anything we consider important and hence feel no desire to seek God. This lack of passion for God is what I mean by indifference.

---

[26]For the connection between the cult of celebrity and the contemporary epidemic of narcissism, see Jean M. Twenge and W. Keith Campbell, *The Narcissism Epidemic* (New York: Free Press, 2009), pp. 89-122.

The agnostic. The agnostic character may seem a bit out of place in a list that includes the esthete, the conformist and the celebrity. Perhaps this is because agnosticism is not a way of life that turns our attention away from God to the world but a theory that contends that we cannot know whether or not God exists. It claims that neither side can marshal decisive evidence to prove its case. According to Thomas Huxley, the thinker who invented the term *agnosticism*, "it is wrong for a man to say he is certain of the objective truth of a proposition unless he can provide evidence which logically justifies that certainty. That is what agnosticism asserts and in my opinion, is all that is essential to agnosticism."[27] Stated in this way, agnosticism sounds like a theory of knowledge or rationality. But that impression is misleading because the agnostic theory entails significant practical implications. Given a commitment to agnosticism, it makes sense to avoid basing our lives on either hypothesis. We would be wiser to turn our attention to the sources of good we know exist, all of which are worldly. Agnosticism, then, implies a life focused on the world and indifferent to God, or even to the question of God. Or, with a little more cynicism, we could say that agnosticism is a theoretical justification for a life of indifference, whether one lives as an esthete, a conformist or a celebrity.[28]

THE INDIFFERENT GOD OF INDIFFERENCE

In previous chapters we noted that the attitudes of defiance and subservience correspond to certain images of God and make sense only as responses to those images. For defiance, God demands all space and sucks up all the air. It sees God as an almighty power bent on domination. We can relate to that Power only with subservience or defiance. The attitude of indifference corresponds to a different image of God and makes sense only as a response to *that* image. But what sort of image of God would allow us to adopt a stance of indifference?

---

[27]Thomas H. Huxley, "Agnosticism," *Secular Web*, www.infidels.org/library/historical /thomas_huxley/huxley_wace/part_02.html.

[28]Agnosticism advocates the permanent undecidability of the question of God. But there is another kind of not knowing. At one time or another, many people have felt doubts about the existence of God. This condition is consistent with recognizing the importance of God and conducting a passionate search for God. The state of doubt for these souls is an agonizing suspension of life. In contrast, the agnostic finds comfort in dispensing with the question of God to focus on the search for pleasure, success or attention.

We are indifferent to things we do not think can (or will) help or harm us, to things that are neither beautiful nor ugly, neither good nor evil. The attitude of indifference implies that God is similarly irrelevant. However, the indifferent do not formulate a thought of God because the essence of indifference is that it does not think about God. In not thinking about God, it thinks of God as one whom it is possible to ignore without loss. Indifference treats God as an impersonal force like gravity or the energy emitted by the sun to which life has long since adjusted. It acts as if God were a boulder on the dark side of the moon. Whether it exists or not makes no difference to our lives. Some people even get as far as thinking of God as the origin and support for the world. But the world itself is what they love. If they discovered tomorrow that God does not exist, the world would still exist and nothing would be lost. The indifferent possess no consciousness of God as personal, that is, as acting, commanding, loving and guiding. Hence, for the indifferent, God is also indifferent.[29] Consequently, as Kierkegaard so poignantly put it, "spiritually understood, they have no self, no self for whose sake they could venture everything, no self before God."[30] The indifferent cannot entertain an idea of God that it would be a loss to lose! Their imagination is so stunted that they cannot imagine greatness or happiness beyond the mundane pleasure of habitual existence with its modulating highs and lows. The French spiritual writer François Fénelon captured this condition so well:

> It is not astonishing that men do so little for God and that the little which they do costs them so much. They do not know Him; scarcely do they believe that He exists; and the impression they have is rather a blind deference for general opinion than a lively and distinct conviction of the Divinity. They suppose it is so, because they do not dare to examine, and because they are indifferent in the matter, their souls being distracted by the inclination of their affections and passions for other objects; but their only idea of Him is of something wonderful, far off and unconnected with us.[31]

---

[29]This is another example of how when we think a certain way about God we exemplify the same characteristic. God and the self are bound together. If you think God is nothing, you will think of the self as nothing. This is why thinking of God as love is so important. To believe God is love implies that the human essence and action is also love. To anticipate future chapters, this is the only way God and the self can coexist happily.

[30]Søren Kierkegaard, *Sickness Unto Death,* ed. and trans. Howard V. and Edna H. Hong (Princeton, NJ: Princeton University Press, 1980), p. 53.

[31]François Fénelon, "Of the Necessity of Knowing and Loving God," in *Spiritual Counsel*

RETROSPECTIVE ON THE THREE ATTITUDES

In the previous chapters I examined three types of attitude toward God: defiance, subservience and indifference. I discussed them separately for the sake of conceptual clarity. In real life, however, we rarely find an individual who conforms wholly to the pure type. We combine these stances in our individual ways. We do not openly defy God, though often enough we pursue our own will secretly even when we suspect that it contradicts the divine will. Even those who would not admit to being moderately or even mildly religious consider themselves at least "spiritual." But I suspect that indifference toward God dominates most people's lives if measured by the duration of attention we give to God or level of our awareness of God. Though mutually exclusive as pure types, these three attitudes can reinforce each other if combined in the right proportions. If the goal of defiance is to do my own will in all things, this attitude harmonizes well with an indifference that puts the thought of God out of its mind better to seek its will. And if a little subservience in areas of lesser concern is the price paid for liberty to pursue my own will in the really important areas, the payoff seems worth the cost. *Hence the desire to realize oneself according to ones' own will underlies and unifies all three attitudes. One defies or obeys or ignores God for the sake of one's own will, which one identifies with one's very self.*[32]

---

on *Divers Matters Pertaining to the Inner Life*, Christian Classics Ethereal Library, www
.ccel.org/ccel/fenelon/progress.iii.iii.html.

[32]Again we find that the modern self secretly understands itself as "pure will." Its essence is unlimited will or ambition but it is burdened with accidental attributes that limit it and circumstances that hold it back from achieving its dreams of unlimited expansion. It conceives God, too, in such terms. Such an understanding of divine and human selfhood inevitably produces competition, conflict, envy and domination. I will address this secret directly in the next chapters.

5

THE GOD OF THE MODERN SELF

In his spiritual autobiography, *My Religious Experience* (1890), Samuel Putnam records his fall into atheism. His condemnation of religion is uncompromising: "The last superstition of the human mind is the superstition that religion in itself is a good thing, though it might be free from dogma. I believe, however, that the religious feeling, as feeling, is wrong, and the civilized man will have nothing to do with it."[1] In Putnam's view, God, or the idea of God, is a moral offense to human dignity and freedom. A good person *ought not* to believe. Hence Putnam announces his objective: "to vindicate liberty, I must dethrone God."[2] What sort of picture of God could generate such antipathy?

In the previous chapters we discovered that contemporary culture pictures God in a way that makes God a threat to our freedom and dignity. Whether we relate to God in defiance, subservience or indifference, we treat God as unworthy of our complete trust and love. In this chapter we will take a closer look at that threatening image of God and describe how it pits us against God. I want to show why this image leads us to resent and envy God.

---

[1]Samuel Putnam, *My Religious Experience* (New York, n.p., n.d.), p. 15, quoted in James Turner, *Without God, Without Creed: The Origins of Unbelief in America* (Baltimore: John Hopkins University Press, 1985), p. 224.

[2]Putnam, *My Religious Experience*, pp. 82-83, quoted in Turner, *Without God, Without Creed*, p. 211.

THE SUPERHUMAN GOD

Consider again my six-year-old thoughts about God. I imagined that God possesses all the good things I lacked and the powers I desired. God gets to do whatever God wants, but we are restricted on every side. *We* can imagine doing infinitely more than we can do, but *God* has power to fulfill every wish. God enjoys unlimited knowledge and wealth. We do not. In short, God is the sum of everything we desire to be, a kind of superhuman being, possessing human characteristics and desires without human limits—an enviable state indeed!

If the superhuman image of God were merely a childhood fantasy most people would grow out of it. It would not be worth discussing. But it is so natural to our minds that it is almost the inevitable beginning point for all thinking about God. The history of the world's religions confirms this theory. In the ancient religions practiced by Israel's ancestors and neighbors—including Mesopotamia, Egypt, Canaan and Greece—religious devotion focused on the powers of nature. For these religions, "nature is but the manifestation of the divine."[3] Living in an age before advanced technology, ancient peoples experienced nature intimately. It was clear to them that the mysterious powers revealed in sun, earth, rivers, mountains, storms, death, oceans and other natural forces were of a higher order than human beings.[4] We obviously depend on natural forces and live at their mercy; hence, these powers demand our worship. For polytheistic religions the divine is whatever is higher than human beings in the order of being. According to Anderson, "the gods and goddesses, whose loves and wars dramatize the conflicts of nature and the cyclical movement of the seasons, are personifications of natural forces."[5] Even today, this view of the divine exerts its attraction on the mind.[6]

---

[3]Henri Frankford et al., *Before Philosophy: The Intellectual Adventure of Ancient Man* (Baltimore: Penguin, 1960), p. 241.

[4]For a classic treatment of the nature of archaic religion still worth reading, see Mircea Eliade, *The Sacred and The Profane: The Nature of Religion* (New York: Harcourt Brace Jovanovich, 1959).

[5]Bernhard W. Anderson, *From Creation to New Creation* (Minneapolis: Fortress Press, 1994), p. 20.

[6]Robert Sokolowski, *The God of Faith and Reason: Foundations of Christian Theology* (Washington, DC: Catholic University of America Press, 1995), p. xi. See especially chapter two, "Pagan Divinity," pp. 12-20.

All things in the universal order, whether higher or lower, tend to be measured from the human point of view. Lower things lack qualities and powers that human beings have, and higher things possess those qualities and powers in greater measure. The Babylonians, Egyptians and Greeks pictured the gods as humanlike beings who were powerful and immortal. Their myths attributed to the gods the moral defects to which human beings are subject. Despite their defects, their power and status were no less enviable than my childhood image of God. Such philosophers as Plato, Aristotle and Plotinus criticized the mythic picture of the gods as too human; nevertheless, these philosophers also grounded their thinking about God in human nature. But they attempted to remove contradictions and evil from the concept of the divine and attribute only humanity's highest qualities to God.[7] God is the most perfect being, possessing to the full the life we want, perfect and eternal. Thus even this refined concept of divinity can excite envy and generate enmity toward God.

Not everything in the pagan view of the divine is false from a Christian point of view, any more than my childhood picture of God is totally false. On the contrary, Greek philosophers performed a great service to all religious people by insisting that religion and theology should learn to appreciate the value of rational consistency. The Bible, however, introduces a new understanding of the divine derived not from observing nature or from humanity's experience of itself. It finds its origin in God's self-revelation in Israel's history and in Jesus Christ. I will reserve fuller explanation of this new way later; for now I want to consider how Christian thinkers used the philosophical methods developed by the Greeks to explain the Christian view of God and thereby unintentionally reinforced a view of God that the modern self finds disturbing.[8]

---

[7]Plotinus, *The Enneads* 5.1.9, 5.4.2, trans. Stephen McKenna, abr. John Dillon (London: Penguin Books, 1991), pp. 358, 389. For further study of Plotinus, see Lloyd P. Gerson, ed., *The Cambridge Companion to Plotinus* (New York: Cambridge University Press, 1996).

[8]Unlike many contemporary theologians I do not believe that patristic and medieval theologians betrayed the original Jewish gospel and substituted Greek metaphysics in its place. The modern form of this view was begun by the nineteenth-century liberal theologian Albrecht Ritschl and was continued by Adolf von Harnack and Wilhelm Herrmann. See Albrecht Ritschl, "Metaphysics and Theology," in *Albrecht Ritschl: Three Essays*, trans. Philip Hefner (Philadelphia: Fortress Press, 1972); Wilhelm Herrmann, *Die Metaphysik in der Theologie* (Halle, 1876); Adolf von Harnack, *History of Dogma*, 3rd ed., vol. 1, trans. Neil Buchanan (New York, 1958). For my criticism of the Ritschl-Harnack theory, see *Great Is the Lord* (Grand Rapids: Eerdmans, 2008), pp. 266-69.

It makes sense from a Christian point of view to think of God as the most perfect being. Augustine of Hippo asserts that God must be the greatest reality conceivable and confesses to God that no one is "capable of conceiving that which is better than you, who are the supreme and highest good."[9] We cannot possibly consider something imperfect and corruptible as God. We reserve the word *God* for the best.[10] In his treatise *On Christian Doctrine,* Augustine observes:

> For when the one supreme God of gods is thought of, even by those who believe that there are other gods, and who call them by that name, and worship them as gods, their thought takes the form of an endeavor to reach the conception of a nature, than which nothing more excellent or more exalted exists. . . . All, however, strive emulously to exalt the excellence of God: nor could anyone be found to believe that any being to whom there exists a superior is God. And so all concur in believing that God is that which excels in dignity all other objects.[11]

Later Christian thinkers in the West followed Augustine and developed his ideas in greater detail. Anselm of Canterbury (c. 1033-c. 1109) spoke of God as the greatest conceivable being. As the most perfect being, God is not limited by space, time, matter and other characteristics of creatures. "God is whatever it is better to be than not be. . . . What good, therefore, does the supreme good lack, through which every good is?"[12] Hence, we must think of God as "just, truthful, blessed, and whatever it is better to be than not to be. For it is better to be just than not just; better to be blessed than not blessed."[13] Thomas Aquinas (c. 1225-1274) argues that since "God is the most noble of beings" God is free from every defect and limitation.[14] For Aquinas,

---

[9]Augustine, *The Confessions of Saint Augustine* 7.4, trans. Henry Chadwick (New York: Oxford University Press, 1991), p. 114. For a study of Anselm's perfect being theology, see Katherine A. Rogers, *Perfect Being Theology* (Edinburgh: Edinburgh University Press, 2002).

[10]Augustine, *Confessions* 7.4, trans. Chadwick. He says, for "had it been the case that you [God] are not incorruptible, I could in thought have attained something better than my God" (p. 114).

[11]Augustine, *On Christian Doctrine* 1.6-7, Nicene and Post-Nicene Fathers 1st ser. (Peabody, MA: Hendrickson, 1994), 2:524.

[12]Anselm of Canterbury, "Proslogium" 3, in *Saint Anselm, Basic Writings,* 2nd ed., trans. S. N. Deane (La Salle, IL: Open Court, 1968), pp. 8-9.

[13]Ibid., p. 11.

[14]Thomas Aquinas, *Summa Theologica* 1.3.1, in *Basic Writings of Saint Thomas Aquinas,* ed. Anton C. Pegis (New York: Random House, 1945), 1:25-26.

every good characteristic derives from God and resembles God, just as every effect resembles its cause.[15]

Later medieval theology emphasized the freedom of God. In an effort to protect divine freedom from encroachment from supposedly necessary laws of being, logic and morality, Duns Scotus (c. 1265-1308) and William of Ockham (c. 1285-1347) and Gabriel Biel (1420-1495) argued for the priority of the divine will over the divine intellect. All agree that nothing can withstand God by a vicious necessity, but some came to think of the divine will as completely arbitrary. In God's omnipotence God exercises absolute freedom and can do anything with no moral or rational restraints. Through these thinkers voluntarism (as this attitude is called) passed over into Protestant theology, thereby having a huge influence on the formation of the modern world. Since the attributes of God are understood as human qualities freed from limitation and perfected, it is easy to see how early modern voluntarism could easily morph into the notion that both God and human beings are essentially "pure willing, pure activity, or pure power."[16] Clearly, such a view of God and humanity pits us against each other as competitors or enemies; for there are no rules or structures to serve as a basis for harmony among arbitrary wills. Sheer power determines the relationship.[17]

Augustine, Anselm, Aquinas and the others were very sophisticated thinkers and as people of deep faith and spirituality were aware of the

---

[15]Aquinas develops this point in *Summa Theologica* 1.4.3, 1.44.1.

[16]Michael Allen Gillespie, *The Theological Origins of Modernity* (Chicago: University of Chicago, 2008), p. 35. Gillespie documents the contributions of Ockham (or Occam) and the nominalist tradition inspired by him to the formation of modernity. In an argument that supports my thesis that our contemporaries tend to place God and humanity in competition, Gillespie contends that modernity, rather than ridding itself of the idea of God, merely transfers "his attributes, essential powers, and capacities to other entities or realms of being" (p. 274).

[17]Gillespie understands Descartes's philosophical project as an effort to defeat the God of pure will and make room for humanity's freedom and knowledge. The voluntarist view of God made it impossible to know that we have freedom or that our knowledge of nature is reliable. For God could change the past or the laws of mathematics or make right wrong or wrong right. Descartes hoped to overcome the threat of the arbitrary will of God by grounding knowledge in the self-certainty of the human mind and will. In doing so, however, he had to give human beings the same pure self-positing will as he understood God to possess. In doing so he laid the ground for the development of modern nihilism, which freed the arbitrary human will to reconstruct the given world in any way it chooses. Since the world is a product of arbitrary will, there are no necessary structures that must be respected or laws that are impossible to change. See Michael Allen Gillespie, *Nihilism Before Nietzsche* (Chicago: University of Chicago Press, 1995).

danger of thinking of God simply as a perfected and unlimited image of ourselves. As Christian believers, they understood that our knowledge of God rests on revelation and that all our language about God is analogous. They would have emphasized as strongly as I will in the coming chapters that God is not a threat to our freedom or dignity and that envy of God makes no sense. But not even the best teachers can protect against every misunderstanding. The image of an all-powerful and all-knowing God puts us in the apparent dilemma discussed in earlier chapters. We seem constrained to choose from among Promethean defiance, lamb-like subservience or sleepy indifference. Some modern thinkers attempt to escape this dilemma by denying the existence of God altogether.[18]

I am not the first to notice our tendency to conceive of God as a superhuman being. Modern atheism uses this observation as one of its chief arguments against the existence of God. In 1770 the French atheist Baron d'Holbach published *The System of Nature*, a book that became known as the "atheist's bible." In volume two of this work he asserted: "Man having placed himself in the first rank in the universe, has been desirous to judge of everything after what he saw within himself, because he has pretended that in order to be perfect it was necessary to be like himself. Here is the source of all his erroneous reasoning upon nature and his Gods."[19] Seventy years later, in the 1840s, Ludwig Feuerbach articulated an ingenious theory in his book *The Essence of Christianity*. Feuerbach argued that we form the idea of God by projecting our own existence into the heavens. Each existing human being is finite but the human essence is infinite. We arrive at the idea of God by imagining that the infinite human essence exists as an actual being. We experience being, knowing, being present, loving, living and other human activities as finite and limited, but we can imagine the infinite maximum of these qualities as possessed by a real being—God. Feuerbach summarizes: "The necessary turning-point of history is therefore the open confession, that the consciousness of God is nothing else than the consciousness of the species . . . that there is no other essence which man can

---

[18]Michael J. Buckley, *At the Origins of Modern Atheism* (New Haven, CT: Yale University Press, 1987), tells the story of how Enlightenment era philosophers and scientists, Christians all of them, prepared the way for atheism by limiting the reasons to believe in God to those directly supported by the new natural science pioneered by Galileo and brought to maturity by Isaac Newton.

[19]Baron d'Holbach, *The System of Nature* (Kitchener, ON: Batoche Books, 1868), 2:30.

think, dream of, imagine, feel, believe in, wish for, love and adore as *absolute*, than the essence of human nature itself."[20] Karl Marx, Sigmund Freud and many others have defended variations of this projection thesis.

I do not raise the projection problem to undermine faith but to warn of the danger of thinking of God exclusively from a center within ourselves. The oppressive image of God makes atheism look attractive because ceasing to believe removes the threat of divine tyranny, and the projection theory makes atheism look likely by explaining away belief with a plausible psychological explanation. With that said, I would be irresponsible if I did not explain why the projection argument fails. Assume that God really exists. Even with this assumption we would still need to form a conception of God by attributing to God the very highest and best qualities we can imagine. Feuerbach's "discovery" that we think of God as possessing infinitely those excellent qualities we find in ourselves reveals nothing theologians did not already know. It cannot count for or against the existence of God. Or, to put it in a slightly different way, suppose you have other reasons for believing that God really exists and really is all-knowing, all-powerful, infinite and loving; for example, suppose that one believes that God spoke and acted in relation to Israel and in Christ, or that nature's power and beauty points to God as its cause. In that case, thinking of God as possessing infinitely qualities that we possess in a finite way would be essentially correct. Hence the mere observation that we construct a concept of God as a being who possesses human qualities to an infinite degree is not enough to prove this belief false. Clearly, the projection theory does not contribute to an argument for atheism unless you presuppose that belief in God is false or undesirable; so unless you agree with that assumption, you will not find the theory very compelling.[21]

---

[20]Ludwig Feuerbach, *The Essence of Christianity*, trans. George Eliot (Amherst, NY: Prometheus Books, 1989), p. 270.

[21]See Alvin Plantinga, *Warranted Christian Belief* (New York: Oxford University Press, 2000), for his response to the Marx/Freud thesis. See also Scott A. Shalkowski, "Atheological Apologetics," in *Contemporary Perspectives on Religious Epistemology*, ed. R. Douglas Geivett and Brendan Sweetman (New York: Oxford University Press, 1992), pp. 58-77. Shalkowski shows that much of modern atheism assumes that belief in God is allied with oppressive and illiberal social powers. This makes atheism's case much easier rhetorically without making it stronger intellectually. He imagines a situation, however, where atheism is allied with such powers. In these circumstances atheism would have the burden of proof.

THE SUPERHUMAN BEING'S POWERS

Let us consider a few of the traditional divine attributes in detail and notice how disturbing they sound when heard as the qualities of a God who is essentially arbitrary power. Most people believe that God possesses perfect freedom and supreme dignity. Nothing sinister or threatening arises from this belief alone. However, most people also tend to think of freedom, divine or human, as the ability to do whatever you want. Conceived in this way, freedom in the fullest sense can be exercised by God alone, for only God is all-powerful. All things depend on God, and nothing can resist God's will.

The modern concept of dignity is closely related to the idea of freedom.[22] We often understand dignity as the right and authority to do as we wish without permission or help from someone in a higher position. Thought of in this way, our dignity is relative to our place in the pecking order. But God's dignity knows no limit, for God relies on no one for authority or power to act. All authority, rights and dignity derive from God. If the view I just described is the true nature of freedom and dignity, only God can exercise genuine freedom and possess true dignity. Other beings have power and authority to do as they wish only within the limits God permits.

Viewing divine and human freedom in this way inevitably places them in tension so that obeying God appears to be surrendering freedom and disobeying God looks like a way of asserting it. Submission to God looks like an affront to our dignity, and defiance feels like an assertion of our dignity. Prometheus returns to tell us again: "None is free but Zeus." And the defiant words of Milton's Satan are given revived plausibility: "To bow and sue for grace with suppliant knee. . . . That were an ignominy and shame beneath this downfall."

Omnipotence feared. Consider how the attribute of omnipotence might strike one who thinks of arbitrary power as the essential quality of God and humanity. Power can be understood as the ability to control the circumstances that produce happiness and to render ourselves invulnerable to threats. The Bible proclaims God's unlimited power:

"My purpose will stand,
 and I will do all that I please." . . .

---

[22]See chap. 6 for further analysis of the modern concepts of freedom and dignity.

What I have said, that I will bring about;
what I have planned, that I will do. (Is 46:10-11)

The Apostles' Creed begins, "We believe in God the Father, Almighty." Augustine says that God

> without doubt can as easily refuse to permit what He does not wish, as bring about what He does wish. And if we do not believe this, the very first sentence of our creed is endangered, wherein we profess to believe in God the Father Almighty. For He is not truly called Almighty if He cannot do whatsoever He pleases, or if the power of His almighty will is hindered by the will of any creature whatsoever. . . . The will of the Omnipotent is never defeated.[23]

While God enjoys omnipotence, we can only dream of such power and must find a way to enjoy life as much as possible without it. But the image of an arbitrary, superhuman God looms as a threat even to finite happiness. Power is the ability to control your circumstances. If God controls God's circumstances completely and *I* am part of God's "circumstances," will not I be robbed of all control and denied any significant human freedom? If happiness requires optimum circumstances and I have no control over my circumstances, happiness may forever remain beyond my reach. The conclusion seems obvious: none but God can be happy. No wonder we sometimes harbor envy and feel resentment toward God. We cannot help but desire freedom, dignity and happiness, yet these appear to be under constant threat from God, who alone possesses them securely.

Omnipresence dreaded. Think about divine omnipresence and omniscience as the attributes of a God whose essence is arbitrary will. As these attributes are described in the Bible and by Christian thinkers, God dwells in all things and knows all things. Nothing can hide from God's gaze or escape God's reach. The writer of Psalm 44 reminds us:

> If we had forgotten the name of our God
> or spread out our hands to a foreign god,

---

[23]Augustine, *Enchiridion* 96 and 102; Augustine, *On The Holy Trinity, Doctrinal Treatises, Moral Treatises*, vol. 3, Nicene and Post Nicene Fathers, 1st ser., ed. Philip Schaff (Grand Rapids: Eerdmans, 1971), pp. 267, 270.

would not God have discovered it,

since he knows the secrets of the heart? (Ps 44:20-21)

And the writer of Hebrews declares, "Nothing in all creation is hidden from God's sight. Everything is uncovered and laid bare before the eyes of him to whom we must give account" (Heb 4:13). In his *Epistle to the Corinthians* (A.D. 96), Clement of Rome asks, "Whither, then, shall any one go, or where shall he escape from God who comprehends all things?"[24] Clement of Alexandria (c. 150-c. 215) explains that "God is very near in virtue of that power which holds all things in its embrace. . . . For the power of God is always present, in contact with us."[25] For Hilary of Poitiers (c. 315-368), God is "infinite, for nothing contains God and God contains all things; God is eternally unconditioned by space, for God is illimitable."[26] Thomas Aquinas tells us that "God is in all things by God's power, inasmuch as all things are subject to God's power; God is by God's presence in all things, inasmuch as all things are bare and open to God's eyes; God is in all things by God's essence, inasmuch as God is present to all as the cause of their being."[27]

These divine characteristics can comfort us with the thought that God is always near to help and guide, but they can also underline God's ability to judge and punish. In either case we are told that God is inescapable, and even if we have no conscious wish to escape God we may not be altogether comfortable with this idea. We can at least hide our thoughts from every other being; we would not give even our most beloved friend access to our

---

[24]Clement of Rome, *The Epistle to the Corinthians* 28, in *Apostolic Fathers, Justin Martyr, Irenaeus*, vol. 1, Ante-Nicene Fathers, ed. Alexander Roberts and James Donaldson (Grand Rapids: Eerdmans, 1971), p. 12. For other references, see Stanislaus J. Grabowski, *The All-Present God: A Study of St. Augustine* (St. Louis: B. Herder, 1954), pp. 33-34. I have substituted the word *God* for the pronoun *Him* in this quote.

[25]Clement of Alexandria, *Stromata* 2.2, cf. 7.2, in *Fathers of the Second Century*, vol. 2, Ante-Nicene Fathers, ed. Alexander Roberts and James Donaldson (Grand Rapids: Eerdmans, 1979), p. 348. I have substituted the word *God* for the pronoun *He* in this quote.

[26]Hilary of Poitiers, *On the Trinity* 2.6, in *St. Hilary of Poitiers and John of Damascus*, vol. 9, Nicene and Post-Nicene Fathers, 2nd ser., ed. Philip Schaff and Henry Wace (Grand Rapids: Eerdmans, 1979), p. 53. I have substituted the word *God* on four occasions for the pronouns *Him* and *He* in this quote.

[27]Aquinas, *Summa Theologica* 1.8.1-4, in *Basic Writings of Saint Thomas Aquinas*, ed. Anton C. Pegis (New York: Random House, 1945), 1:67-69. For a developmental view of Aquinas's thinking on divine omnipresence, see Adrian Fuerst, *An Historical Study of the Doctrine of the Omnipresence of God in Selected Writings Between 1220-1270* (Washington, DC: Catholic University of America Press, 1951), pp. 171-200. I have substituted the word *God* or *God's* for the pronouns *Him*, *He* and *His* in this quote.

every whim. We guard our privacy as closely as we guard our very selves. We view our "self" as that mysterious reality of our most intimate and private being. We associate existing with being independent, with having our own unique space that excludes other existing things. We want a place that no one else can enter, fortified against invasion, so it would not be strange if we regarded a loss of privacy as a loss of the self's integrity. If God is omniscient and omnipresent, however, we have no control over God's knowledge of us or presence in the intimate details of our lives. Who has not felt some resentment at this suggestion!

THE SUPERHUMAN GOD'S INNER SELF

One last aspect of the image of the arbitrary God demands our attention. In our dealings with each other we distinguish between others' inner selves and their characteristics and powers. I can imagine being myself even if I were smarter, faster, stronger or younger. I would remain me even if I had better eyesight or keener hearing. Would I become a different person if I became more compassionate and gained greater patience? Having a completely different body would not change my inner self.[28] Chapter six will be devoted to the human self, but it will help us to make a preliminary observation here: I understand my inner self to remain self-identical through all external changes. Put otherwise, I think of my real "self" as having no unchangeable characteristics. Nothing I *possess* defines me. And what I *am* seems to be a mysterious self without defining qualities. So, what am I and who am I, and what makes me myself?

The empty self. We tend also to distinguish between God's unchanging self and God's characteristics. We imagine that God has an inner self and to that self are added those attributes and powers that enable God to act as God. God's inner identity is not determined by God's added qualities. We think that God would still have the same inner self if God were not as free or powerful or compassionate or knowledgeable as God is. We may believe that God securely possess those characteristics and powers. We may be

---

[28]This understanding of the self, which seems so natural to us, became plausible only after the creation of the "modern self," which can think of itself as buffered, isolated and insulated from external reality. Premodern people did not exist as selves only in this inner world. For this contrast, see Charles Taylor, *A Secular Age* (Cambridge, MA: Harvard University Press, 2007), pp. 25-89.

certain that God will never die, lose power or commit a sin, but we still think of God as a "self" distinct from the powers God possesses. Like a human self, God's "self" possesses no unchangeable characteristics, no essential attributes. In principle, God's "self" could possess a completely different set of attributes.

This way of thinking explains why a six-year old might get the idea that he could have been born God. God is a mysterious "self" without essential characteristics, *and so am I*. There is no difference between our inner selves. The difference lies in the external powers and characteristics we possess. So why does God possess them and not us? How did God come by them? These questions remind us of the theologies of Prometheus and Milton's Satan. According to Prometheus, mere chance and necessity made Zeus great. And for Milton's Satan, God has no intrinsic right to the power God wields. God is merely one "whom thunder hath made greater." Whether in defiance or subservience, as long as we understand God in this way, we cannot help but envy and resent God.

The self as will. One more issue remains. As I said earlier, we tend to view the human and divine selves as having no essential attributes because we want to maximize the self's freedom. Possessing essential characteristics appears to restrict freedom because it limits our ability to choose an identity for ourselves. But upon reflection we can see that a self must possess at least one essential quality. If the self had no essential characteristics we could say nothing about it; nor could we explain why the self possesses the characteristics and powers it does or why it acts as it does. It would be nothing at all. Under all conditions, with or without other attributes, *we treat the self as having will*. It wills to be, to expand, possess and control. The self's one essential attribute, then, is unlimited will or desire.[29] If it is empty in every

---

[29]Will is more fundamental than desire. Desire is occasional and focuses on a particular object, whereas will is constant and omnidirectional. Arthur Schopenhauer (1788-1860) brought this intuition to metaphysical expression in his theory of will. He argued that will is the metaphysically fundamental reality and that each and every being exists and acts as a manifestation of that will. And this drive is the source of all conflict and suffering. Under the influence of Buddhism, he argued that the solution to conflict and suffering was rooting out the will to live. Early in his career Friedrich Nietzsche became a disciple of Schopenhauer but later abandoned him. Nietzsche retained the idea that the reality of all things is will. Unlike Schopenhauer and in opposition to him, Nietzsche attempted to develop a positive philosophy of life to overcome the nihilism he saw on the horizon. For Nietzsche's relationship to Schopenhauer, see Julian Young, *A Philosophical Biography of Friedrich Nietzsche*

other respect, it is full of desire to bring all other things into itself. It is easy to see that this definition of the self guarantees competition and conflict among selves—among human beings and between human beings and God. If the essential goal of a self is to expand itself to infinity, only one self can achieve its essential fullness. Others must defy, submit or hide. By definition, God is a barrier, a limit, a competitor or at best a means to our ends. This way of understanding God and humanity sets the divine will against the human will, "which appears to achieve independence only in the kind of arbitrary self assertion which appears to be the mark of divinity."[30]

Now we can see in greater depth that the common image of God as a superhuman being is exclusionary and competitive. According to the view I wish to challenge, if God has complete freedom, other beings can have no freedom. If God has all power, other beings can have no say. If God is everywhere, there is no place for us. If God knows all, we can have no privacy. God seems to be at the center of all things, pulling them into himself like some gigantic black hole, not allowing even one atom to escape. If Samuel Putman lay awake at night contemplating the all-consuming superhuman being we have considered in this chapter, no wonder he concluded: "to vindicate liberty, I must dethrone God."[31]

(Cambridge: Cambridge University Press, 2010). For brief but helpful summaries of the careers and thought of these two thinkers, see R. Audi, ed., *The Cambridge Dictionary of Philosophy*, 2nd ed. (New York: Cambridge University Press, 1999).

[30]Colin Gunton, *The One, the Three and the Many: God, Creation and the Culture of Modernity* (Cambridge: Cambridge University Press, 1993), p. 58.

[31]Putman, *My Religious Experience*, pp. 82-83, quoted in Turner, *Without God, Without Creed*, p. 211.

6

THE SECRET ASPIRATIONS
OF THE MODERN SELF

As Plato and Aristotle observe, human beings seek what they think is good and resist whatever they think blocks access to this good.[1] Desire and ambition drive us from one apparent good to another with no obvious stopping place. One achievement becomes a platform from which to strive for another. When I was a child I wanted to be a teenager. After I became a teen I wanted to be twenty-one. After I got my baccalaureate degree I immediately set my sights on a master's degree, then a Ph.D. and then . . . At each stage we delude ourselves into thinking the next thing will satisfy. But there is no reason to believe that a little more freedom or power or wealth or honor will end the striving. Our ambitions are insatiable.

In chapter five I described a perspective that pictures God as a threat to the dearest goods of life: freedom, dignity and happiness. In this chapter I want to depict the image of humanity that corresponds to this divine image, the human being for whom it is natural to envy and compete with God. Not surprisingly, the two images look very much alike, for just as we tend to think of God as the idealized essence of humanity, we conceive of humanity as a potential God. We strive to become what God is already. Our ambition to catch up with God explains much of what we do and defines our relationship with God and others.

---

[1]Aristotle, *Rhetoric* 1.10, in *The Basic Writings of Aristotle*, ed. Richard McKeon (New York: Random House, 1941), pp. 1360-61. For studies of both Plato's and Aristotle's thinking on desire for the good, see Sergio Tanenbaum, ed., *Desire, Practical Reason, and the Good: Classical and Contemporary Perspectives* (New York: Oxford University Press, 2010).

What Is Freedom?

In my previous discussions of freedom I assumed a commonsense understanding of freedom. It is now time to think more precisely about it. In his
monumental study of the idea of freedom in Western thought, Mortimer
Adler shows that thinkers have held three distinct views of freedom: (1)
circumstantial freedom of self-realization, (2) natural freedom of self-
determination, and (3) acquired freedom of self-perfection.[2] We will now
consider each of these.

Self-realization. Circumstantial freedom of self-realization is the most
commonsense view of freedom. It defines freedom as the power to realize
our desires if circumstances permit. This view is more typical of modern
authors than of ancient ones. The seventeenth-century political philosopher
Thomas Hobbes (1588-1679), for example, says that "a freeman is he that, in
those things which by his strength and wit he is able to do, is not hindered
to do what he has the will to do."[3] John Locke asserts that freedom is "the
idea of a power in any agent to do or forebear any particular action, according to the determination of thought of the mind, whereby either of
them is preferred to the other."[4] And for David Hume, the eighteenth-
century Scottish philosopher, freedom means "a power of acting or not

---

[2]Mortimer Adler, *The Idea of Freedom: A Dialectical Examination of the Conceptions of Freedom,* 2 vols. (Garden City, NY: Doubleday, 1958). Adler finds two other forms of freedom, but
they are variations of the other more fundamental forms: political liberty is a variant of self-
realization and collective freedom is a variant of self-perfection. Isaiah Berlin, in his influential essay "Two Concepts of Liberty" (1969), in *Freedom: A Philosophical Anthology,* ed. Ian
Carter, Matthew H. Kramer and Hillel Steiner (Malden, MA: Blackwell, 2007), divides ideas
of freedom into "negative" and "positive" freedom. Negative freedom understands freedom
to exist "to the degree to which no man or body of men interferes with my activity" (p. 39).
Berlin's negative freedom clearly corresponds to Adler's "circumstantial freedom of self-
realization." "Positive" freedom is the condition under which "my life and my decisions . . .
depend on myself, not on external forces of whatever kind" (p. 44). Positive freedom clearly
corresponds to Adler's "natural freedom of self-determination." I have chosen to use Adler's
typology because I think his threefold distinction is clearer than Berlin's twofold one. Berlin
discusses Adler's "acquired freedom of self-perfection" and "natural freedom of self-
determination" as two forms of positive freedom. Adler (I believe) is correct to bring out their
distinctiveness. Gerald C. MacCallum Jr. criticizes the adequacy of differentiating between
positive and negative freedom as two kinds of freedom ("Negative and Positive Freedom,"
Philosophical Review 76 [July 1967]: 312-34).
[3]Thomas Hobbes, *Leviathan* 2.21, ed. Michael Oakeshott (New York: Collier Books, 1962),
p. 159.
[4]John Locke, *Essay Concerning Human Understanding* 2.21, ed. and abr. Maurice Cranston
(London: Collier-Macmillan, 1965), p. 149.

acting, according to the determinations of the will; that is, if we choose to remain at rest, we may; if we choose to move, we also may."[5]

As far as circumstances limit the number of wishes you can realize, your freedom is limited. To whatever degree circumstances improve, your freedom is increased. This theory does not try to explain the origin of our desires; it takes them for granted and focuses on our ability to achieve them. Slaves cannot do as they wish; they are controlled by the will of their masters. Prisoners' circumstances keep them from fulfilling their desires. To become free, a slave's or a prisoner's circumstances must change. According to this theory of freedom, any circumstance that keeps you from doing what you wish— even a divine or just human law—limits your freedom. Complete freedom would require removing all external obstacles to realizing our desires.

Self-determination. Natural freedom of self-determination identifies freedom with the power to decide what you do and become. This type of freedom takes center stage in most contemporary discussions of free will and has been held by thinkers from Aristotle and Cicero to Charles Hartshorne and Jean-Paul Sartre. According to René Descartes, human beings possess total control over what they will, which "renders us like God in making us masters of ourselves."[6] In criticizing the circumstantial view of freedom and defending natural freedom, Sartre declares, "In addition, it is necessary to point out to 'common sense' that the formula 'to be free' does not mean 'to obtain what one has wished' but rather 'by oneself to determine oneself to wish' (in the broad sense of choosing). In other words, success is not important to freedom."[7]

Whereas the circumstantial view does not investigate the origin of our desires, natural freedom of self-determination understands freedom as the power to choose our own character or self. According to this view, we are free only insofar as we create and possess ourselves. The nature of natural freedom is somewhat difficult to grasp, perhaps, because it seems to lift itself by its own bootstraps. That is, in order to escape determination by an outside source—God or natural forces—the self decides for itself its char-

[5]David Hume, *Enquiry Concerning Human Understanding* 8.1.73 (Kitchener, ON: Batoche Books, 2000), p. 66.
[6]René Descartes, *Passions of the Soul,* quoted in Adler, *Idea of Freedom,* 1:474, n. 32.
[7]Jean-Paul Sartre, *Being and Nothingness,* trans. Hazel E. Barnes (New York: Citadel Press, 1969), p. 459.

acter and actions. The self creates itself. The "self" exists in two states, as the creator and the created. Self-creation seems irrational to many thinkers, and the critics of natural freedom attack the theory at this point.

Self-perfection. Acquired freedom of self-perfection views freedom very differently. According to this view, freedom cannot be identified with having favorable circumstances or with power to choose your nature. Instead, true freedom is the state of willing the good perfectly. This theory has been held by thinkers from Plato and Marcus Aurelius to Hegel and Karl Barth. In his *Meditations* (7.68), Marcus Aurelius, the Stoic Roman Emperor, defined freedom as the virtuous man's "power to live free from all compulsion in the greatest tranquility of mind, even if all the world cry out against you as much as they choose."[8] Plotinus (A.D. 204-270) also advocates the freedom of self-perfection: "Soul becomes free when it moves without hindrance, through the Intellectual-Principle, towards The Good; what it does in that spirit is its free act."[9] And Philo, in his treatise *Every Good Man Is Free*, explains that "those who are under the dominion of anger, or appetite, or any other passion, or of treacherous wickedness, are in every respect slaves; and those who live in accordance with the [divine] law are free."[10]

According to the theory of self-perfection, many of our wants and wishes arise from ignorance of good. Our undisciplined desires conflict with each other, and attempting to realize them puts us in conflict with other people and with reality itself. Surely freedom is too noble a word to describe acting on immediate impulse or from blindness, confusion or malice. True freedom is the state of knowing and willing the good. We are not born with this power but acquire it by education or divine grace. Only when our inner condition of ignorance and confusion is overcome do we attain genuine freedom. You can be free in this sense even if you are a slave or a prisoner. The freedom of self-perfection is foreign to our common way of thinking about freedom and comes nearest to the highest of Bernard of Clairvaux's levels of love, love of God for God's sake. More than Adler's other types of freedom, it escapes the trap of envy and competition between God and hu-

---

[8]Marcus Aurelius, *Marcus Aurelius and His Times* (Roslyn, NY: Walter J. Black, 1945), p. 78.
[9]Plotinus, *The Enneads* 6.8, trans. Stephen McKenna, abr. John Dillon (London: Penguin Books, 1991), p. 518.
[10]Philo, *Every Good Man Is Free* 7.45, in *The Works of Philo (Complete and Unabridged)*, trans. C. D. Yonge (Peabody, MA: Hendrickson Publishers, 1993), p. 686.

manity. I will delay further discussion of this view until I have developed a noncompetitive view of the human-divine relationship.

The general idea of freedom. Adler makes a convincing case that, even though these three views conceive of freedom in very different ways, a common (if general) understanding of freedom unites them. In each case a self is understood to have the power to act exempt from the compulsion of some other force. Adler defines this general sense as follows: *"A man is free who has in himself the ability or power whereby he can make what he does his own action and what he achieves his own property."*[11]

In the following comparison Adler shows that his general definition expresses the essential features of all three basic types, where (A) is circumstantial freedom of self-realization, (B) is acquired freedom of self-perfection, (C) is the natural freedom of self-determination and (X) is the general definition of freedom:

A man who is able

(A) under favorable circumstances, to act as he wishes for his own
     individual good as he sees it

or

(B) through acquired virtue or wisdom, to will or live as he ought in
     conformity to the moral law or an ideal befitting human nature

or

(C) by a power inherent in human nature, to change his own character
     creatively by deciding for himself what he shall do or shall
     become

is free in the sense that he

(X) has in himself the ability or power whereby he can make what he
     does his own action, and what he achieves his property.[12]

According to Adler, one theory of freedom differentiates itself from others by the way it uses these central terms: "self, other, power, and

---

[11]Adler, *Idea of Freedom*, 1:614 (italics original). MacCallum offers a similar general concept of freedom. "Such freedom is thus always *of* something (an agent or agents), *from* something, *to* do, not do, become, or not become something; it is a triadic relation. Taking the format '*x* is (is not) free from *y* to do (not do, become, not become) *z*,' *x* ranges over agents, *y* ranges over such 'preventing conditions' as constraints, restrictions, interferences, and barriers, and *z* ranges over actions or conditions of character or circumstance" ("Negative and Positive Freedom," p. 314).

[12]Adler, *Idea of Freedom*, 1:616.

exempt."[13] Different understandings of freedom can be mapped by speci-
fying the different ways these terms are defined in each. In all theories, the
self is the principle of freedom and the "other" is the principle of un-
freedom.[14] A free act is something the self does. The power to act freely is
something the self has. The "other" is whatever challenges the self's possession of the power to act. To be free, then, the self must be exempt from
control by the "other" and have power over its own action.

Competitive freedom. These three views of freedom are not necessarily
incompatible. Some thinkers have harmonized them by making one
primary and the others subordinate. In our unreflective moments, however,
most of us act as if circumstantial freedom of self-realization were the only
real freedom. We feel our desires and wishes immediately and we very
quickly detect obstacles to their realization. Since in principle there is no
limit to our desires and wishes, this view of freedom guarantees that, in a
world with many free beings, no one can realize their will completely and
attain perfect freedom. This perspective is intrinsically competitive and
guarantees that envy will be a permanent fixture of human relations and of
the human-divine relation.

Most people do not bother with the issue of natural freedom. They do
not wonder why they want what they want; they are too busy trying to *get*
what they want. But we resent it when we are told that we do not have free
will, that even if we can *do* what we will, we cannot *will* what we will. It
would bother us to think that we are avidly trying to fulfill wishes and desires implanted in us by space aliens, subliminal advertisements, chemicals,
evolution or Satan—or God.

As we can see, natural freedom also lends itself to a competitively structured existence. If I insist on being the absolute cause of my existence, desires and actions, how can I acknowledge that I am God's creature, pre-
served by his power, obligated by his law and in need of his grace? Would

---

[13]Ibid., p. 611.
[14]Ibid., p. 610. Isaiah Berlin confirms Adler's observation when he says, "Conceptions of free-
     dom directly derive from views of what constitutes a self, a person, a man. Enough manipu-
     lation of the definition of man, and freedom can be made to mean whatever the manipulator
     wishes" ("Two Concepts of Liberty," p. 45). Berlin criticizes those who like the Stoics and
     the Apostle Paul distinguish between a true or transcendental self and an empirical self. To
     indicate the special sense of the word *other* I will place it within quotes throughout this book.

not such admissions imply a limit to my natural freedom, if not its complete annihilation? Søren Kierkegaard, clairvoyant as always, shines the spotlight on the rebellious heart of the modern self when he observes:

> Serfdom's abominable era is past; so there is the intention to go further with the help of this abomination: to abolish man's serfdom in respect to God, to whom every man not by birth, but by creation from nothing, belongs as a bondservant, and in such a way as no bondservant has ever belonged to an earthly master, who nevertheless concedes that thoughts and feelings are free. But he belongs to God in every thought, the most hidden, in every feeling, the most private, in every motion, the most inward. Yet men find this bondservice to be a burdensome imposition and are more or less openly intent upon deposing God in order to enthrone man.[15]

Even if we are not as defiant as Henley, we feel the appeal of the last refrain of "Invictus": "I am the master of my fate: I am the captain of my soul."[16]

THE MODERN CONCEPT OF HUMAN DIGNITY

The English word *dignity* still retains overtones of the Latin words *dignus* (worthy) or *dignitat* (merit or worth).[17] Dignity, like worth, comes in degrees. People in positions of authority deserve more deference and honor than those under them; hence they are called dignitaries. When we speak of human dignity we are contrasting the worth of human beings to inanimate objects and lower animals. We are taught to treat people differently than we treat a pot of soil, a hammer or a rat. To treat humans according to their dignity is to treat them as if they owned themselves and had a right to determine their own actions. As I argued earlier, the concept of dignity as it is commonly used is related to the idea of freedom, usually understood as a combination of circumstantial freedom and natural freedom. A being's dignity increases or declines with their level of independence. The more self-sufficient and self-defining we are, the more dignity we have. This understanding of human dignity began to gain dominance in Western thought

---

[15]Søren Kierkegaard, *Works of Love*, trans. Howard and Edna Hong (New York: HarperCollins, 2009), p. 119.

[16]William Ernest Henley, "Invictus," *Modern British Poetry*, ed. Louis Untermeyer (New York: Harcourt, Brace, 1950), p. 53.

[17]*Oxford English Dictionary*, s.v. "Dignity." In Greek, the idea of dignity is expressed by *axiōma* (worth, dignity or weight) and *timē* (honor, respect, recognition).

during the Renaissance. Prior to that time, human dignity was understood as rooted in the twin honors of having been created in God's image and the Son of God having become one of us.[18]

Typical of this Renaissance shift is Pico Mirandola's essay *Oration on the Dignity of Man* (1486). Whereas Mirandola still thinks of humanity as a divine creation and uses the incarnation as proof of human dignity, he prepares the way for those who would assert a human dignity independent of a theological foundation. After surveying past estimations of the human dignity, Mirandola offers his reason for thinking of human beings "as the most fortunate of creatures and as a result worthy of highest admiration." As his words below will attest, humanity's worth rests in its power of self-creation.[19] Putting words into the mouth of the Creator, Mirandola praises human beings:

> We have given thee, Adam, no fixed seat, no form of thy very own, no gift peculiarly thine, that thou mayest feel as thine own, have as thine own, possess as thine own the seat, the form, the gifts which thou thyself shalt desire. A limited nature in other creatures is confined within the laws written down by Us. In conformity with thy free judgment, in whose hands I have placed thee, thou art confined by no bounds; and thou wilt fix limits for thyself. . . . Thou, like a judge appointed for being honorable, are the molder and maker of thyself; thou mayest sculpt thyself into whatever shape thou dost prefer. Thou canst again grow upward from thy soul's reason into the higher natures which are divine.
>
> O great liberality of God the Father! O great and wonderful happiness of man! It is given him to have that which he chooses and be that which he wills.[20]

---

[18]See Charles Trinkaus, *In Our Image and Likeness: Humanity and Divinity in Italian Humanist Thought* (Notre Dame, IN: University of Notre Dame Press, 1995), 1:179-99. In these pages Trinkaus surveys patristic and medieval thinkers' views on human dignity. While thinkers of these periods were aware of the "misery" of humanity, they extolled the dignity bestowed on humanity by the Creator.

[19]According to John Webster, Mirandola treats God's creation as the act of "producing a free-standing reality, not the establishment of relations." Pure will and unlimited imagination rather than a divine vocation characterize the "dignity of man" ("The Dignity of Creatures," in *The God of Love and Human Dignity: Essays in Honour of George M. Newlands*, ed. Paul Middleton [New York: T & T Clark, 2007], p. 21).

[20]Pico Mirandola, *Pico Della Mirandola: On the Dignity of Man and Other Essays*, trans. Charles Glenn Wallis et al. (Indianapolis: Bobbs-Merrill, 1965), pp. 4-5. For a thorough study of Mirandola in the context of Italian humanism, see Charles Trinkaus, *In Our Image*

Perhaps the most influential proponent of autonomy-based dignity is the champion of enlightenment, Immanuel Kant. According to Kant, a person is free only insofar as he "obeys laws which he gives to himself" through his reason. Since this law-giving power creates all value and determines what is worthy of our efforts, this power itself must be of supreme worth. "Hence autonomy is the ground of the dignity of human nature and of every rational creature."[21] In addition, Kant reverses the classic relationship between God and dignity. We do not have dignity *because* of our relationship to God; to the contrary, God must judge us worthy because of our inherent dignity. Kant pronounces, "The essence of things is not altered by their external relations; and whatever without reference to such relations alone constitutes the absolute worth of man is also what he must be judged by, whoever the judge may be, even the Supreme Being."[22]

Contemporary secular discussions of human dignity omit reference to a transcendent ground and hence give the impression of mere assertions without foundation. The "United Nations Universal Declaration of Human Rights" (1948), for example, begins by asserting that "the inherent dignity" and "equal and inalienable rights" of all human beings is the "foundation of freedom, justice and peace in the world." Article 1 of the Declaration states, "All human beings are born free and equal in dignity and rights. They are endowed with reason and conscience and should act towards one another in a spirit of brotherhood."[23] Other international documents follow suit. Article 1 of "The Charter of Fundamental Rights of The European Union" (2000) states simply, "Human dignity is inviolable. It must be respected and protected."[24] The Charter's explanation of article 1 appeals not to a transcendent ground but to the United Nations Declaration to support its assertion that "human dignity is not only a fundamental

---

and Likeness: Humanity and Divinity in Italian Humanist Thought (Notre Dame, IN: University of Notre Dame Press, 1995), 2:505-26.

[21]Immanuel Kant, Grounding for the Metaphysics of Morals, 3rd ed., trans. James W. Ellington (Indianapolis: Hackett, 1981), p. 41.

[22]Ibid., p. 44. I shall argue the opposite.

[23]Walter Laqueur and Barry Rubin, The Human Rights Reader (New York: Meridian Books, 1979), pp. 197-98.

[24]"The Charter of Fundamental Rights of The European Union," European Parliament, www .europarl.europa.eu/charter/default_en.htm.

right in itself but constitutes the real basis of fundamental rights."[25] One author assesses the contemporary discussion in these words: "Generally speaking, contemporary theories about human dignity are, in one way or another, vulgar forms of Kantian moral philosophy."[26] That is, they remove all references to God but retain the idea of autonomy and dignity, groundless though they have become.

In many contemporary discussions it is difficult to assess whether freedom or dignity is held to be foundational. Do we have inherent dignity, which gives us a claim to independence? Or are we free by nature and therefore have a right to assert our dignity?[27] European political and legal philosophy tends to make dignity foundational for freedom, whereas American political and legal thinking tends to make freedom foundational for dignity.[28] In either case, human beings strive toward maximum freedom and dignity. Any abridgment of our freedom would diminish our dignity, and any diminishment of our dignity would reduce our freedom. We think of our dignity like we think of our freedom, as potentially infinite.

Though unlimited dignity is our ambition, it seems unlikely we can ever achieve it. We suspect that we are dependent on something outside of us and have no real control over our circumstances and fate. We have no memory of causing ourselves to come into being and have no sense that we sustain our being by our wills. We rarely think about this truth. On the contrary, we do everything we can to escape it and to convince ourselves that we have escaped it. In our insecurity we assert our independence vociferously and proclaim our autonomy in eloquent phrases. Most of all, however, we attempt to assert control over the external world. We kick a stone, utter a curse or build a house. We buy a toy, build a monument or go on a diet. We thrust ourselves into the world and long to see the effects of

---

[25]"Draft Charter of the Fundamental Right of the European Union," European Parliament, October 11, 2000, www.europarl.europa.eu/charter/pdf/04473_en.pdf.

[26]Marc D. Guerra, "The Affirmation of Genuine Human Dignity," *Journal of Markets and Morality* 4.2 (Fall 2001), www.thefreelibrary.com/The affirmation of genuine human dignity.-a0186469526.

[27]The answer to these questions depends on which of Adler's concepts of freedom you have in mind in each instance.

[28]Guy E. Carmi, "Dignity—The Enemy from Within," Oxford University Comparative Law Forum, 2007, http://ouclf.iuscomp.org/articles/carmi.shtml. See also Georg Nolte, ed., *European and American Constitutionalism* (New York: Cambridge University Press, 2005), pp. 83-134.

our actions. If we can affect the external world or cause a reaction of some kind, we prove that we matter and are not helplessly dependent. As long as we do not notice that we act in dependence on the world even as we declare our independence from it and that our little changes make no difference in the long run, we can imagine that we are asserting a godlike independence.

In viewing ourselves as potentially infinite, we doom ourselves to perpetual restlessness and insatiable ambition. However high we climb, infinite heights will tower above us. Our true worth will always be in doubt, and in our wounded pride we will proclaim our lofty status even more assertively to avoid despair. Humanity so defined cannot love God; it can only envy and resent God.

AMBITIONS OF THE EMPTY SELF

What is the human essence or self that strives to master circumstances and fulfill its desires? Who are those that seek to establish their infinite dignity so that they can rule over all things? In chapter five I suggested that by envying God we treat the divine self as a pure will that just happens to possess the divine attributes that allow it to gain everything it desires. Now I am suggesting that by envying God we act as if the human self were also a pure will that could possess divine attributes. On this level, the human self does not differ in essence from the divine self. But in fact, we do not possess divine attributes and hence cannot gain everything we desire. Our desire is infinitely greater than our capacity to satisfy it. What an unhappy state!

What is this envious human self? Emptiness or empty desire seems an apt description. The self is *empty* because it defines itself apart from its relationships with others. It finds itself alone, without identity and unhappy. It is *desire* because it must move out of itself to find other things to support, accompany and satisfy it. We attempt to inflate our empty selves by consuming other things and drawing them into us. This strategy is doomed to futility, however, for no finite thing can satisfy an infinite desire. Our desire is insatiable.

The "other" is anything that does not submit to be a means to our ends. Anyone, God or other people, who intentionally blocks our attempt to fulfill ourselves limits our freedom and slights our dignity. Even if hard experience teaches us to accept our limits, we only grudgingly admit them and secretly resent them. We preserve our dignity by refusing to be conquered in spirit even if we are crushed in fact. We reserve a space inside where we reign supreme. We can at least think to ourselves:

> What though the field be lost?
> All is not lost; the unconquerable Will,
> And study of revenge, immortal hate,
> And courage never to submit or yield.[29]

Clearly, as long as we understand freedom, dignity and the self in these ways we will find ourselves in competition with all other beings, human and divine.

---

[29]Milton, *Paradise Lost*, 1.105-8.

7

SOME UNWELCOME LIMITS ON
FREEDOM AND DIGNITY

If we learned about the human condition only from the high-flying rhetoric of the modern self, we would imagine humanity a race of gods. Given only the descriptions of Mirandola, Descartes and Rousseau, beings from another galaxy might imagine human beings as winged creatures in graceful flight, their noble faces shining with cool pride as they survey their broad domain. Their freedom knows no limit, their dignity exceeds all bounds and their power dwarfs all competitors. Ah, but we know the human condition too well for such illusions! The little biped comes into the world naked and helpless, bounded by nothingness as its origin and destined for nothingness as its end. Anxiety, weakness, suffering, sadness, futility and despair mark its path from start to finish. What a contrast!

In this chapter we will explore the strange disparity between the inflated self-concept of modernity and the truth of the human condition. Confronting the limits of human freedom and dignity will serve as the beginning of a transition from me-centered identity to God-centered identity. It will show that the competitive understanding of the God-human relationship has lured me-centered culture into a labyrinth from which there is no exit. We must make a new beginning.

Freedom's Finitude

Take our existence and our native powers for granted for a moment and focus on what we can do with them. We cannot remain satisfied with bare existence. Some force propels us outside of ourselves to seek what we do not have within. We can think of the propelling force as desire or will that reaches out in search of some as-yet-unidentified object, or we can think of the moving force as external things that lure us toward them, promising pleasure or happiness. From either perspective, it is clear that we do not have within ourselves everything we need.

Since our desires cannot be satisfied by merely feeling them, they force us to look for means through which to fulfill them. Perhaps we secure a ladder so we can get at those juicy apples on the tree. Or we go back to school for more training so we can buy that sports car we've always wanted. The need for means raises the issue of power, which is the measure of our ability to fulfill our desires. Our greatest power is reason, which we use to discover ways to get what we want. We feel our power or powerlessness as we strive to achieve our goals. Although we use power primarily as a means to the good things we want, exercising power can be pleasurable in itself. We want to enjoy that new car but we also enjoy the thrill of purchasing it.[1]

In striving to fulfill our needs and desires we face resistance, and sometimes we find our way blocked completely. Seeking to evade barriers we encounter the concept of freedom. Freedom appears in our consciousness first not as an abstract concept denoting the absence of all limits but as desire for the removal of a particular obstacle. A fence, a concrete wall or a law stands between us and achieving of our goals. We were focusing on the object of desire but now the obstruction commands our attention. Getting past the barrier becomes our aim. We want to be *free* from that impediment. Notice that freedom, as I have used the word so far in this section, is wholly negative and refers to the absence of barriers. Freedom itself is desirable only because the good we seek is desirable. Because our desires are limitless, however, we come to think of freedom itself as a good thing. When we overcome one barrier and acquire the sought-after object, desire immediately sets its sights on other goods and encounters other obstacles. This

---

[1]For an overview of various views of power, see Kyle A. Pasewark, *A Theology of Power: Being Beyond Domination* (Minneapolis: Fortress Press, 1993). Hannah Arendt argues that power is a property of groups rather than of individuals. She asserts, "Power corresponds to the human ability not just to act but to act in concert. Power is never the property of an individual; it belongs to a group and remains in existence only so long as the group keeps together" (*On Violence* [New York: Harcourt, Brace & World, 1970], p. 44).

process leads us to think of freedom itself as an object of desire. It stands for all the goods that would become available were all limits removed.

Since desire knows no limit, we cannot be satisfied with anything but maximum freedom, that is, the removal of all limits. Only such freedom would make available all the goods we crave. However, thinking of freedom in this way guarantees that God will appear before us as an obstacle, a competitor, a limit; and by definition freedom cannot coexist with limits. Even worse, in confrontation with God we become acutely aware of our lack of freedom and the utter impossibility of achieving it. In this unhappy state we cannot help but view God as an object of envy, for God alone possesses our heart's desire.

As this analysis shows, ordinary experience leads us to think of freedom as the freedom to do as you wish (Adler's first type). It also enables us to see its defects.[2] As we observed earlier, we want this "freedom" only because we want to fulfill our desires. We want a new car, better health or more respect from our peers. And given the right conditions these things are attainable. But we need to ask a further question: *Why do we want the things we want?* Perhaps we desire them because other people enjoy them or because they enable us to get to work or give us more leisure time. But ultimately all those things are desirable because we believe they can contribute to our happiness. Our desire for happiness is more fundamental than our desire for new carpet or fashionable clothes. And it is more fundamental than our desire for circumstantial freedom to do what we want. Circumstantial freedom, then, is valuable only as a means to happiness.

But as everyone knows, simply having circumstances favorable to fulfilling our desires cannot guarantee happiness. Charles Taylor reminds us that even if external obstacles are absent "there may also be internal ones."[3] And as William Temple observed, we need freedom not only from "external control, but freedom from internal compulsions . . . [from] a chaos of impulses."[4] We can desire something, plan for it and work toward it, thinking it will add to our happiness, but experience disappointment or

---

[2]For a thoughtful critique of the negative view of freedom, see Charles Taylor, "What's Wrong with Negative Liberty," in *Freedom: A Philosophical Anthology*, ed. Ian Carter, Matthew H. Kramer and Hillel Steiner (Malden, MA: Blackwell, 2007), pp. 177-93.

[3]Ibid., p. 162.

[4]William Temple, *The Nature of Personality* (London: Macmillan, 1915), pp. 30-31.

regret once we acquire it. We begin to question whether we know ourselves at all. We wonder, *How could I have thought that this would make me happy?* Kierkegaard recommends that we remind ourselves often of the limits of insight and foresight. He says,

> I will call to mind that even if I had my soul concentrated in one single wish and even if I had it concentrated therein so desperately that I could willingly throw away my eternal salvation for the fulfillment of this wish— that still no one can with certainty tell me in advance whether my wish, if it is fulfilled, would still not seem empty and meaningless to me. And what is more miserable, that the wish would not be fulfilled and I would retain the sad and painful ideas of the—missed good fortune—or that the wish would be fulfilled and I would retain it, embittered by the certainty of how empty it was![5]

Confronting our lack of self-knowledge proves the powerlessness of circumstantial freedom to provide happiness, which is the very reason we want freedom. What advantage does being able to do what we want bestow when we cannot know we will be glad we did it? Our immediate wants do not reliably give us self-knowledge. Of course, we know what we want while we feel our desire for it, but feeling a desire does not guarantee that it arises from our deepest self so that fulfilling it will give expression to our true identity and never be regretted. On the contrary, our desires, wishes and daydreams pull us in a thousand directions. They contradict each other and put us at odds with ourselves and with the fabric of reality. I cannot be all those selves clamoring for satisfaction. Which is my *true* self?

I am not saying that having circumstantial freedom is of no advantage at all. Without favorable circumstances we could do nothing; indeed, we could not even exist. But it should be clear that it makes no sense to seek circumstantial freedom as if it were the sure gateway to happiness. It is not. We need more than favorable external circumstances; we need inner freedom, a freedom attained by coming to know ourselves and what is truly good for us. As Taylor puts it, I need to be "able to overcome or at least neutralize my motivational fetters . . . to achieve a certain condition of self-

---

[5]Søren Kierkegaard, *Christian Discourses*, trans. Howard V. Hong and Edna H. Hong (Princeton, NJ: Princeton University Press, 1997), pp. 256-57.

clairvoyance and self-understanding. I must be actually exercising self-understanding in order to be truly free."[6] We need more than the ability to do what we want; we need to acquire the right wants. Only then will we gain the ability to act in harmony with our true selves. These are the minimum conditions necessary for happiness.

Unfortunately, circumstantial freedom's quest for happiness faces a second challenge even more insurmountable than the first: the problem of finite knowledge or the limited power of reason. Circumstantial freedom envisions using reason to discover means to achieve our wants.[7] Reason is a torchlight that illuminates the path far in front of us, but the darkness is greater still. Perhaps circumstances permit and reason figures out a way to fulfill our desires. Does this guarantee that we will find happiness? Sadly, it does not. In constructing means, reason surveys possible consequences of different courses of action. Everything we do has incalculable consequences. Should I drive to work or take a bus? Should I take the red eye or the 8 a.m. flight from Los Angeles to Washington, DC, next month? However good we are at assessing the data we have, there is much more unknown than known. Even if circumstances permit and I choose to take that 8 a.m. flight, it is not within my power to guarantee that I will arrive safely. I could exercise my circumstantial freedom perfectly and still die as a result of my choice. Having circumstantial freedom, then, does not give me the power to achieve my wants, much less to attain my true good.[8]

Circumstantial freedom cannot give us the very thing for which we treasure freedom. We need the inner freedom of self-knowledge so that we know what is good for us. And we need sufficient knowledge of our actions' consequences so that we know what we are getting when we choose. Asking for these conditions to be fulfilled moves us beyond the range of human possibilities. So, should we give up on freedom or settle for the best we can

---

[6]Taylor, "What's Wrong with Negative Liberty," p. 162.

[7]Circumstantial freedom does not consider reason's function of disciplining and enlightening our wants (or ends).

[8]Isaiah Berlin expresses skepticism about including such natural limitations among the conditions that limit freedom. He restricts freedom to the part "played by other human beings . . . in frustrating my wishes" ("Two Concepts of Liberty," in *Freedom: A Philosophical Anthology*, ed. Ian Carter, Matthew H. Kramer and Hillel Steiner [Malden, MA: Blackwell, 2007], p. 40). Berlin's restriction is understandable since he thinks of freedom primarily in political terms.

get? I believe there is another possibility. The promise of freedom is at the heart of the Christian hope. Paul encourages us to expect to share in the "glorious freedom of the children of God" (Rom 8:21 NIV 1984). But we are not ready for that story yet.

IN SEARCH OF DIGNITY

As I pointed out in chapter six, we make a close connection between dignity and freedom. The freedom we associate most often with dignity is self-determination. In our demand for certain freedoms or rights we often appeal to our self-determining nature. Because we are aware of ourselves, cherish hopes and dreams for the future and to a degree control who we are and what we want, we think of ourselves as our own possession. We demand respect and reject the idea of being treated as the property of another person. We assert our "inherent" worth and invoke humanity's "inviolable" dignity. These claims translate into the principle that we should never violate someone's person. The human person must be valued above other things and never treated as a mere means to other ends.

Examining the notion of self-determination a bit more closely, we find that there have always been philosophers and theologians who deny that human beings possess the power of self-determination. Such diverse thinkers as Thomas Hobbes, Jonathan Edwards and Bertrand Russell agree on the vast difference between the power to *do* what you will and the power to *will* what you will. Hobbes objects that "nothing taketh beginning from itself, but from the action of some other immediate agent without itself."[9] How could I decide to change my will, since that by which I decide is also my will? My will would have to become its own cause, which is absurd. Edwards makes essentially the same point in saying that "if that first volition is not determined by any preceding act of the Will, then that act is not determined by the Will, and so is not free . . . [in the sense of being] the Will's self-determination."[10] In other words, how can we determine our wills without willing to do so? But willing to determine our wills shows that they

---

[9]Thomas Hobbes, *The Questions Concerning Liberty, Necessity, and Chance, Clearly Stated and Debated Between Dr. Bramhall and Thomas Hobbes*, objection 2, quoted in Adler, *The Idea of Freedom: A Dialectical Examination of the Conceptions of Freedom* (Garden City, NY: Doubleday, 1958), 2:262.

[10]Jonathan Edwards, *Freedom of the Will* (Morgan, PA: Soli Deo Gloria, 1996), p. 39.

have already been determined—before we thought of determining them! According to these thinkers we may have some control over our actions but we have none over our willing.

These critiques of self-determining free will are significant and very interesting.[11] I am not sure they can be answered to the satisfaction of all, but neither do I think they prove the power of self-determination nonexistent. I do not want to get bogged down in this debate because my goal is not to deny or defend a particular version of free will but to show its inadequacy as a basis for human dignity. Assume that we possess the power of self-determination to some degree. I want to show that even with this freedom we cannot achieve full self-determination, much less complete happiness.

If our claims to dignity rest on our complete possession of ourselves and control over what and who we are, it rests on a shaky foundation indeed. As the philosopher Hegel points out, even if we can choose freely among available alternatives, we cannot choose which alternatives are put before us. We must choose from within a situation we did not create, from whatever is given to us before our choice. Hegel observes, "if you stop at the consideration that, having an arbitrary will, a man can will this or that then, of course, his freedom consists in that ability. But if you keep firmly in view that the content of his willing is a *given* one, then he is determined thereby and in that respect at all events is free no longer."[12] Being able to choose from among alternatives thus does not give us complete self-possession and hence proves an inadequate foundation for our dignity. How can I demand that others refrain from restricting my choices when they are already restricted in countless ways by the very structure of reality? Why should I feel compelled to make way for your choices when space, time and physical and biological laws already constrain your choices to a narrow area? If the rest of the universe does not bow to your supposedly "infinite" dignity, why should I?

Our natural freedom is even more restricted than Hegel argued if we consider our existence as such. We did not choose to exist or to be human

---

[11]In contemporary discussions self-determining free will is usually termed *libertarian* free will. Those who hold the circumstantial self-realization view usually adhere to what is today called *compatibilist* free will, that is, the will is free in the sense that in its willing it really wills what it wills. The will cannot be coerced.

[12]Georg W. F. Hegel, *Hegel's Philosophy of Right*, trans. T. M. Knox (New York: Oxford University Press, 1967), pp. 230-31.

or to possess the power of free will. Our genetic codes, the time and place of our birth or the identities of our parents are not within our power to choose. Possessing countless qualities we did not select, we endure innumerable limitations we did not take on and would not have chosen. Of course, we enjoy great powers compared to creatures with no power of choice. But when you compare the number and significance of goods we can attain by choice to the number and significance of circumstances over which we have no such command, our control over our lives appears small indeed. We simply awake in the world to find ourselves already defined and largely determined.

This truth is so deep-seated that its force cannot be evaded, and attempts to escape it make this impossibility even clearer. In book five of *Paradise Lost* Abdiel, one of God's most faithful and zealous angels, rebukes Satan for his ingratitude and rebellion against his Creator. Satan, however, will not admit Abdiel's basic assumption that God created him, for this would imply that Satan owes God something and concede Abdiel's major point. So the devil contends that he has always existed or came into being by fate:

> who saw
> When this creation was? rememberest thou
> Thy making, while the Maker gave thee being?
> We know no time when we were not as now;
> Know none before us, self-begot, self-raised
> By our own quickening power.[13]

C. S. Lewis astutely observed the futility of Satan's evasion. To admit ignorance of your beginnings proves that your origin "lies outside" yourself. Lewis concludes, "The being too proud to admit derivation from God, has come to rejoice in believing that he 'just grew' like Topsy or a turnip."[14]

Karl Marx also attempts to circumvent the truth that we are not our own origin. He explains:

> A *being* only considers himself independent when he stands on his own two feet; and he only stands on his own two feet when he owes his *existence* to himself. A man who lives by the grace of another regards himself

---

[13] Milton, *Paradise Lost*, 5.856-61.
[14] C. S. Lewis, *A Preface to Paradise Lost* (London: Oxford University Press, 1942), pp. 95-96.

as a dependent being. But I live completely by the grace of another if I owe him not only the sustenance of my life, but if he has, moreover, *created* my *life*—if he is the *source* of my life; and if it is not of my own creation, my life has necessarily a source of this kind outside of it. . . . Since for the socialist man the *entire so-called history of the world* is nothing but the begetting of man through human labor, nothing but the coming-to-be of nature for man, he has the visible irrefutable proof of his birth through himself, of his *process of coming-to-be*.[15]

Clearly, it is just as important for Marx's purpose as it was for Satan's self-concept to evade the obvious truth that we did not create ourselves and endow ourselves with freedom. Not many of us, I venture to say, will think Marx's assertion of human self-creation any more plausible than Satan's explanation of his spontaneous generation.

In light of our analysis, the bold claims of natural freedom for complete self-possession and inherent dignity appear highly exaggerated. If my existence, my human nature, all my powers and my free will itself are not my own achievements, how can they found my claim to unlimited dignity? How can I claim to own them if I did not create them, earn them or find them in a ditch? Why do I have an obligation to respect your existence and freedom when you came by them in such a strange way? A dignity founded on self-determining freedom must be limited to the extent of self-determining freedom. This diminished dignity falls infinitely short of the unlimited worth for which we long.

THE FRAGMENTED SELF

In chapters five and six I painted pictures of the divine and human selves that are at work in the competitive view of the relationship between God and humanity. Now I want to look at the human self that is disclosed by my analysis of freedom and dignity. The self at work in our decisions and acts turns out to be fragmented, changeable and restless. Postmodern philosopher Richard Rorty describes the empty and fragmented self as "a network

---

[15]Karl Marx, "Economic and Philosophic Manuscripts of 1844," in *Marx-Engles Reader*, ed. Robert C. Tucker, 2nd ed. (New York: W. W. Norton, 1978), pp. 91-92 (italics original). For further discussion of these ideas, see David Walsh, *After Ideology: Recovering the Spiritual Foundations of Freedom* (Washington, DC: Catholic University of America Press, 1995), p. 122.

of beliefs, desires and emotions with nothing behind it—no substrate behind the attributes. . . . [A] person just *is* that network."[16] Even if in one moment the self does what it wants, it may regret this act in the next. It is happy, sad, vain, angry and arrogant all in one day in response to changing external circumstances. This fragmented self does not have the self-knowledge or integrity to withstand being pulled apart by the many enticing things that come within its view.

Vast energy is required to sustain the illusion that the self is in control, that its dignity is rooted in its own powers. It must suppress the knowledge that it did not choose its existence, nature and powers. It must push aside any feeling of dependence on a reality greater than itself and focus only on those small areas where it can hope to exert some control. Even here it must ignore the fact that its options are limited to those at hand. Because the fragmented self cannot always do as it pleases and never feels it receives the honor it deserves, it will always feel that its freedom is hindered and its dignity slighted. Augustine labeled this condition a "state of disintegration," and Kierkegaard called it despair. Before his conversion Augustine found himself "tossed about and split, scattered and boiled dry . . . incapable of rest in my exhaustion."[17] Should we describe this condition as a state of having no self except in response to something external or as having many selves all vying for control? Either way, it is a miserable condition far removed from the happiness and rest we seek.

---

[16]Richard Rorty, *Objectivity, Relativism, and Truth* (Cambridge: Cambridge University Press, 1991), p. 199.

[17]Augustine, *Confessions* 2.2, in *The Confessions of Saint Augustine*, trans. Henry Chadwick (New York: Oxford University Press, 1991), pp. 24-25.

Part Two

THE GOD-CENTERED SELF

IN PART ONE we explored the identity of the modern self and laid out its strategies for dealing with its uneasy feelings about God. I explained how modern people view God, freedom and dignity, and demonstrated the inadequacy of this understanding. We discovered that the pain and paradox of the human condition is that our potential is so much greater than we can actualize, that our imaginations can envision so much more than we can achieve and that we long for so much more than the world can offer. What shall we do? Shall we give up on God, let go of freedom and settle for limited dignity? No. We dare not do this because in these issues our essential humanity is at stake. To be human, to feel one's humanity awake is to seek God, desire freedom and long for dignity.

In part two I want to show that the view of God, freedom and dignity brought to light in Jesus Christ addresses the pain and paradox of the human condition and secures the hope that we will experience our true greatness and inherit our promised glory. Jesus Christ reveals a God whose very being is love and whose every act is self-giving. God's power gives life and freedom, God's omnipresence opens a place for us and touches us with infinite love, and God's knowledge of us roots our identity in God's eternal life. Jesus pioneers a new way of being human, enabling us to think of ourselves as God's beloved children whose life task is to embody God's love for the world. The Christian picture of humanity empowers us for true selfhood, perfect freedom and the highest dignity conceivable. In Christ we find an identity rooted not in others' changing thoughts about us, but in God's eternal knowledge of us. The Spirit leads us toward the perfect freedom of life in harmony with our truest identity.

8

THE SELF-GIVING GOD
OF THE GOSPEL

The cross is the most universally recognizable emblem of Christianity. An instrument of a cruel and shameful execution, the cross was transformed by Jesus Christ into a symbol of the infinite love of God and the uncountable cost of our salvation. Christianity sees in the cross the deepest revelation of the divine life: God is love—self-giving, eternal love. What a contrast to Zeus and the enviable God of our imaginations! These gods burst through every limit and overwhelm every foe. They enjoy every pleasure and possess riches beyond measure. Their subjects seethe with defiance, cringe in terror or burn with envy. But Zeus cannot inspire gratitude, nor can a god whose essence is arbitrary power evoke love and praise. As we shall see in this chapter, the God whom Jesus reveals lives a very different life from those of Satan's "Almighty" or my object of envy. God does not exist by crowding out other beings or live by absorbing other things. The Christian story of creation and redemption portrays God as a fountain from which flow all good things in abundance. Infinite in goodness, God wills that there are creatures with whom to share his goodness. Even when we depart from the divine example and turn inward, God does not give up on us. God longs for our restoration and salvation so much that God becomes one of us and pours out God's life that we may live. There is no competition here, no grounds for envy.

THE GIFT OF CREATION

We can think of God as a threat to our freedom and dignity only if we forget
that God is our Creator. If God had not created there would be nothing. We
would not exist to exercise freedom or enjoy dignity. But God did create the
world and is the source of every good and beautiful thing in it. Everything
we need comes from God. Bernard of Clairvaux brings all his rhetorical
skill to bear on this truth: "Why should not the creature love his Creator,
who gave him the power to love? Why should he not love Him with all his
being, since it is by His gift alone that he can do anything that is good? It
was God's creative grace that out of nothingness raised us to the dignity of
manhood."[1] How could we mistake the gracious giver of existence for an
enemy of life?

According to traditional Christian teaching, God created the world
"from nothing." Even if Bernhard Anderson is correct that the full doctrine
of creation from nothing is not found in the Old Testament, it is certain that
the author of Genesis emphasizes the "absolute sovereignty" and "perfect
freedom" of God in relation to creation.[2] The later doctrine of creation from
nothing merely articulates this "absolute sovereignty" in another vocabu-
lary.[3] The phrase *from nothing* does not mean that God created the world
using "nothing" as a building material. Instead it means "not out of anything." God simply wanted the world to be and it was. God loved it and it
came to be. Another way to say this is that God made the world freely. God
faced no constraints. God needed no matter, no blueprint other than God's
will and Word, and no means and no reason outside of God.[4] God met no
resistance. And, most important, God was not compelled or motivated to
create the world by any lack that the world could fill or any good that the
world could add to his infinite goodness. God did not create the world to
have something to eat and drink or to have a place to sleep at night; nor did

---

[1]Bernard of Clairvaux, *On Loving God*, chap. 5, Cyber Library, www.leaderu.com/cyber
/books/onloving/onlovo5.html.

[2]Bernhard W. Anderson, *From Creation to New Creation* (Minneapolis: Fortress Press, 1994),
p. 30.

[3]For a thorough study of the origins of the doctrine of creation from nothing in the early
church, see Gerhard May, *Creatio Ex Nihilo: The Doctrine of "Creation Out of Nothing" in
Early Christian Thought*, trans. A. S. Worrall (London: T & T Clark, 1994).

[4]In trinitarian thought the Word or Son of God serves as the archetype for the world, a role
Plato reserved for the world of forms, which the creator needed as a pattern.

God need worshipers to make him feel worthy. God was not lonely or bored.

Why did God create us? The only answer that makes sense of the biblical story is that God created us because of love for us. God's grace, kindness and goodness overflow into the world. Paul assures us of this in the book of Ephesians: "for [God] chose us in [Christ] before the creation of the world. . . . In love [God] predestined us to be adopted as his sons through Jesus Christ" (Eph 1:4-5 NIV 1984). In Karl Barth's words, "God is the One who is free in his love. In this case we can understand the positing of this reality [creation]—which otherwise is incomprehensible—only as the work of his love."[5] For the Romanian Orthodox theologian Dumitru Staniloae, "God shows us his love through the world as a gift, so that a progressive dialogue with us in love may come to be."[6] But why did God love us? It could not have been for anything lovable in us because we were nothing, and "nothing" is not lovely. Again we find the answer best stated in Barth's words: "He loves because he loves."[7] There is no deeper answer. Our lovableness is not the motivation for God's love but its goal. God's love makes us lovable. But even as I write I find myself wondering if this could be true. God loves me for no reason other than that God loves me? God created me because God wanted me to know God's love for me? God called my name from desire for me to experience infinite joy? I confess I do not always feel God's love, but when I feel it I am overwhelmed and know that nothing else matters.

But we have a thousand ways of keeping ourselves from believing this. We subtly mistrust God and think that somehow God must need us and want something from us. We apply the logic of human gift giving to God. In his radical analysis of gift giving, Jacques Derrida speaks of the gift as "not impossible but *the* impossible. The very figure of the impossible. It announces itself, gives itself to be thought as the impossible."[8] He continues to explain why gifts are impossible:

---

[5]Karl Barth, *Church Dogmatics*, vol. 3., pt. 1, ed. G. W. Bromiley and T. F. Torrance, trans. J. W. Edwards et al. (Edinburgh: T & T Clark, 1958), p. 95.

[6]Dumitru Staniloae, *The World: Creation and Deification*, vol. 2, *The Experience of God*, trans. and ed. Ioan Ionita and Robert Barringer (Brookline, MA: Holy Cross Orthodox Press, 2000), p. 21.

[7]Barth, *Church Dogmatics*, 2.1, p. 279.

[8]Jacques Derrida, *Given Time: I, Counterfeit Money*, trans. Peggy Kamuf (Chicago: University of Chicago Press, 1992), p. 7.

> For there to be a gift, there must be no reciprocity, return, exchange, coun-
> tergift, or debt. If the other *gives* me *back* or *owes* me or has to give me
> back what I owe him or her, there will not have been a gift, whether this
> restitution is immediate or whether it is programmed by a complex calcu-
> lation of a long-term deferral or difference. . . . It is thus necessary, at that
> limit, that he not *recognize* the gift as a gift. If he recognizes it *as a gift*, if
> the gift *appears to him as such*, if the present is present to him *as present*,
> this simple recognition suffices to annul the gift. Why? Because it gives
> back, in the place, let us say, of the thing itself, a symbolic equivalent.[9]

Even if Derrida cannot convince us that giving is impossible, we can
admit the difficulty of escaping the logic of giving and reciprocating. Hence
we can see why some people find it difficult to believe that God's gifts are
really free. What human giver gives only for the good of the recipient?

The thought of such one-sided grace may even trouble us. Can a love that
feels no need for the beloved really be love? If you say to someone "I need you,"
it could be taken in different ways depending on circumstances. If you have
fallen down, you may be letting your neighbor know how badly you are hurt.
If you are speaking to your employee, you may be giving an order with a
touch of sarcasm. If you are speaking to your special beloved, you may be
expressing a bond of attachment so strong that the thought of losing it causes
pain. In each case, the one expressing the "need" is giving a type of significance to the one "needed." If someone "needs" you, you are not useless, superfluous or rejected. Being needed in this way can be very important to our
sense of self-worth, and this makes the idea of being needed by God attractive.
But consider this: you can be needed without being cared for. In need, we
view things as *means* to our happiness. Of course, being a means to someone's
satisfaction gives you a sort of significance, but it is easy to see how this need-
satisfaction relationship could descend into some very dehumanizing ar-
rangements. We must, I think, conclude that being needed in the absence of
being cared for does not measure up to the Christian ideal of love. At
minimum, need-love must be accompanied by care-love or benevolence.[10]

---

[9]Ibid., pp. 12-13.

[10]C. S. Lewis's *The Four Loves* (New York: Harcourt, 1960) is a classic statement on divine love.
   See especially p. 127, where he says, "God, who needs nothing, loves into existence wholly
   superfluous creatures in order that He may love and perfect them." Gary D. Badcock accuses
   Lewis of portraying God as "a simple fool, or worse again, a masochist." For "who or what,

Can God really love us if he does not need us? Would not his love be enhanced if his care were accompanied by need? It should be clear from what I said earlier that the answer to this question is no. If God needed us we could never know for sure whether the attention paid to us is for our good or is designed to meet God's needs. It is precisely because God does not *need* us that we know God really *loves* us. This makes God's love unique, amazing and reliable. Philip Rolnick states this idea well: "To recognize God as creator is to recognize ourselves as recipients of creation, that our very existence and the world in which we live it are gifts."[11]

But would not God's needing us give us more significance? Not at all! If God needed us our significance would be as a *means* to satisfy a need and it would be measured by the greatness of the need we satisfy. In contrast, if God bestows significance on us by loving us even when God does not need us, we gain our significance as an *end* rather than as a means. Of course, we are not God's end in the same sense that God is our end. God is our end in that we were created to know, love and glorify God forever. We cannot be complete or happy apart from God. When I say God treats us as ends I mean that the good he gives us is for *our* help and joy rather than for some other purpose. God does not love us to increase God's joy; God loves us that we might share in the joy that God is eternally. God delights in loving us because God is love. *Hence the measure of our significance is the greatness of the one who loves us and depth of the love with which God loves rather than the greatness of the need we satisfy.* We are significant *because* God loves us for no reason other than that God has freely chosen to love us.

THE SACRIFICE OF DIVINE LOVE

Contemplating God's gift of creation alone should be enough to show us that God does not threaten our freedom and dignity. But there is more to consider. The creatures to whom God gave existence and all good things do

---

after all, in all the universe gives itself up for nothing?" See Gary D. Badcock, "The Concept of Love Divine and Human," in *Nothing Greater, Nothing Better: Theological Essays on the Love of God*, ed. Kevin J. Vanhoozer (Grand Rapids: Eerdmans, 2001), p. 43. Vincent Brümmer also disagrees with the perspective I am offering in this section. See his *The Model of Love: A Study in Philosophical Theology* (Cambridge: Cambridge University Press, 1993); *Speaking of a Personal God: An Essay in Philosophical Theology* (Cambridge: Cambridge University Press, 1992). According to Brümmer, God needs us.

[11]Philip Rolnick, *Person, Grace, and God* (Grand Rapids: Eerdmans, 2007), p. 167.

not always respond to God's kindness with gratitude, love and praise. Instead, they turned away from their benefactor in rebellion, immersing themselves in the things of the world. Genesis 3–11 tell this sad story of rebellion, murder, arrogance and inhumanity. In Romans 1, Paul describes the degeneration that followed the rebellion. People became filled with "every kind of wickedness." "Murder, strife, deceit and malice" mark their behavior. They are "senseless, faithless, heartless and ruthless." But Paul does not make us aware of anything we cannot see on the evening news, in our fellow workers, classmates and, yes, in our own hearts.

What would you expect God to do in response to such ingratitude and wickedness? What would you do? God could let creation cease to be as easily as God created it, or God could enforce the full weight of justice against our injustice. But God does something unexpected. God patiently prepares a people, and when the time is right sends his beloved Son to become one of us. Jesus Christ lives a fully human life, exposed to the same dangers, temptations and suffering we are subjected to. Through it all Christ does what Adam would not do: he trusts God and lives only to do the Father's will. And when God requires him to give up everything, to suffer and die on a cross, Jesus places himself completely in God's hands. In the incarnation and cross of Jesus Christ the New Testament writers see a most unexpected act of divine love. John writes that "God so loved the world that he gave his one and only Son" (Jn 3:16). In another place John writes, "This is love: not that we loved God, but that he loved us and sent his Son as an atoning sacrifice for our sins" (1 Jn 4:10). Paul speaks eloquently of God's love for the unworthy: "You see, at just the right time, when we were still powerless, Christ died for the ungodly. Very rarely will anyone die for a righteous person, though for a good person someone might possibly dare to die. But God demonstrates his own love for us in this: While we were still sinners, Christ died for us" (Rom 5:6-8). Peter also takes up this contrast between the one who died and those for whom he died: "For Christ died for sins once for all, the righteous for the unrighteous, to bring you to God" (1 Pet 3:18 NIV 1984). We could extend Peter's list by adding holy for the unholy, immortal for the mortal, faithful for the unfaithful, divine for the human and so on, indefinitely. No wonder Bernard of Clairvaux, when asked why we should love God, said:

Could any title be greater than this, that He gave Himself for us unworthy wretches? And being God, what better gift could He offer than Himself? Hence, if one seeks for God's claim upon our love here is the chiefest: Because He first loved us (I John 4.19). Ought He not to be loved in return, when we think who loved, whom He loved, and how much He loved? . . . In the first creation He gave me myself; but in His new creation He gave me Himself, and by that gift restored to me the self that I had lost. Created first and then restored, I owe Him myself twice over in return for myself. But what have I to offer Him for the gift of Himself? Could I multiply myself a thousand-fold and then give Him all, what would that be in comparison with God?[12]

If the New Testament writers are correct that Christ's self-sacrificial love represents how God really feels about us, what sense does it make to think of God as against us? God's interactions with us are all designed to give us being, save us from destruction or bring us to glory. Why hold back from placing ourselves in God's hands? Paul asks us a similar question: "He who did not spare his own Son, but gave him up for us all—how will he not also, along with him, graciously give us all things?" (Rom 8:32). The answer is obvious. He will give us everything we need and more.

DIVINE DIGNITY

Does the Christian faith have something unique to say about God's dignity? What is the foundation and what are the qualities of divine dignity? How does God express and guard it? In this section and the next I want to show that God's dignity is perfectly compatible with human dignity and understood rightly gives no grounds for envy. We now move into the heart of the Christian message, the revelation and reality of God in Jesus. What kind of dignity do we find?

Thinking about God's dignity likely brings to mind God's power, majesty, holiness and glory. We think of such passages as Isaiah 6:3: "Holy, holy, holy, is the LORD Almighty; / the whole earth is full of his glory." Or we might call to mind a definition like that of Puritan theologian Thomas Ridgley (c. 1667-1734), who observes that holiness is the attribute "whereby God is in-

---

[12]Bernard of Clairvaux, *On Loving God*, chaps. 1, 5, Cyber Library, www.leaderu.com/cyber /books/onloving/onlov01.html.

finitely opposite to every thing that tends to reflect dishonour or reproach on his divine perfections . . . a harmony of all his perfections, as they are opposed to sin."[13] As I defined it in my book on the doctrine of God, God's glory is the "manifestation and perception of the greatness, splendor and excellence of God's being and actions."[14] Karl Barth speaks of divine glory as "the self-revealing sum of all divine perfections. It is the fullness of God's deity, the emerging, self-expressing and self-manifesting reality of all that God is. It is God's being in so far as this is in itself a being which declares itself."[15] In speaking of God's glory Edward Leigh makes a distinction that also applies to God's dignity. God's glory may be understood as "the inward excellence and worth whereby he deserves to be esteemed and praised" or as "the actual acknowledging of it, for glory is defined as clear and manifest knowledge of another's excellence; therefore the glory of God is two-fold."[16] Understood exclusively in these ways, God's dignity puts God at a distance from us, transcendent and exalted.

It would not occur to most of us to see divine dignity in the death of Christ. In the cross we see shame, indignity and weakness. We can envy a God of wealth, glory and power, but the dying Jesus we cannot envy. Yet according to the Christian faith, God's true dignity is revealed in the cross of Christ. Christ crucified is the "power of God and the wisdom of God," proclaims Paul (1 Cor 1:24). In the Gospel of John, Jesus points to the cross as the place where God will be glorified. "I, when I am lifted up from the earth," Jesus says, "will draw all people to myself" (Jn 12:32).[17] The cross represents the act of one who was rich, yet for our sakes became poor (2 Cor 8:9). The "Lord of glory" allowed himself to be crucified by the "rulers of this age" so that we could share in his glory (1 Cor 2:8).

---

[13]Thomas Ridgley, *Body of Divinity*, ed. Rev. John M. Wilson (New York: Robert Carter, 1855), 1:103.

[14]Ron Highfield, *Great Is the Lord: Theology for the Praise of God* (Grand Rapids: Eerdmans, 2008), p. 391.

[15]Barth, *Church Dogmatics*, 2.1, p. 643.

[16]Edward Leigh, *Treatise of Divinity*, 2.15 (London: 1647), pp. 111-12. We can see here that *glory* is a relative term. Glory is excellence perceived and acknowledged. I will argue later that dignity must also be understood as in an important sense relative.

[17]See Søren Kierkegaard's beautiful commentary on this verse in *Training in Christianity*, trans. Walter Lowrie, ed. John F. Thornton and Susan B. Varenne (New York: Vintage Book, 2004), pp. 135-238. Kierkegaard emphasizes that these words were spoken by Jesus in his humiliation and not by the exalted Jesus. It is the dying Jesus that "draws all people" to himself.

Apart from the cross we cannot know the deepest ground of God's dignity. In Christ's act of self-giving, obedience and supreme love for God and humanity, he achieved creation's redemption from bondage to sin and death. No greater accomplishment can be imagined. He worked a genuine second creation, no longer simply "good" but now perfect. No lesser wisdom could have planned and no weaker power could have accomplished this great deed. Though hidden from mortal eyes at the time, there has never been and there never will be a more glorious victory. Where then is the glory that befits such a victory?

It is often said that Christ laid aside his glory and dignity to give himself on the cross. Though not altogether wrong, this idea can be misleading. In the darkness and shame of the cross God revealed a glory and dignity far deeper than the superficial glory and dignity the world seeks. Christ glorified and dignified the Father by giving himself completely and freely into the Father's hands. And the Father glorified and dignified God's beloved Son by accepting his offering and raising him from the dead. The Son of God grounds his worth in the Father's love for him, and the Son bestows dignity on the Father by giving himself in return. God's dignity, then, is the power, wisdom and glory of his love and is manifested most fully in the self-giving of Jesus on the cross.

The glory and dignity of a human being follows the same pattern. In the footsteps of Jesus and in the power of the Spirit we can give ourselves absolutely into the hands of the one whom the Son enabled us to call "our Father." Our dignity consists in being loved by the Father of our Lord Jesus Christ. God's love makes us worthy. We live up to our dignity not by defying God and dominating others but by loving God and loving others because God loves them. The power of love *not the love of power* is "the ground of the dignity of human nature and of every rational creature."[18]

THE TRUE DIVINE SELF

In chapter five I described the "self" of the enviable God, the image of God we create in our own unredeemed likeness. The essential attribute of this

---

[18]Immanuel Kant, *Grounding for the Metaphysics of Morals*, 3rd ed., trans. James W. Ellington (Indianapolis: Hackett, 1981), p. 41. Kant, as we noted earlier, speaks of *autonomy* as the ground of human dignity.

divine self is arbitrary will. Like the false human self, the imaginary divine self wills only its own good, expansion and happiness. God's dignity set in this framework would be constituted by absolute independence from the world. We on the other hand are absolutely dependent on God. On what foundation, then, does our dignity rest? This way of thinking places the human and divine selves into competitive tension and guarantees that God will be the object of our envy. But if the cross of Jesus really manifests the true character of God, we must rethink our understanding of the divine self. This necessity forces us to think about God in a trinitarian way.

No teaching is more central to Christianity than the doctrine of the Trinity.[19] It constitutes the "fundamental grammar of Christian dogmatic theology."[20] The reason is this: the doctrine of the Trinity asserts that the revelation of God's love enacted in Jesus Christ and put into our hearts by the Holy Spirit is the unveiling of the very being of the eternal God. The doctrine of the Trinity assures us that when, in the power of the Spirit, we look at Jesus, at his love, compassion and self-sacrifice, we are seeing into the very heart of God. When Jesus says to you, "Do not be afraid" or "in my Father's house are many rooms" or "I will be with you always," you can take it as God's word because Jesus *is* God's very Word (Jn 1:1). God was always like Jesus, because Jesus is the exact image of God (Heb 1:1-3). The Spirit can draw us into God because the Spirit knows "the deep things of God" (1 Cor 2:10). The Spirit can sanctify and give life and put God's love into our hearts because the Spirit comes from the Father and is sent by the Son (Jn 15:26).

When John says "God is love" (1 Jn 4:8), we can embrace it with our minds as well as our hearts. The Father, Son and Spirit loved each other from all eternity. The doctrine of the Trinity teaches us to understand that the relationships displayed among the Father, Son and Spirit in the drama of our salvation enact in time their eternal relations. The Father has always been giving himself to the Son in the Spirit, and the Son has always returned the Father's love in the Spirit. The Father has always been

---

[19]For those readers interested in the development of the doctrine of the Trinity, see John Behr, *The Formation of Christian Theology*, 2 vols. (Crestwood, NY: St. Vladimir's Seminary Press, 2001); and R. P. C. Hanson, *The Search for the Christian Doctrine of God: The Arian Controversies, 318-381* (New York: T & T Clark, 1998).

[20]Thomas Torrance, *The Christian Doctrine of God: One Being Three Persons* (Edinburgh: T & T Clark, 1996), p. 82.

breathing the Spirit through the Son. Each divine person lives by giving, receiving, returning and sharing. There is no taking and keeping. As Dumitru Staniloae said, "In God the love between 'I's is perfect and therefore the unity between them is surpassing."[21] When we think of divinity as an enviable superhuman God, we cannot be thinking of the Trinity we meet in the Bible. The superhuman God does one thing: he wills himself. He seeks to dominate and absorb everything to which he relates. The God of Christian faith does *nothing* for God! In a sense God does not even love self. For God has no "self" in the sense of an isolated center of will and action in competition with other isolated selves.[22] One church father stated this faith in bold terms when he declared, "But when I say God, I mean Father, Son and Holy Spirit."[23]

The members of the divine Trinity love themselves only in their love for each other.[24] They will themselves only by willing each other. The Father gives freely to the Son and Spirit. The Son and Spirit joyfully receive the Father's love and give themselves freely to the Father in return. The fullness of God's being, which apart from a trinitarian understanding we are tempted to envy, is the fullness of loving freely and being freely loved, of giving, receiving, returning and sharing. God's dignity is founded and expressed in the loving and being loved among Father, Son and Spirit. God gains worth not from exercising unlimited freedom to act arbitrarily or by making the whole world serve and cringe; God is infinitely worthy because each infinite divine person loves and is loved by the others infinitely. By loving, each gives worth to the others.

Hence when the Son of God becomes a human being, washes feet and dies on a cross in obedience to the Father, he does not act in a way contrary to his divine dignity, for the Son of God has always been receiving

---

[21]Dumitru Staniloae, "The Holy Trinity: Structure of Supreme Love," in *Theology and the Church*, trans. Robert Barringer (Crestwood, NY: St. Vladimir's Seminary Press, 1980), p. 79.

[22]God "is personal as being three persons in relation, of having his being in what Father, Son and Holy Spirit give to and receive from each other in the freedom of their unknowable eternity" (Colin Gunton, *The Promise of Trinitarian Theology*, 2nd ed. (New York: T & T Clark, 1997), p. 195.

[23]Gregory of Nazianzus, *Oration 38*, chap. 8, in *St. Cyril of Jerusalem and St. Gregory of Nazianzen*, vol. 7, Nicene and Post-Nicene Fathers, 2nd ser., ed. Philip Schaff and Henry Wace (Grand Rapids: Eerdmans, 1979), p. 347.

[24]Wolfhart Pannenberg argues this point in *Systematic Theology*, trans. Geoffrey Bromiley (Grand Rapids: Eerdmans, 1991), 1:426.

and returning himself to the Father. He does in his human life in time exactly what in his divine life he does in eternity. In his cross he overturns the world's idea of dignity and shows dignity's true nature. Our dignity cannot be measured by our authority or wealth or coercive power. It is not revealed by our capacities, inner qualities or intrinsic nature. It is measured only by greatness of the one who loves us. We act consistently with our dignity when we love God and our neighbor in the freedom given to us by God's love for us. As a human, the Son of God loved the Father in the way we ought to have loved him. In the cross, Jesus shows the true meaning of both divine and human worth. No one can envy the dignity of the self-giving God!

9

THE IRONY OF DIVINE "WEAKNESS"

When we think of God's greatness we usually call to mind such awe-evoking qualities as omnipotence, omnipresence, omniscience and immortality. As we confront death, fate, chance and other powerful forces that threaten us with annihilation or slavery, we may rejoice in God's power to deal with them. On the other hand, we may find it difficult to suppress suspicion that these attributes may also be turned against us, that God's greatness may leave us little room to live. We worry that to shield ourselves against our powerful enemies we have had to sell ourselves to an even more powerful—if more benevolent—being. I believe these thoughts arise because we think of these attributes as the characteristics of a self-centered being, a being it makes sense to envy. We are thinking of that divine self discussed earlier, the self of pure will. But a far different picture emerges when we consider God in light of Jesus Christ. Through Christ we come to know God as the eternal Trinity who lives by loving.

Misunderstanding God's Omnipotence

Several misconceptions plague the competitive view of divine power. The first concerns the definition of omnipotence. Many think of God's power in quantitative terms, that is, that affirming God's omnipotence implies that God possesses all power. Thinking of it this way naturally leads us to consider God as a threat. If God possesses all power, we are left with none, and if we possess some power God cannot have all. Of course, the doctrine of omnipotence teaches that God can do anything he wants. The Lord questioned Abraham, "Is anything too hard for the LORD?" (Gen 18:14). Abraham knew the answer. The Apostles' Creed begins, "We believe in God the Father, *Almighty*." And Augustine says that God "without doubt can as easily refuse to permit what He does not wish, as bring about what He does wish. . . . [T]he will of the Omnipotent is never defeated."[1] But this is only the beginning point for reflection on God's power. The final word is that God's power is not quantifiable at all, because power is not something God *has*—this would make God into Zeus—but something God *is*. One ancient writer explains, "God is power because in His own Self He contains all power beforehand and exceeds it."[2] God does not need power. He does not gain, lose, hold or even *use* power. God *is* power, just as God *is* love and wisdom.

Since we call God "powerful" in analogy to our power, we need to remember that God's power is unlike as well as like our power. We use energy to get things done, and in using it we exhaust it. For us, power comes in megawatts and horsepower. But power is more than physical energy even for us. Energy without direction is destruction. Getting something done requires know-how or wisdom, and wisdom is not depleted by its accomplishments. In wisdom we imagine a bridge to the moon or a machine in which to travel to the stars. We need energy to make our dreams exist but God does not. Energy applies to changes within our space-time world, changes in place, form or state. It does not apply at all to God's relationship to the world. God's creations exist merely because God wills them. If we think of God's power like we think of his wisdom, we can see that God's power is not exhausted—or even affected—by using it. Do we make God less wise because we grow in wisdom? And does God's unlimited wisdom render us incapable of wisdom? Of course not. In the same way, exercising the power given to us does not make God less powerful, and recognizing that God empowers our power does not make it any less our power.

---

[1]Augustine, *Enchiridion* 96 and 102, in *St. Augustine: On the Holy Trinity, Doctrinal Treatises, Moral Treatises*, vol. 3, Nicene and Post-Nicene Fathers, 1st ser., ed. Philip Schaff (Grand Rapids: Eerdmans, 1979), pp. 267, 270.

[2]Dionysius the Areopagite, *The Divine Names* 8, in *Dionysius the Areopagite on the Divine Names and the Mystical Theology*, trans. C. E. Rolt (Berwick, ME: IBIS Press, 2004), pp. 154-57.

The second misunderstanding of God's omnipotence is related to the first. The doctrine of omnipotence affirms that although there are created powers, none escapes dependence on God's power. No power can act apart from God's continual sustaining and empowering. This perpetual dependence and lack of autonomy provokes some to modify the doctrine of divine omnipotence and assert that we can do some things "on our own." For example, Clark Pinnock asserts, "Thinking of God as literally *all*-powerful divests the finite universe of a degree of power."[3] Instead of exercising all power, God shares power. Pinnock explains, "The Lord of the universe has chosen to limit his power by delegating some to the creature."[4] Most often, changes such as the one Pinnock proposes are motivated by fear that God's empowering power poses a threat to our freedom and dignity. It is another manifestation of the competitive model of the divine/human relationship.

This view mistakenly assumes that doing things on your own is the essence of freedom and dignity. Being able to act only with the help of something other than ourselves lessens us. I will deal in greater detail with the nature of freedom in chapter fourteen. For now, consider that wanting to be able to do something on our own with respect to God is asking for the impossible. We cannot even exist on our own, and everything else we do depends on our existence. Strictly speaking, we can do nothing on our own.

The idea of doing something on our own applies in a limited way to our ordinary experience. To prove his strength a weightlifter may lift his car on his own rather than using a jack. To prove her mastery of a concept a student refuses a teacher's help in solving a math problem, choosing to do it on her own. But these examples show only a relative independence. We can momentarily assert independence from one thing by depending all the more

---

[3]Clark Pinnock, "Between Classical and Process Theism," in *Process Theology*, ed. Ronald Nash (Grand Rapids: Baker, 1989), pp. 316-17. See also Pinnock, *Most Moved Mover: A Theology of God's Openness* (Grand Rapids: Baker Academic, 2001), pp. 53-55. Process philosopher Charles Hartshorne denies that the concept of divine omnipotence is coherent (*Omnipotence and Other Theological Mistakes* [Albany: State University of New York, 1984], p. 26). For a similar view from another process thinker, see David Ray Griffin, *God, Power and Evil* (Louisville, KY: Westminster Press, 1976), and his *Evil Revisited: Responses and Reconsiderations* (Albany: State University of New York Press, 1991).

[4]Clark Pinnock, "Systematic Theology," in *The Openness of God: A Biblical Challenge to the Traditional Understanding of God*, ed. Clark Pinnock et al. (Downers Grove, IL: InterVarsity Press, 1994), p. 115.

on others. The weightlifter still needs solid ground on which to stand and even the accomplished student relies on past lessons learned. But asserting that we can do something independent of God would declare an absolute independence because there is no ground left onto which to shift our dependence—every other thing also depends totally on God for its existence.

Far from being a threat to our freedom and dignity, God's empowering power is their most secure foundation. We do not resent the air we breathe because we depend on it for all we do, and we do not curse the ground beneath our feet because it enables us to walk. In the same way, God's gracious power empowers us to walk and breathe and accomplish everything else we achieve. Far from suppressing our freedom, God's power frees us from nothingness into existence, from death into life and from paralysis into activity. Without his power we can do nothing, but with it we can do whatever God wants us to do.

In a third misunderstanding, we often think of God's power as force. While God's power is not wholly unlike force, we need to be very careful in applying this concept to God. The word *force* evokes the idea of destruction and coercion. In our experience we need power not only to build but to destroy. Demolishing a skyscraper requires less subtlety but no less energy than building one. But God's power is very different. God's power lets things be by thinking and willing them. God has no need to compel them to be, for before they come into being nothing exists to be compelled. Creation requires no energy and involves no change; for change is alteration in something that exists as it moves from one state to another. Nor does annihilation require energy or change. God does not have to demolish and haul things away. If God ceases to will something's existence, it ceases to exist without residue.

DIVINE PERSUASION

If God does not accomplish goals by force, how does God get things done? We have seen that God creates the world and everything in it simply by willing it to be. This act certainly qualifies as power because a power's greatness is measured by what it can achieve. What achievement could be greater than creating this beautiful and vast universe from nothing? Letting things be is just the beginning of God's work, however. It is but one di-

mension of the Bible's story of God's relationship with his creatures. The
Bible also tells the story of the fall, reconciliation and redemption of creation. From our perspective the act of creation looks like a one-way relationship. God willed that creatures exist, and they came to be. They had no
choice. But once they exist, some of God's creatures possess wills and minds
of their own. God wants human beings not only to exist and reflect his glory
simply by being there but also wants them involved in their growth and
salvation. God wants us to know love and to love in return, to know God's
will and desire it. God gave us existence before we could do anything, but
God will bring us to perfection through our own freedom. In the words of
Dumitru Staniloae, "The things given us by God can become our own gift
to God by the fact that in the return of these things to God we are free."[5] But
how can God accomplish this? What kind of power will it take?

Scripture spends comparatively little space on creation and gives most of
its attention to the story of redemption. Unlike creation, the story of salvation is full of pathos and surprises: the call of Abraham, the exodus, the
covenant with Israel, the giving of the law, the exile and return, and the
birth, ministry, death and resurrection of Jesus Christ. It is a story of God's
love, grace and corrective discipline. The response of the people was a combination of faithfulness and unfaithfulness, of some gratitude and much
ungratefulness, of a few who loved the Lord and the many who worshiped
other gods. The Old Testament closes without reaching the goal or showing
the way to it.

The New Testament proclaims that God has accomplished the goal in
one Israelite, Jesus Christ. Jesus became the first human being to reach the
end God had set for all creation. He lived in faithfulness to God and loved
God with all his heart, mind, soul and strength. He gave himself utterly to
his Father, even unto death, as our representative. In Jesus' resurrection
God raised our human nature to eternal life, and through the power of the
Holy Spirit we can be united to Jesus so that we share in his righteous actions and affections. In this way God accomplishes for us and for all creation what is already real in Christ.

---

[5]Dumitru Staniloae, *The World: Creation and Deification*, vol. 2, *The Experience of God*, trans.
and ed. Ioan Ionita and Robert Barringer (Brookline, MA: Holy Cross Orthodox Press, 2000),
p. 22.

What kind of power do we see displayed in the salvation God has accomplished? We see creation power, for God let Christ become incarnate through the womb of Mary. Creation power was also at work in Jesus' miracles and in the resurrection. Even in the atonement we see creation power at work, for Jesus was a human being who shared human nature with us. Christ transformed human nature by his holiness and resurrection. But we also see another type of power at work, which we can call gospel power. This power works by a kind of persuasion. We cannot be transformed into the likeness of God in the same way we were created. It is one thing to build a house, but it is quite another to create a saint! A house does not become a house because it wants to become a house, but people cannot become saints unless they will to be saintly. Willing with one's whole heart to be saintly is the substance of being a saint. The power of the Spirit to free our hearts from sin, enable us to believe and participate in Christ's holiness is a matter of persuasion. We need to consider, then, the nature of persuasion within our experience and how God's persuasion power might differ from ours.

In his book *Rhetoric*, Aristotle defines rhetoric as "the faculty of observing in any given case the available means of persuasion."[6] The speaker uses three "modes" or "sources" of persuasion: *ethos* or character, *pathos* or emotions, and *logos* or reason. People can be persuaded by the good or beautiful character of the speaker or by appeal to such natural emotions as pity, envy, anger and friendship. They can also be moved by reasonable arguments.[7] In keeping with his definition of rhetoric Aristotle spends most of this work exploring ways speakers can establish rapport with the audience, appeal to their emotions and argue effectively to prove a point. In looking for means of persuasion, however, the orator must take into consideration certain natural tendencies all human beings possess. We have a natural affinity for truth and justice. Aristotle explains, "Rhetoric is useful (1) because things that are true and things that are just have a natural tendency to prevail over their opposites."[8] Or he says a few paragraphs later, "Things that are true and things that are better are, by their

---

[6]Aristotle, *Rhetoric* 1.2, in *The Basic Writings of Aristotle*, ed. Richard McKeon (New York: Random House, 1941), p. 1329.
[7]Ibid., pp. 1329-30.
[8]Ibid., 1.1, p. 1327.

nature, practically always easier to prove and easier to believe in."[9] Additionally, human beings want to be happy and desire whatever they think will facilitate happiness:

> It may be said that every individual man and all men in common aim at a certain end which determines what they choose and what they avoid. This end . . . is happiness and its constituent parts. For all advice to do things or not do them is concerned with happiness and with things that make for or against it; whatever creates or increases happiness or some part of happiness, we ought to do; whatever destroys or hampers happiness or gives rise to its opposite, we ought not to do.[10]

For Aristotle, then, effective persuasion must take account of the natural tendency toward truth, justice and goodness. For "nobody wishes for anything unless he thinks it good. . . . To sum up then, all actions due to ourselves either are or seem to be either good or pleasant."[11]

In book four of his work *On Christian Doctrine* Augustine reflects on the use of rhetoric by Christian teachers. The Christian preacher must teach, delight and persuade. Teaching is the most important of the three. But pleasing and persuading are often useful, for sometimes people hear truth and are still unmoved. "As the hearer must be pleased in order to secure his attention, so he must be persuaded in order to move him to action."[12] The goal of persuasion is not to inform people of what ought to be done—that is the function of teaching—but to "urge them to do what they already know ought to be done."[13] "For if a man be not moved by the force of truth, though it is demonstrated to his own confession, and clothed in beauty of style, nothing remains but to subdue him by the power of eloquence."[14] Persuasive speech, according to Augustine, moves people by promises of good and threats of destruction. Such persuasion is not always necessary, for sometimes the hearer assents to truth immediately upon hearing it. And it

---

9Ibid., p. 1328.
10Ibid., 1.4, p. 1339.
11Ibid., 1.10, pp. 1360-61.
12Augustine, *On Christian Doctrine* 4.12, in *St. Augustine's City of God and Christian Doctrine*, vol. 2, Nicene and Post-Nicene Fathers, 1st ser., ed. Philip Schaff (Grand Rapids: Eerdmans, 1979), p. 583.
13Ibid.
14Ibid., 4.13.

is not always necessary to please the hearer because occasionally "the truth itself, when exhibited in its naked simplicity, gives pleasure, because it is the truth."[15] Augustine, like Aristotle, assumes that we were created with the natural need for truth, goodness and beauty, even if in our fallen condition we are blinded by falsehood and weighted down by bad habits.

Considering the thought of these ancient theorists enables us to see that persuasion makes use of four forms of natural affinity: (1) the desire for good, (2) the attractiveness of beauty, (3) the just demand of the right and (4) the power of truth. We are naturally repelled by their opposites: evil, ugliness, falsehood and injustice. Coercion moves people against their wills whereas persuasion moves people to move themselves freely. To persuade people, we hold up a truth before them that exerts its attraction on their minds and wills. God created us for truth, goodness, beauty and rightness; we cannot re-create ourselves otherwise. By inclination we seek what appears pleasant, but our God-created nature cannot thrive except upon the truly good. Our minds seek truth and our consciences tell us we ought to do right. We can be deceived by fictions and overcome by bad habits, but our underlying constitution remains. Persuasion addresses this basic structure of human nature and makes no sense apart from it. If we can convince people of something's goodness or harmfulness we go a long way toward persuading them to seek goodness and avoid injury.

What is divine persuasion? As a way to clarify this concept I will contrast my thinking on divine persuasion with process theology, a contemporary viewpoint that has made divine persuasion central to its understanding of God's relationship to the world. Indeed, this system of thought understands God's power as wholly persuasive and rejects completely the idea of divine coercion. In the words of John Cobb and David Griffin, "God seeks to persuade each occasion toward that possibility for its own existence which would be best for it; but God cannot control the finite occasion's self-actualization."[16] Lewis Ford affirms that "divine persuasive power maximizes creaturely freedom, respecting the integrity of each creature in the

---

[15]Ibid., 4.12.
[16]John B. Cobb and David Ray Griffin, *Process Theology: An Introductory Exposition* (Philadelphia: Westminster John Knox, 1976), p. 53.

very act of guiding that creature's development toward greater freedom."[17] Taken by itself one could hardly quibble with Ford's statement. However, when we take into account process thought's rejection of the doctrine of creation from nothing—what I called "creation power"—and its designation of any divine act of "efficient causality" within the world as coercive, it becomes problematic.[18] These views make sense only within a worldview that considers freedom to be something that "cannot be derived from any external agency, including God."[19] For process theology, the world exists and exercises freedom by its own inherent power of existence. This makes it difficult if not impossible to conceive a way for divine persuasion to achieve perfectly the goal at which it aims. For, since God is not the origin of the creature's nature or its capacity for freedom, God cannot be the end of that freedom, that for which it was made. And if creatures are not made for God, they may continually find reasons to reject God's persuasion. In process thought, then, divine persuasion is fallible and imperfect.[20] In my view we need to develop a different model of divine persuasion.[21]

Divine persuasion must be distinguished from human persuasion in

---

[17]Lewis S. Ford, "Divine Persuasion and the Triumph of Good," *Christian Scholar* 50 (Fall 1967): 236.

[18]Lewis S. Ford, *The Lure of God: A Biblical Background for Process Theism* (Philadelphia: Fortress Press, 1978). Ford defines coercion as "any restriction on the range of real possibility which would otherwise be available (pp. 17-18).

[19]Ibid., p. 18. The traditional view I am defending understands freedom to be a gift God bestowed on us through his creation power. Hence, God's acts of "efficient causality" do not contradict freedom; rather, they are foundational for freedom.

[20]This problem is illustrated in Thomas Jay Oord's attempt to appropriate the process view of divine power for evangelical theology. See his "Divine Power and Love: An Evangelical Proposal," *Koinonia* 10, no. 1 (Spring 1998): 1-18. He proposes numerous examples biblical and extra-biblical where God was not able to achieve his will through persuasion or "indirect physical force" (p. 12). Oord gives no assurances that God can in the short or long term achieve his goals. Nor can he provide such assurances given his commitment to the basic principles of process philosophy.

[21]Deists and supernatural rationalists developed another view of divine persuasion in reaction to orthodox views of the work of the Spirit on the human heart. Matthew Tindal (1655-1733) expresses a position typical of this outlook: "The Holy Ghost can't deal with men as rational creatures, but by proposing arguments to convince their understandings, and influence their wills, in the same manner as if proposed by other agents; for to go beyond this would be making impressions on men, as a seal does on wax; to the confounding of their reason, and their liberty in choosings; and the man would then be merely passive, and the action would be the action of another Being acting upon him; for which he could be in no way accountable" (*Christianity as Old as Creation*, quoted in John Martin Creed and Boys Smith, *Religious Thought in the Eighteenth Century* [Cambridge: Cambridge University Press, 1934], pp. 33-34).

several respects. First, human persuasion reflects the strengths and weaknesses of the persuader. People sometimes attempt to persuade us to do things without having our best interests at heart. Occasionally, they have only their own interests in mind or they are even malicious. Even with the best intentions persuasion is burdened by uncertainty. We should not, however, attribute to God anything less than ideal persuasion, which is moving someone to move themselves wholly toward goodness, truth, beauty and justice.

Second, even apart from the question of motives, persuasion is problematic. The ideal persuader knows two things: (1) the truth, goodness and beauty of the thing to be communicated, and (2) how to place this thing clearly before the minds and hearts of the listeners so that illusions are dispelled and habits are broken. Unfortunately, in human communication both parties are fallible and inept—as well as morally flawed. We may not know the truth well enough to articulate it clearly. Even if we have an adequate grasp of what we wish to communicate, we do not know others well enough to get past their fears, false opinions, illusions, wounds and bad habits.

But God is the perfect persuader. Through the Spirit, God can move us *without coercion* by enabling us to move ourselves toward our perfect joy and fulfillment. God knows perfectly the truth and goodness we need because God *is* the truth and goodness we need! God knows our nature and how to bring it to perfection because God created us. God knows our thoughts and wishes, our sins and illusions, our habits, fears and wounds. And God can place himself right in front of the eyes of our hearts because God is the Spirit. What does God place before our spirits to move us to move ourselves? God's own self. But not the self we sometimes imagine him to be, blindingly glorious and thunderously powerful—and self-centered. God appears as a lamb slain, as Jesus Christ crucified, as perfect love and goodness and joy. It is not true, as is commonly said, that God hides God's glory and power so that we can make a free decision, as if seeing that glory would overwhelm our freedom. God appears in weakness not to protect our freedom but to win our love. Jesus shows us how much God loves us, and the Spirit says to our hearts: "Behold the man Jesus! He is what you were meant to be from the beginning. He is your future and your true self." As a human being, Jesus gave himself to God as our representative and pioneered the way we can become our true selves. Because he binds himself to our human nature, Jesus' deed counts as ours. His obedience can become our own free act through the Spirit's power. This power enables us to become like the crucified and risen One, to will God's will perfectly in the glorious freedom of the children of God (Rom 8:21) and to act with the love of God put in our hearts by the Spirit (Rom 5:5).

The view of divine persuasion I am advocating, though a minority view, is not foreign to mainstream Christian theologians. The great medieval theologian Duns Scotus, in his commentary on Peter Lombard's *Sentences*, distinguishes himself from the views of Thomas Aquinas by advocating a type of infallible persuasion that God exerts in grace. God moves without fail those whom he chooses to will his good will.[22] Many may find it surprising that the early post-Reformation Reformed theologian Girolamo Zanchi (1516-1590) argues that God's grace never acts by coercion on the human will. Instead, God leads the will persuasively: "For even when he [God] changes it and makes it good out of bad, and willing out of not-willing, he does not exert power onto it but persuasively leads it so that it, being led, spontaneously even moves itself immediately."[23]

Hence we need not fear that God's omnipotence somehow threatens our freedom and dignity. On the contrary, God's creation power gives us being, life, freedom and all good things. Apart from it we could will nothing and do nothing. The Spirit places the love of God before our hearts and persuades and empowers us to move ourselves beyond the futility and despair of sin. These two powers do nothing against us. They do not overwhelm us, restrict us or weaken us in any way. They liberate us from our real enemies,

---

[22]According to Reginald Garrigou-LaGrange, Thomists reject this theory as impossible apart from the vision of God. I am not convinced by their criticism, however. Indeed, only the vision of God is absolutely persuasive, but persuasion does not need to be absolute to be infallible. Perhaps there are no subjects whom God desires to persuade for whom only the vision would suffice. For further discussion, see Reginald Garrigou-LaGrange, *Predestination: The Meaning of Predestination in Scripture and the Church* (Rockford, IL: Tan Books, 1998), pp. 113-14.

[23]This remarkable statement breaks the stereotype of the Reformed doctrine of conversion as divine coercion. The editors in commenting on this text point out that only after the Remonstrants began to employ the concept of "moral persuasion" (i.e., a fallible and imperfect type of persuasion very much like human persuasion) did the Reformed theologians cease using the idea of persuasion to explain God's action in conversion. (*The Fall of the First Man, Sin and the Law of God*, bk. 1, chap. 6, cited in *Reformed Thought on Freedom: The Concept of Free Choice in Early Modern Reformed Theology*, ed. Willem J. van Asselt, J. Martin Bac and Roelf T. te Velde [Grand Rapids: Baker Academic, 2010], pp. 74, 92).

which do overwhelm, restrict and weaken us. They free us from illusions and fears and addictions. They raise us from undignified slavery to fantasy, pride and lust to the glorious station of the children of God. With this view of divine power in mind we can understand why the psalmist exclaims, "The LORD reigns, let the earth be glad" (Ps 97:1).

10

THE AWAKENING PRESENCE

As children, one of the first things we learn about God is that God is present everywhere and knows everything. As I noted in an earlier chapter, these qualities strike both positive and negative chords in us. It can be very comforting to believe that God is always near and knows our every need. Of what comfort would God's power be if God were not near enough to help or if God were unaware of our plight? On the other hand, some people find the idea of God's all-knowing nearness very troubling. Someone is always watching. You can never close the door for a moment alone, not even inside your most private self. There is no encryption technique sophisticated enough to render your thoughts unreadable.

Perhaps the most disturbing thought about God's perfect knowledge of us is fear of losing our sense of self. Above all things, we want to preserve our integrity as persons. We want a real self, our own sphere of will and action, a space in the center of our being where we control who gets admitted. But can we be a real self if we are pervaded by another, even if that other is God? How can you have a sense of identity if you cannot think about yourself? And how can you think about yourself when you are always aware of someone else's knowing presence? How can you possess yourself without freedom, yet how can you exercise freedom under the watchful eye of God?[1]

---

[1]The sense of self I am describing in this paragraph is a very modern notion. It is what Charles Taylor calls the "buffered" self. The modern self possess a boundary that marks it off from the outside world, giving it the distinctly modern sense of integrity and privacy. In contrast, the premodern self was "porous," susceptible to the influence of magical objects, spirits, de-

ANOTHER LOOK AT POWER

The first thing to notice about these concerns is that they raise in another form the issue of power. The one who knows has an advantage over the one who does not. We value our privacy if for no other reason than because we value our safety. The more others know about us the more vulnerable we are. You do not want everyone to know you are carrying $10,000 in your briefcase. We keep our debit card access codes to ourselves. Under certain circumstances it can be very important to keep your thoughts to yourself. At an auction you do not want everyone else to know how high you are willing to bid. If knowledge bestows power and God knows everything, it follows that God has all the power.

Chapter nine, on God's power, sheds much light on this issue as well. There we learned that God's power is noncompetitive. God does not over-power but empowers us for our own free action. God's knowledge, like God's power, differs greatly from human knowledge. We can know things only because they exist and impress themselves on our knowing faculties. God's knowledge, on the contrary, is creative. Nothing can exist unless God knows it and wills it to exist. Thomas Aquinas denied that God knows things because they exist, asserting rather, that things exist because God knows them.[2] To grasp this counterintuitive idea consider Aquinas's thought on the nature of God's self-knowledge. It cannot be right to say that God's existence causes God's self-knowledge because this would imply that God is not the cause of God's own existence, that something other than God causes God to exist. This is true of us—we must exist before we can do anything or know that we exist—but this is not true of God. But it makes even less sense

---

mons and God. The closing of the self to these forces is seen by modern people as an advance for human dignity and freedom. The idea of God's omnipresence then is associated with a return to this earlier age. See Charles Taylor, *A Secular Age* (Cambridge, MA: Belknap Press, 2007), pp. 35-41.

[2]Thomas Aquinas, *Summa Theologica* 1.14.8, in *Basic Writings of Saint Thomas Aquinas*, ed. Anton C. Pegis (New York: Random House, 1945), 1:147. Augustine also speaks of God's way of knowing in this way: "Nor did God become acquainted with them [creatures], so as to know them, at any definite time; but He knew beforehand, without any beginning all things to come in time, and among them also both what we should ask of Him, and when; and to whom He would either listen or not listen, and on what subjects. . . . He does not know them because they are, but they are because he knows them" (Augustine, *On the Holy Trinity* 15.13, in *St. Augustine: On the Holy Trinity, Doctrinal Treatises, Moral Treatises*, vol. 3, Nicene and Post-Nicene Fathers, 1st ser., ed. Philip Schaff [Grand Rapids: Eerdmans, 1979], p. 212).

to reverse the relationship and say that God exists because God knows God. But what alternative is left?

Such traditional theologians as Anselm of Canterbury and Thomas Aquinas argue that we can do justice to God's divinity only if we understand God to be the cause of God's own existence. Anselm argues in his *Monologium* that it is absurd to say that God is self-created, but on the other hand it is a denial of God's divinity to say that God was created by another power. Even if we cannot grasp fully what we are saying, argues Anselm, we must insist that "God exists through himself."[3] Now, if God exists "through himself"—that is, if God's existence is God's own free act—since God knows what God is doing, God also possesses self-knowledge through the act of existing. So in a sense we could say that God is the cause of God's being *and* of God's knowledge of God in one life act. Another way to say this is that knowing and existing are inseparable aspects of God's eternal life.[4] Now let us apply this lesson to God's knowledge of creatures. Aquinas's assertion that God's knowledge of something causes its existence is simply a shorter way of saying that *God* is the cause of God's knowledge of other things and their existence in the same act. We cannot separate them. In knowing us God gives us being and freedom. We exist because of God's creation power, and we can know ourselves and other things because God knows us and them first. Hence God's knowledge of us is a sign of his grace and love.

God's complete knowledge of us and all things is very important to persuasion power. If God did not know us thoroughly God could not set before us the true, good and beautiful in ways that are persuasive. But God knows why God made us and how to help us achieve that end. God knows all the ways these things are hidden to us and how to break through these illusions. God loves in knowing and knows in loving. God's complete knowledge of us should be very good news to us because it assures us that God knows how to love us.

---

[3] Anselm of Canterbury, *Monologium*, chap. 3, in *Saint Anselm: Basic Writings*, trans. S. N. Deane, 2nd ed. (LaSalle, IL: Open Court, 1968), pp. 42-49.
[4] For my thinking on God's freedom or aseity, see my *Great Is the Lord: Theology for the Praise of God* (Grand Rapids, Eerdmans, 2008), pp. 222-54.

PRESENCE

Think of the importance we attach to being seen, known and acknowledged by others.[5] Even as we claim to desire our privacy, we crave the presence of others. Imagine removing every human action and practice whose main function is to attract the attention of others. What are wealth and fashion and beauty but means by which people seek to be admired or envied? How much of your wealth can you eat? Clothes do not need to be expensive to keep us covered and warm. And cars do not have to be elegant to function as means of transportation. We want to be known and acknowledged by others. Most of all, we want to love and be loved. But this cannot happen unless we become present to each other in honest revelation and respect. For many reasons, however, we find such genuine presence very difficult to achieve. First, we do not know ourselves well enough to present ourselves fully to others. Second, we are afraid of "otherness," that quality in others that is mysterious, unpredictable and not under our control. This fear compels us to withhold ourselves. The "other" might harm us, reject us or absorb us. What we need most, the loving presence of other people, eludes us.[6]

The pain and frustration of our failed attempts to be with others may drive us to want to be alone. Of course, sometimes we need to withdraw to work or to sort our feelings undisturbed by the presence of other people. It is often difficult to distinguish our own thoughts about ourselves from other people's thoughts about us. But no one wants to be absolutely alone. Without the presence of others we would lose ourselves, for we would have nothing from which to distinguish ourselves. Hence the desire to be "alone" is better interpreted as our need to be away from things that disturb us, and with things that give us peace. Perhaps we need a walk in a park with birds singing and chattering squirrels at play, or some time in our favorite chair with our dog curled at our feet. Being with these things restores a sense of identity.

Becoming aware of the difficulty of establishing loving relationships puts the teaching of God's omnipresence in a new light. This thought assures us that God knows us even though we do not know ourselves or have the

---

[5]Recall the section on the celebrity view of human existence in chap. 4.
[6]See John Zizioulas, *Communion and Otherness* (New York: T & T Clark, 2006) for a thoughtful study of the issues treated in this section.

courage to let ourselves be known. God does not depend on us for knowledge of us. We do not have to struggle to make ourselves present to God. There is no need to fear that God might harm, reject or absorb us if we reveal ourselves. God knows all about us. Without confidence in God's omniscience we could not be certain that God loves us. We could always doubt that God would love us *if* God really knew what we are like.

God's knowledge of us can be the foundation of a new way of relating to God and others. First, by believing that God knows us and yet loves us we are given courage to confess our sins and fears to God and receive forgiveness. Openness to God in turn gives us the courage to reveal ourselves to others, and this courage may embolden others to reciprocate. Second, God's omnipresence gives new meaning to our desire to be alone with ourselves. As I noted earlier, we cannot be—nor would we want to be—absolutely alone with ourselves, but we want to be with something that enables us to distinguish our true selves from the disturbing noise that clouds our minds. The divine presence does not create the noise and confusion that we experience in the presence of human beings. Hence, I think our need for time alone arises ultimately from our need to withdraw from other things into God's presence. God is always there, so we need never feel alone; yet, since God is all-knowing, we never need to withdraw from his presence to find ourselves. God's thoughts about us reflect who we truly are, so in God's presence we are fully with ourselves.

DIVINE KNOWLEDGE AND HUMAN SELFHOOD

In the beginning of this chapter I posed the question of the self and God's omnipresence. On the surface it would seem that preserving the identity and integrity of the self requires it to be alone or at least to be in control of its inner space. In other words, the self is defined by itself and so must have the capacity to exist in absolute solitude. If this were true, God's omnipresence would indeed compromise the integrity of the human self. But as I explained in chapter seven, the self has no such independence. We were created by God, and we remain dependent on God for our being. We cannot achieve our true selves except by arriving at the destination God has set in the way God provides. We are ourselves only in relation to God. Apart from him we are nothing and no one.

When you lay aside the illusion of total independence, God's knowledge of us becomes good news rather than an insult to our dignity. To help us grasp why this is so, consider the distinction between human nature and a unique person. A nature is defined by a set of attributes that answers the question What is it? In answer to a space alien's question, "What are you?" I would have to answer, "I am a human being." The common noun *human* refers to the nature I share will others. Insofar as I am human, I am like other human beings. As an individual I do not add anything to human nature.

My name, Ron, designates my person, something I share with no one. The question Who are you? asks for this unique aspect of our being. If you asked me this question I would first give my name, which stands for my unique identity as a whole. As I continue to explain who I am, I would let you know that I am the firstborn son of Curtis and Josephine. I am father, teacher, husband and friend. I love to run and hike and read. These are roles I play and relations that define me, and I am *who* I am only in relation to these things. But how essential are these relations and roles to my being? Are they merely accidental and contingent? After all, I might never have been born. Would my identity be different if I had a different body? Are the names of my parents and my name essential? My parents might never have married. I might never have married or have had children. So who am I really? Is my identity merely the sum total of all these unessential relations? Am I merely individual human number 65,000,000,001, who happens to have all the accidental relations I have? Or do I have an identity rooted in something deeper?[7]

Søren Kierkegaard's thinking about the nature of the self and God in *Sickness Unto Death* sheds important light on this discussion. Kierkegaard conceives of the self as a complex set of relations. We are in one sense (objectively) the sum total of the events and relations of our lives. But this complex reflects on itself, duplicates itself by forming an image of itself and

---

[7]According to Charles Taylor, these questions could not have been asked in earlier ages. Premodern people were "embedded" in a social matrix that gave them identity. They lacked the presuppositions to enable them to ask such questions. Only with the rise of modern "disembedding" from these relations could this new sense of self arise (*Secular Age*, pp. 148-50). This new sense of self, however, leads to loneliness and loss of identity and raises again the question of meaning.

hence becomes conscious of itself.[8] This relation of the self to itself raises another question: how will the self-conscious self relate itself to itself in a value judgment? Will it accept or reject itself, love or hate itself, approve or disapprove of itself? At this point the self faces a crisis and tends to fall into one of the two basic forms of despair: (1) the despair "not to will to be oneself" (i.e., the self does not will to be the finite, limited and imperfect self of which it is conscious) and (2) the despair of being unable "to will to be oneself" (i.e., the self wants to accept itself as the finite, limited and imperfect self it is before God, but cannot achieve it).[9] The first form of despair manifests itself in our dreams of moving beyond all limitations, in our tendency to live in our imaginations and in our futile efforts to remake ourselves according to our daydreams.[10]

The second form of despair overtakes us when we despair of the first despair, when we fall exhausted from our first attempts to escape from ourselves.[11] We realize we need to accept ourselves as we are before God, but we cannot do it. Only by relying completely on God's love, acceptance, grace and forgiveness can we escape from second form of despair.[12] Consciousness of being known and loved by God enables us to confess our sin and acknowledge our limitations without despairing of actualizing the infinite possibilities with which we have been created. And confession allows us to get to know ourselves at a deeper level. "Much that you are able to keep hidden in darkness, you first get to know by your opening it to the knowledge of the all-knowing One."[13] Kierkegaard expresses the state of having rooted out despair this way: "in relating itself to itself and in willing

---

[8]This self-transcendence is possible and conceivable only where the self is involved in a relationship between the finite and the infinite.

[9]Søren Kierkegaard, *Sickness Unto Death*, ed. and trans. Howard V. and Edna H. Hong (Princeton, NJ: Princeton University Press, 1980), pp. 13-14. Kierkegaard here speaks in psychological terms. In religious terms the former is the futile desire to become God and the latter is the futile desire to obey God on one's own power.

[10]This type of despair corresponds to the esthetic stage described in exquisite detail in volume 1 of Kierkegaard's *Either/Or*.

[11]The second form of despair corresponds to Kierkegaard's ethical stage, which is the theme of volume 2 of *Either/Or*.

[12]The first form of despair can be escaped only by being transformed into the second form. In religious terms, the self becomes aware of God, comes to see itself as God's creature and under his judgment.

[13]Søren Kierkegaard, *Purity of Heart Is to Will One Thing* (Radford, VA: Wilder, 2008), p. 17.

to be itself, the self rests transparently in the power that established it."[14]
Hence in Kierkegaard's thinking the very structure of the self includes a
relation to God that must be positively acknowledged before the self can
know and accept itself. By resting in God we can accept ourselves by accepting God's acceptance of us; that is, we relate to ourselves indirectly by
relating to God, who relates to us in love.

In part two of *Sickness Unto Death*, where he considers explicitly the
"theological self" or the "self before God," Kierkegaard enables us to see the
importance of awareness of God for self-awareness.[15] Here Kierkegaard
traces out the path to fuller and fuller self-awareness that leads ultimately to
consciousness of being responsible to God. If we could experience only
ourselves, we would not even be able to experience ourselves. We must be
awakened by contact with something other than ourselves. Only when
awake can we differentiate ourselves from the other and become aware of
ourselves. The first level self-awareness can be achieved through sense experience. And experiencing different things awakens different aspects of
the self. Tasting salt, dark chocolate, scrambled eggs brings to awareness
different possibilities latent within the self. Hence we love variety in foods,
smells, sights, textures and sounds. With each new thing we experience
something in ourselves that we had not known before. Try as we may we
cannot get these experiences through our imaginations or memories alone.
We must encounter other things.

The esthete wants to remain at this first level, forever exploring the infinite possibilities of the sensual self stimulated by a continual series of new
experiences. But the self cannot experience all of itself through sensual experience. And, if it attempts to do this, sooner or later it will experience
boredom or fragmentation. Boredom befalls the self when it can find
nothing by which to stimulate itself in a new way. In this condition the
deeper dimension of the self remains untouched and unfulfilled, and its
unhappy longing renders further repetition of sensual experience uninter-

---

[14]Kierkegaard, *Sickness Unto Death*, p. 14. This state of being rid of despair is also the state of
  freedom where, empowered by God's freedom, one wills what one truly is before God. I
  should point out that only in part two ("Despair Is Sin") does "the power that established"
  the self become known as God.
[15]Ibid., pp. 79-82. In what follows I have expanded Kierkegaard's basic insights and chosen
  different examples.

esting, boring. In boredom, despair finds another form in which to plague the soul. Fragmentation overcomes the self when it finds itself pulled in many directions without an inner basis for self-identity and hence can no longer differentiate itself from other things. It loses its sense of self by being absorbed and dissipated into the many things demanding attention. Instead of ruling as a master over many slaves, it labors in slavery to many masters.

The second level of self-awareness arises when the self encounters other selves or persons. In relating to human beings a level of experience becomes available beyond the reach of sensual experience. Others possess inner selves, minds, desires, interests, experiences, pains and sorrows. The possibility of being known and loved by what you experience presents itself. The other person is like you, a subject with infinite interiority, but also other, mysterious and fascinating. Relating to other selves gets us in touch with regions of ourselves we could not otherwise experience and enjoy. Encountering other people brings into our awareness such deeply moving feelings as compassion, feeling understood and valued, and love and desire to be loved. At this level there is a great expansion of the self over what is possible at the sensual level. Nevertheless, encountering other human beings, however deep and lasting the relationships we form, cannot bring into awareness or actualize all the possibilities of the self. For other people too lack full self-awareness and actuality, and though they possess infinite potential, the *actual* self we encounter in them is finite. We must have more.[16]

Only at the third level can the self be brought into full actuality and self-knowledge. God is the infinite source of every created good. When we encounter God we meet the one who contains all the possibilities for good and joy found within the world in their fully actual form. But God is also the greatest mystery and differs from us more than anything within the world; hence meeting God awakens us to the deepest possible self-awareness. Only before God can we know ourselves as we truly are. Hence, to anticipate the next section, knowing God and knowing ourselves are inextricably bound together. The quest for self-awareness must fail unless it is also a search for God.

After thinking with Kierkegaard about the self, perhaps we can better see

---

[16]Hence some individuals are driven onward from person to person in their futile search for their "soul mate."

how God's eternal knowledge of us is relevant to our lives. God's relationship to us is the most fundamental fact about us. Our existence is rooted in God's creative will. Our personal identity is founded on God's love for us. Everything we come to be grows out of this soil. Moreover, God's relationship to us is the most stable thing about us. Nothing else can secure us from changes of time and chance. God's eternity encompasses our time, and God has always known our names. Hence when God created us, he did not simply create humans number 65,000,000,001 and 65,000,000,002. God created *you* and *me*, the ones whom God had always known.

Thus our true identities are founded in an eternal relationship with God. This relationship defines us by giving us a permanent and unique role to play. It constitutes our most intimate and personal being. It gives unique character to our existence; that is, it is *who* we really are. The other relationships and roles we acquire in the course of our lives are encompassed within this eternal relation and are covered within God's providential care. Hence, although these relationships and roles remain contingent, they are not merely accidental. It is not true that you or I might have been someone else and so have no real identity. I do not have to wonder wistfully who I would have been had this or that not happened to me or what I am missing because I did not do this or that. In God's eternal knowledge I am who I shall be, and with God I lack nothing.

DIVINE KNOWLEDGE AND SELF-KNOWLEDGE

In the previous section we considered our true self as an objective relation to God, real even if we are not aware of it. But God wants us to become aware of our identity so that we can live it in every act. God wishes not only to know and love us, but also wants us to know and love God in return. Now we come to the crucial point: *it is only in knowing God that we can know our true name or identity or self, and in this knowledge we also gain self-awareness and self-possession.* From self-awareness come determination, confidence and the will to live according to our divinely given identity. Far from being a threat to our integrity, God's complete and eternal knowledge of us is the ground of our unique personhood and the only hope of ever knowing our true selves.

According to Adler, the self is the principle of freedom; that is, in freedom the self expresses itself in its acts and remains self-identical in its deeds.[17] If this is so, we need to know ourselves before we can act in freedom and achieve happiness. But as we discovered in chapter seven, we do not have the self-knowledge we need. There is a difference between the *I* of my present consciousness and my real self. The *I* of my present awareness apparently cannot bring to self-consciousness all of my true self. Additionally, the *I* of awareness includes things other than my true self. We discover this by making mistakes, experiencing disappointment and regret. These experiences make us feel alienated from ourselves. How can I remove the difference between the *I* of my awareness and my true self? How can I overcome self-alienation and become an integrated, self-aware self?

In this context the idea that God knows us completely becomes a very exciting thought. First, just believing that you are known makes a huge difference in the way you feel about yourself. We need to know ourselves so that we can make ourselves known to others. We desperately want to be known by others because only then can we feel loved and accepted. If God knows us, we can be sure that we really exist even though we cannot grasp ourselves completely. We are not merely darkness, chaos and confusion. The goals of self-knowledge and self-revelation make sense, for there is something there to know and reveal.

Second, God's knowledge of us gives us hope that we can come to know ourselves fully. If God knows us, perhaps God will show us to ourselves. In God's providence God can lead us in paths of self-discovery. Augustine begins book ten of his *Confessions* with this prayer: "May I know you, who know me." Augustine voices hope that in knowing God he may come to know himself as well: "To hear you speaking about oneself is to know oneself" and "For what I know of myself I know because you grant me light."[18] When we read the Scriptures in faith, we hear God speak about us and to us. In prayer we can speak with our Creator and Redeemer, one who knows and loves us. And God is not silent: "The Spirit himself testifies with our spirit that we are God's children" (Rom 8:16).

---

[17]Mortimer Adler, *The Idea of Freedom: A Dialectical Examination of the Conceptions of Freedom* (Garden City, NY: Doubleday and Company, 1958), 1:610.

[18]Augustine, *Confessions* 10.3, 7, in *The Confessions of Saint Augustine*, trans. Henry Chadwick (New York: Oxford University Press, 1991), pp. 180, 182-83.

A Backward Glance and a Forward Look

In the preceding chapters we have learned that the image of God revealed in Jesus Christ differs radically from the egocentric God of Prometheus or of Milton's Satan. The way Jesus related to his Father in the Spirit reveals an inner trinitarian relation of self-giving, receiving, returning and sharing. God loves us with this same love. God's great power gives life and frees us from illusions and death. God's complete knowledge of us roots our identity in his unchanging and eternal love. Whatever divine attribute or action we consider, we should begin with the confidence that God is always for us and never against us. God always wills our true good, that is, what we would will for ourselves if we knew ourselves truly.

But sadly we do not yet know ourselves truly. We still imagine that we are potential gods chained like Prometheus to a mountain of divinely imposed limits. Until we break out of this illusion we will not be able to grasp God's love for us. However tenderly God speaks to us we will continue to suspect that God finally reserves genuine freedom and dignity for God alone. Hence, to complete the picture of a noncompetitive divine-human relationship, we must find a new image of humanity to replace the envious and empty self. We need a persuasive answer to the anxiety and resentment with which we guard our freedom and dignity. Where shall we turn to find an image of humanity that affirms our true freedom and dignity without placing them in competition with God's freedom and dignity?

11

A NEW WAY OF BEING
HUMAN BEING

Where can we find a new image of humanity, a plausible understanding of the self for whom it is alien to compete with God or harbor envy toward God? We will not find it in Prometheus, Milton's Satan or in Kant's "autonomous" individual. Looking to the esthete, the conformist or the celebrity will only lead us away from that for which we seek. Descartes, Rousseau or Nietzsche cannot serve as reliable guides. No. Only Jesus Christ knows the way. Only he can lead us out of the labyrinth of our own self-contradiction and alienation, and into harmony with ourselves and God. For Christianity the way Jesus relates to God and humanity reveals not only God's true nature and character but humanity's as well. Jesus trusted God and submitted to God's will. He thanked and glorified God in all things. In love he endured suffering and death to save his fallen creation, and his resurrection brought humanity to its ultimate goal of eternal life in union with God. Jesus revealed a noncompetitive image of humanity and marked out a way of living that embodies in this world the eternal life of the Trinity.

Considering every aspect of Jesus' humanity would require not one chapter but several volumes, so I will concentrate on a few of those events that touch most directly on humanity's freedom and dignity. Mainstream Christianity has always taught that Christ is fully human as well as fully divine. Jesus was just as human as you or I. He was body, soul and mind. As the book of Hebrews puts it, "Since the children have flesh and blood, he too shared in their humanity so that by his death he might break the power of him who holds the power of death—that is, the devil" (Heb 2:14). It is important to note, however, that though Jesus was *fully* human from his conception by the Holy Spirit, his humanity was *perfected* only through his death, resurrection and ascension. Theologians often recognize this distinction by designating the first as the state of humiliation and the second as the state of exaltation.[1]

THE TEMPTATIONS OF CHRIST

In chapter four we considered the original sin by which Adam and Eve fell. The snake managed to define God and humanity as competitors. According to the tempter, God's interests may compete with ours or at least blind God to our needs. Hence we cannot trust God absolutely and must rely instead on our own instincts about what is good for us. Since that time we have identified our freedom and dignity with our capacity to decide for ourselves what is good for us.

Jesus too was tempted, especially at the beginning of his earthly ministry and at the end. Yet unlike Adam he did not fall but continued to trust God. According to three of the Gospels, Jesus was tempted by the devil at the beginning of his ministry. The Gospel of Mark notes briefly that Jesus was tempted by Satan (Mk 1:13), but Matthew and Luke detail three temptations. The Gospel accounts may not be contrasting Jesus and Adam, but they probably did see a contrast between Jesus' forty-day temptation and the faithless Israelites, who wandered in the desert for forty years.[2] I will follow Matthew's account (Mt 4:1-11).

It is very important to remember that though Jesus was God's eternal Son, he was also fully human. Everything he did in his flesh he did as a human being in reliance on his Father through the Spirit. As human he had to learn his identity and mission. We know little about this process, but we can assume that he listened to Scripture, prayed and heard God's special call. At Jesus' baptism, the Spirit came on him and a voice from heaven

---

[1]For discussion of the "states of Christ" and related issues, see Otto Weber, *Foundations of Dogmatics*, trans. Darrell L. Gruder (Grand Rapids: Eerdmans, 1983), 2:135-42.

[2]Robert H. Gundry, *Matthew: A Commentary on His Literary and Theological Art* (Grand Rapids: Eerdmans, 1982), pp. 53-54.

said, "This is my Son, whom I love; with him I am well pleased" (Mt 3:17). Matthew presents this event as a turning point in Jesus' life. According to Ulrich Luz, Matthew sees in this event the true meaning of Jesus' divine "sonship," obedience to the Father.[3] Now Jesus' faith and willingness to obey is tested. Jesus is forced in a dramatic way to ask, *Am I really God's Son? Does God really love me, and is he really pleased with me?*

Each of the Gospels says that the Spirit led Jesus into the desert to be tempted. In the desert he fasted forty days. In this vulnerable condition the devil came to him with the first temptation: "If you are the Son of God, tell these stones to become bread" (Mt 4:3). We can see a twofold appeal in this temptation. Notice how the tempter begins. Just as the snake did with Adam and Eve, the devil places the voice from heaven in question and attempts to undermine Jesus' confidence in God. It might have been tempting for Jesus to perform the miracle just to reassure himself of his identity.[4] But the devil also appeals to Jesus' desire to satisfy his hunger and to sustain his life. Matthew informs us that Jesus fasted forty days *and forty nights.*[5] This may be the writer's way of emphasizing that this was not a sunrise to sunset fast. At the end of it he was hungry, life-and-death hungry. In this dire situation, the devil suggests that God cannot be trusted to provide for Jesus. God sent you out into this godforsaken place, the devil says in effect, and it seems that he has forsaken you. If you are to survive you must take care of yourself. In this suggestion the devil puts a particular twist on the nature of Jesus' special relationship to God. Clearly in Satan's theology, being the Son of God means having Godlike powers and using them for yourself. It means being a super-human being with superhuman powers, the desire and envy of humanity.

Jesus did not enter into discussion with the devil. He gave his answer in the words of Scripture without commentary: "It is written: Man shall not live on bread alone, but on every word that comes from the mouth of God" (Mt 4:4, cf. Deut 8:3). Jesus must have been thinking of the larger context of this statement in Deuteronomy. In the previous verses the Israelites are re-

---

[3]Ulrich Luz, *Matthew 1-7: A Commentary* (Minneapolis: Fortress Press, 2007), p. 144. Luz makes the further point that those disciples who would be "sons of God" must also follow the way of obedience.

[4]According to Alan Hugh McNeile, "the first temptation is to doubt the revelation just received" (*The Gospel According to St. Matthew* [1915; reprint, Grand Rapids: Baker, 1980], p. 37).

[5]Moses fasted forty days and nights on the mountain as he received the law from God (Deut 9:9).

minded that God sent them into the desert for forty years to test them and to teach them that "Man does not live on bread alone." The ancient Israelites refused to trust God, so they failed to enter the land. But Jesus asserts complete trust in God, who sent him into the desert. I place my life in God's hands, Jesus says, and I will not assert a right against God even to save myself from death. God's word is the source of life because God's word is the source of everything, including bread. Jesus' answer implicitly corrects the devil's skewed view of Jesus' special relationship to God. For Jesus, being God's Son is a matter of absolute trust and obedience to his Father.[6]

In the second temptation, the devil takes Jesus to the highest wall of the temple in Jerusalem and suggests, "If you are the Son of God, throw yourself down" (Mt 4:6). Perhaps learning from his earlier failure, the tempter quotes a Scripture (Ps 91:11-12) that promises that God's angels will protect the Messiah and keep him from all harm, even from stubbing his toe on a stone. Why the devil thought this temptation would appeal to Jesus is somewhat unclear. It has one element in common with the first temptation, however, appeal to doubt and mistrust. If you are the Son of God, what sense does it make to remain hidden? Allow God to demonstrate care and approval of you for all to see. Of course, the temple was a very public place and such a demonstration would be sure to gain the attention of all Jerusalem. It may be that the tempter was recommending that Jesus take his ministry into his own hands instead of patiently following the way God opened up step by step. Again, Jesus answers in the words of Scripture: "Do not put the Lord your God to the test" (Mt 4:7; cf. Deut 6:16). In the event to which Deuteronomy refers, the Israelites were grumbling against God and Moses. Instead of trusting God, they wanted to see God's provision ahead of time. They demanded a miracle as proof of God's trustworthiness. Jesus quotes this text to say that we must trust God even when God hides himself, when no miracles are forthcoming. We should never attempt to

---

[6]Commenting on Hebrews 5:8 ("Though he was a Son, he learned obedience through what he suffered"), Wolfhart Pannenberg explains, "The status of sonship and obedience to the Father go together. Obedient subordination to the Father characterizes Jesus as the Son. As Paul puts it, he lets himself be guided by the Spirit of God (Rom. 8:14). His obedience, then, is not the alien obedience of the slave. It is an expression of his free agreement with the Father" (*Systematic Theology*, trans. Geoffrey W. Bromiley [Grand Rapids: Eerdmans, 1994], 2:316).

force God's hand.[7] We must wait on the Lord. The glory of being God's children, divine and human, is to let God be God.[8]

Trying for the third time, the devil took Jesus to the peak of a high mountain to show him all the kingdoms of the world.[9] "All this I will give you if you will bow down and worship me," he promised (Mt 4:9). The appeal of this temptation is obvious. Power brings wealth, pleasure and glory. Jesus responds immediately, "Away from me, Satan! For it is written, 'Worship the Lord your God, and serve him only'" (Mt 4:10). Notice that the devil defined worship of him as a means to an end: "If you worship me I will give you all these things." The devil has to use God's creation to entice people to worship him. After all, why would one worship the devil as an end in itself? But the command to worship God alone is an absolute command. God is the only being worthy of worship simply because of God's surpassing worth. By quoting the first commandment, Jesus shows not only that worshiping Satan would be disobedience but also that the devil is not worthy of worship. It is not worship but flattery to praise a being merely as a means to an end.

The world is full of beautiful and good things. Each of them comes from the hand of God, but none is worthy of worship. They were created to be used and enjoyed under the right conditions and at the right time. But everything in God's creation points beyond itself to God, who made it. Only as a gift from God can a created thing be used and enjoyed rightly. The devil is a master at presenting out of order and isolated from God something that God made for our use and enjoyment. Jesus reminds us that the good things of creation are good only if used and enjoyed in the right order and for the right reasons.

In refusing these temptations Jesus rejects Prometheus's rebellion and Satan's ambition. He resists the lure of Kantian autonomy, Nietzsche's will to power or Rousseau's inner voice. He will not succumb to the siren song of celebrity or be seduced by conformity's comforts or beguiled by esthetic

[7]Several times during his ministry the Pharisees and others asked Jesus for a "sign from heaven," a request that Jesus consistently refused. Luz sees this episode as looking forward "to the obedience of the Son of God in his life and especially during his passion" (*Matthew 1-7*, p. 153).

[8]Donald Miller argues that the three temptations represent three alternatives to the suffering Messiah: the economic, miracle-working and political messiahs (*The Gospel of Luke* [Louisville, KY: John Knox Press, 1971], pp. 52-55).

[9]At the end of the Gospel of Matthew the risen Jesus explains to the disciples that "all authority in heaven and on earth" has been given to him (Mt 28:18).

pleasures. Instead, Jesus trusts his Father and obeys. He counts his life a gift given for the sake of his mission. He will not use it for himself but determines to return it to his God.

THE LAST TEMPTATION

After three temptations at the beginning of Jesus' ministry, the Gospels narrate no further direct confrontations with the devil. However, Luke adds that the devil left Jesus "until an opportune time" (Lk 4:13). What more opportune time could there have been than in the Garden of Gethsemane as Jesus prayed to his Father?[10] Clearly, Jesus has heard his Father's command: "You must give your life as a ransom for many. You must drink the cup of suffering to the last dregs." But this command goes against every human instinct, so Jesus prays for the "cup" to be removed. Perhaps God will find another way at the last minute, as he did in Abraham's and Isaac's case. Perhaps it is only a test. But here there is no ram caught in the bushes, for the roles are different. Jesus is the lamb and we are Isaac. He must take Isaac's place. We will follow Matthew's narrative of these events (Mt 26:36-46).

After predicting that one of his disciples would betray him, Jesus took them to the secluded olive grove where he often prayed. He told the rest to sit down and wait for him, but Jesus invited Peter, James and John to join him a little further in. He said to these three, "My soul is overwhelmed with sorrow to the point of death. Stay here and keep watch with me" (v. 38). Jesus went a little further and fell on his face and prayed, "My Father, if it is possible, may this cup be taken from me. Yet not as I will, but as you will" (v. 39). After praying, he returned to find Peter and the others asleep. Scolding them, he said, "Watch and pray so that you will not fall into temptation. The spirit is willing, but the flesh is weak" (v. 41). Jesus continued to pray, "My Father, if it is not possible for this cup to be taken away unless I drink it, may your will be done" (v. 42). He returned a second and a third time to find the disciples sleeping. By this time the betrayer is approaching. The contrast between Jesus and the disciples is a major feature of the narrative. Jesus warned

---

[10]In his Christology Karl Barth treats the temptation narratives in intimate connection with the Garden of Gethsemane narratives. For Barth, the question at issue is whether the Son of God will remain true to his mission to identify with sinners for their salvation (*Church Dogmatics*, vol. 4., pt. 1, ed. G. W. Bromiley and T. F. Torrance, trans. G. W. Bromiley [Edinburgh, T & T Clark, 1956], pp. 259-73).

them to "watch and pray" so that they would not fall to temptation. The tempter cannot succeed without using lies and deception. Withstanding temptation requires keeping your mind focused on truth and reality. Jesus says watch your enemy, keep your eyes open for the tempter's approach and maintain awareness of God's presence through prayer. But the disciples gave in to their weariness; they were not ready when the time came.

Jesus' sorrow and agony were very real. He prayed in total concentration on his Father. Though he prayed for escape, Jesus never willed anything contrary to his Father's will. There is a difference, however, between willing the will of God and willing suffering and death, even if suffering and death are the will of God. God willed Jesus' death not as an end but as a means to the salvation of the world. We should rejoice in God's willing, even if for the moment we cannot rejoice in what God wills. In this life, acceptance is sometimes as close as we can get to willing God's will in a specific situation. But, as his prayer indicates, it was not absolutely clear to Jesus that God willed his suffering and death. The test in the garden was whether Jesus would continue to will God's will when it became crystal clear that there was no other way to do God's will than to take up the cross.

I am reminded of the book of Job. God says to Satan, "Have you considered my servant Job?" (Job 1:8). Satan responds, "Does Job fear God for nothing?" (Job 1:9). Clearly, Satan does not consider human beings capable of love, trust and loyalty toward God. Take away his possessions and his health, Satan reasons, and you will see what Job really loves and why he pretends to serve you! The Lord gave Satan permission to crush Job, but Job maintained his integrity:

> Naked I came from my mother's womb,
>   and naked I will depart.
> The LORD gave and the LORD has taken away;
>   may the name of the LORD be praised. (Job 1:21)

Does Jesus serve God for nothing? Or does Jesus serve God only when God pours out the good things we all desire? The last temptation answered this question once and for all: to be a child of God means to love and trust God to whatever end.

Jesus passed this test by placing himself utterly into the hands of his

Father to use as he pleased. From a human point of view only failure, shame and annihilation awaited him. Even so, Jesus knew that everything we have, every moment, every good and our existence itself is God's gift. We did not create them, we do not deserve them, and we do not own them. When God asks us to give everything back to him, we have no grounds to think God unjust or unkind. We exist only because of God's grace, and we can affirm our existence rightly only by our gratitude. In gratitude we acknowledge both our dependence and God's grace. We prove our gratitude and our belief in God's grace by placing ourselves into God's hands and trusting completely in his goodwill.

In Jesus' temptations we see clearly what a human being should be in relation to God. Jesus related to God as his Father, and God related to Jesus as his beloved Son. As I will show in chapter twelve, Jesus enables us to also relate to God as our Father and understand ourselves as God's dearly loved children. Following Jesus, we should treat our human existence as a gift through which we experience God's grace. Being a good human being means reverencing God above all other things, trusting God utterly and entrusting ourselves completely into our Father's care. Or, in Kierkegaard's words quoted earlier, "in relating itself to itself and in willing to be itself, the self rests transparently in the power that established it."[11] In the following chapters we will see in what ways this understanding of our humanity and these basic human acts embody our true freedom and dignity.

---

[11]Søren Kierkegaard, *Sickness Unto Death*, ed. and trans. Howard V. and Edna H. Hong (Princeton, NJ: Princeton University Press, 1980), p. 14.

12

THE DIVINE ADOPTION

The great nineteenth-century British preacher Charles Haddon Spurgeon (1834-1892) marveled at the profound message of 1 John 3:1: "See what great love the Father has lavished on us, that we should be called children of God!" He searches for words to help his listeners get past the familiar phrases to the revolutionary meaning of this joyful exclamation:

> Consider who we were, and who we are now; ay, and what we feel ourselves to be even when divine grace is powerful in us. And yet, beloved, we are called *"the sons of God."* It is said that when one of the learned heathens was translating this, he stopped and said, "No; it cannot be; let it be written 'Subjects,' not 'Sons,' for it is impossible we should be called 'the sons of God.'" What a high relationship is that of a son to his father! What privileges a son has from his father! What liberties a son may take with his father! and oh! what obedience the son owes to his father, and what love the father feels towards the son! But all *that,* and more than *that,* we now have through Christ. "Behold!" ye angels! stop, ye seraphs! here is a thing more wonderful than heaven with its walls of jasper.[1]

Spurgeon was right, I think, to sense the importance of this theme for our self-understanding and for living as a Christian. Hence in this chapter we will examine Jesus' and the rest of the New Testament's teaching that God is our Father and we are his dear children for further insights into our true identity.

---

[1]Charles Haddon Spurgeon, "Exposition of 1 John 3:1-10," The Spurgeon Archive, www .spurgeon.org/sermons/0062.htm.

OUR FATHER IN HEAVEN

Although Jesus' teaching ranges over many topics, I will concentrate on the theme that we are God's dear children, created to image God's character and do his will. The Gospel of Matthew places special emphasis on the fatherhood of God. In Matthew's account Jesus refers to God as "my Father" or "your Father in heaven" scores of times. The greatest concentration of these references occurs in the Sermon on the Mount (Mt 5–7). In these three chapters God is called "Father" fifteen times. Apparently Jesus wants his disciples to develop a relationship to God similar to his own. So how did Jesus relate to God?

Abba, Father. The first three Gospels do not provide many direct windows into Jesus' awareness of his special relationship to God. However, the account of his baptism offers a glimpse of this bond when Jesus heard God's voice from heaven declare, "This is my Son, whom I love; with him I am well pleased" (Mt 3:17). He heard this voice and these words again at the transfiguration (Mt 17:5). Additionally, there is a remarkable passage in Matthew 11. In a moment of joy Jesus addresses God: "I praise you, Father, Lord of heaven and earth. . . . All things have been committed to me by my Father. No one knows the Son except the Father, and no one knows the Father except the Son and those to whom the Son chooses to reveal him" (Mt 11:25, 27).

The Gospel of Mark preserves an Aramaic word from Jesus' agonized prayer in the Garden of Gethsemane. According to Mark, Jesus cried, *"Abba,* Father, everything is possible for you. Take this cup from me. Yet not what I will, but what you will" (Mk 14:36). Some scholars argue that this word *Abba* resonates with the familiarity of the home. A child jumping into its father's arms after an absence or crying over a scraped knee might say *"Abba."* Whether this way of speaking to God represents something totally new in the history of religion is not central to my point.[2] Jesus does not approach

---

[2]On the Jewish forms of address to God, see Joachim Jeremias, *The Prayers of Jesus* (Philadelphia: Fortress Press, 1967), pp. 57-65. In his later work *New Testament Theology: The Proclamation of Jesus* (New York: Charles Scribner's, 1971), p. 67, Jeremias cautions that the term *Abba* was not limited to small children but was used by older children in reference to their fathers. See Gordon D. Fee, *Pauline Christology: An Exegetical-Theological Study* (Peabody, MA: Hendrickson, 2007), pp. 217-20, for his comments on the *Abba* statement in Galatians 4:6. Fee also records the debate about the meaning of Abba that occurred in the wake of Jeremias's studies. Fee argues that Paul's usage confirms the "basic soundness" of Jeremias's thesis (p. 218).

God as a distant Creator, Lord and Judge, much less an impersonal cosmic force. His way of speaking to God, according to Jeremias, "expresses the heart of Jesus' relationship to God. He spoke to God as a child to its father: confidently and securely, and yet at the same time reverently and obediently."[3] Jesus brings us into the intimate family room of God, where with childlike boldness we hear him address the Lord of the universe as *Abba*.

Jesus does not reserve this intimacy with God for himself alone. He initiates his disciples into this new relationship with God. In Jeremias's estimation, "For the disciples, being children means sharing in Jesus' sonship."[4] In the Sermon on the Mount Jesus repeatedly refers to God as "your Father in heaven" and to his disciples as God's children. Peacemakers will be blessed because they will be called "children of God" (Mt 5:9). We are urged to let the light of our good deeds shine so that others may praise "your Father" (Mt 5:16). Jesus teaches the disciples to "love their enemies" so that they may be "children of your Father in heaven" (Mt 5:45). Indeed, he calls us to "be perfect, therefore, as your heavenly Father is perfect" (Mt 5:48). Do not do the right thing just to make an impression on other people, for then "you will have no reward from your Father in heaven" (Mt 6:1). Three times Jesus says that the audience for our prayers should be the Father alone (Mt 6:6-8). Then he gives a model prayer, which begins, "Our Father in heaven" (Mt 6:9; see also Mt 6:14-15, 18). We need not worry about food and clothes, Jesus teaches, for "your heavenly Father" feeds even the birds, and "are you not much more valuable than they?" (Mt 6:26). Seek first the things of God and "your heavenly Father" will provide the other things you need (Mt 6:32-34). Even earthly parents, imperfect and sinful, provide for their children. "How much more will your Father in heaven give good gifts to those who ask him!" (Mt 7:11). In summary, then, Jesus teaches that God is our Father and we are the Father's children. But what does this teaching say about our humanity?

What does being a child of God mean? Let us first deal with a common misunderstanding. The idea that God is our Father and we are his children has become so familiar that it has almost lost all meaning. At most it says that God is kindly toward us, and this translates into a warm feeling without

---

[3]Jeremias, *New Testament Theology*, p. 67.
[4]Ibid., p. 181.

much conceptual content. Of course, Jesus teaches that God cares for us as a good father cares for his children. God wants us to enjoy this sense of intimacy and security. But there is more. The feeling or consciousness of being God's child must be rooted in the reality of what we are.[5]

In Jesus' discussion of the resurrection in response to the challenge of the Sadducees, he asserts that the resurrection life will be very different from life here and now (Lk 20:27-38; cf. Mt 22:23-33; Mk 12:18-27). There will be no death and, hence, no need for marriage and procreation. The resurrection will transform human beings into angel-like beings who cannot die.[6] Jesus continues, "They are God's children, since they are children of the resurrection" (Lk 20:36). Clearly the category "sons of God" (the Greek word *huios* [son] is often translated "child" in the NIV) here designates a mode of life available to us in its fullest form only after the resurrection.[7] The resurrection is a sort of second birth in which we take on such divine qualities as immortality and holiness. As N. T. Wright expresses it, "God's true children are like their father, and cannot die."[8]

We find similar ideas in the Gospel of John and in 1 John. The Word was made flesh and came to give people who believe in him "the right to become children of God—children born not of natural descent, nor of human decision or of a husband's will, but born of God" (Jn 1:12-13). Being a child of God means more than merely being a creature of God. We become God's children by being "born" of God, a supernatural transformation that begins with faith in the unique Son of God. This theme is expanded in 1 John. John

---

[5]For a survey of the way the term *sons of God* was used before the New Testament era as well as in the New Testament itself, see Brendan Byrne, "Sons of God," in *Anchor Bible Dictionary*, ed. David Noel Freedman (New York: Doubleday, 1992), 6:156-59.

[6]In this text "eschatological divine sonship obviously derives from the description of the angels as God's sons . . . so that the 'sons of the resurrection' . . . are defined as beings in the heavenly sphere immune from death and corruption" (Eduard Schweitzer, "υἱός, υἱοθεσία," in *Theological Dictionary of the New Testament*, ed. Gerhard Friedrich, trans. Geoffrey W. Bromiley [Grand Rapids: Eerdmans,1972], 7:390).

[7]I. Howard Marshall, *Commentary on Luke: A Commentary on the Greek Text* (Grand Rapids: Eerdmans, 1978), pp. 741-42.

[8]N. T. Wright, *The Resurrection of the Son of God* (Minneapolis: Fortress Press, 2003), p. 23. Wright considers the likeness to angels referred to in this text to be "functional" rather than "ontological." When he specifies the likeness as not being able to die, one wonders why he rejects the ontological label. Being changed from a mortal being to an immortal being represents some sort of ontological change. Wright is certainly correct that the phrase "for they are like the angels" does not mean that resurrected humans become angels. They are like angels in that "they cannot die" (pp. 22-23).

rejoices in God's love, through which we are not only called but have become God's children. We are God's children even now, but "when Christ appears, we shall be like him, for we shall see him as he is" (1 Jn 3:2).

Romans 8 highlights each of these aspects of our relationship to God.[9] God's Spirit works in us both to make us holy and to give life to our "mortal bodies" (Rom 8:11). We do not have to be controlled by "flesh," that is, "the sinful nature" (Rom 8:6), because the Spirit leads us and makes us "children of God" (Rom 8:14). The Spirit enables us to cry *Abba* to the Father and "testifies with our spirit that we are God's children" (Rom 8:16). Douglas Moo contends that Paul's use of *Abba* in these verses "shows that Christians have a relationship with God that is like (though, of course, not exactly like) Christ's own relationship to the Father."[10] We are in a sense already "children of God," but the future promises a more dramatic transformation and revelation of the children of God: "The creation waits in eager expectation for the children of God to be revealed" (Rom 8:19). On that day creation will share in "the freedom and glory of the children of God" (Rom 8:21). Paul compares waiting for this event to groaning in childbirth. The first stirrings of the Spirit make us eager for "our adoption to sonship, the redemption of our bodies" (Rom 8:23).

The teaching of Jesus and the rest of the New Testament is clear. Human beings do not come into this world in their final state. The God-given goal of human life is the glorious freedom of the children of God. The truth of our nature is revealed not by our present sinful, blind and mortal state but by our final end. In view of our identity and destiny as "children of God," J. I. Packer recommends that the Christian repeat every day, *"I am a child of God. God is my Father; heaven is my home; every day is one day nearer. My Saviour is my bother; every Christian is my brother too."*[11]

Be Perfect as Your Father in Heaven Is Perfect

So far we have been looking for the explicit Christian teaching about human nature. We have seen that Jesus and the Spirit enable human beings to relate

---

[9]See Douglas J. Moo, *The Epistle to the Romans* (Grand Rapids: Eerdmans, 1996), pp. 496-504, 512-15, for his comments on the present-future and ethical-eschatological dimensions of sonship in Romans 8.

[10]Ibid., p. 503.

[11]J. I. Packer, *Knowing God* (Downers Grove, IL: InterVarsity Press, 1973), p. 207. In this classic work, Packer writes a fine chapter on the subject of sonship (pp. 181-208).

to God as children to their *Abba*, Father. We are invited into the intimate home life of God. Our destiny is to become children of God in another, fuller sense of participating in the divine nature. I want now to consider this issue from another angle, using the commonsense principle that we know what something is by what it does. Jesus transferred this rule into the ethical sphere when he said, "By their fruit you will recognize them. Do people pick grapes from thornbushes, or figs from thistles?" (Mt 7:16). If it is true that people's deeds reveal their character and nature, then it is also true that every ethical command implies a certain understanding of human nature. In other words, if Jesus commands us to act like children of God it is because he knows this is our true destiny. Implicit in Jesus' ethical teaching is a view of what human beings really are.

In Matthew 5:17-48, Jesus lays out a sweeping ethical vision in which he demands that his disciples achieve a higher moral level than even the experts in the law had achieved. He sums up that vision with an extraordinary demand: "Be perfect, therefore, as your heavenly Father is perfect" (v. 48).[12] The first question we are inclined to ask is, How is this possible? How can a human being treat others with the same justice and love that God does? As important as this question is, there is another that must be answered first: What *are* we if we can fulfill our nature only by living the way God lives? The answer is obvious. We are God's children, created images of the divine nature. Let us look at these verses in detail and see how this is so.

In this section Jesus addresses six ethical principles held up by the best moral thinkers as representing the highest ethical life.[13] In each case Jesus shows the imperfections of a life that rises only to this level and urges his

---

[12]According to T. W. Manson, Jesus' teaching is not new that our relationship to God as his children requires us to manifest his moral character. The rabbinic writings taught this. However, Jesus moves this teaching to the center of the life of discipleship (*The Teaching of Jesus: Studies in Form and Content* [London: Cambridge University Press, 1963], p. 93).

[13]According to Hans Dieter Betz, Jesus refutes "both a specific interpretation and the claim by present advocates that it came down straight through the authoritative chain of tradition" (*The Sermon on the Mount* [Minneapolis: Fortress Press, 1995], p. 217). According to Ulrich Luz, we should not exaggerate the difference in content between Jesus' moral teaching and that of contemporary Judaism. However, Jesus does "something special" by setting the divine law and the accepted moral application against each other. "The OT legal system is not radical enough, and it does not yet completely reflect God's will; it is the radically formulated wisdom admonition that is actually his will" (*Matthew 1-7: A Commentary* [Minneapolis: Fortress Press, 2007], pp. 237-38).

disciples to achieve perfection. First, the good person will obey the command not to murder:

> You have heard that it was said to the people long ago, "You shall not murder, and anyone who murders will be subject to judgment." But I tell you that anyone who is angry with a brother or sister will be subject to judgment. Again, anyone who says to a brother or sister, "Raca," is answerable to the court. And anyone who says, "You fool!" will be in danger of the fire of hell. (Mt 5:21-22)

Murder deserves "judgment" or punishment by a criminal court. If God's command to respect the lives of others rises only to this level, people who control their anger just enough to avoid murdering an adversary can think of themselves as a good people. However, Jesus responds, "I say that anyone who is angry with a brother or sister will be subject to judgment" (v. 22). Even if anger lashes out with words only (*raca* or "fool"), one places oneself in danger of "the fire of hell" (v. 22)! Jesus thus declares that anger, which is the root cause of murder, is just as evil to God as murder is to us. Anger arises from jealously and envy, and these arise from pride and ingratitude. Pride and ingratitude are directed at God.

Second, Jesus deals with adultery and lust:

> You have heard that it was said, "You shall not commit adultery." But I tell you that anyone who looks at a woman lustfully has already committed adultery with her in his heart. If your right eye causes you to stumble, gouge it out and throw it away. It is better for you to lose one part of your body than for your whole body to be thrown into hell. And if your right hand causes you to stumble, cut it off and throw it away. It is better for you to lose one part of your body than for your whole body to go into hell. (Mt 5:27-30)

Here Jesus addresses the common opinion that if you have not literally slept with another man's wife or another woman's husband, you can consider yourself righteous. Jesus' teaching on this subject was not utterly unique. In both Judaism and Hellenism desire was seen to be the root problem of the sinful act.[14] According to Ulrich Luz, Jesus teaches that "not only legal facts but the inner feelings of the human . . . heart are affected by it [i.e., the lustful

---

[14]For examples, see Luz, *Matthew 1–7*, p. 245.

look]. The Torah lays such a total demand on the whole person that its function as the basis of Israel's legal system becomes completely irrelevant."[15] To reinforce his point, Jesus urges us to discipline ourselves to the point of removing our eyes or cutting off our hands if these lead us into sin. Better to enter heaven blind and mutilated than to land in hell with a whole body! Even if Jesus is using hyperbole, his point is still radical: we should treat anything as an enemy that pulls us even one inch away from God's perfect holiness. Even if one restrains oneself from committing the external act of adultery, the lustful heart has already lost touch with God's holiness. The two greatest commandments are both matters of the heart: to love God and one's neighbor.[16] The lustful heart banishes both loves.

Third, Jesus addresses divorce: "It has been said, 'Anyone who divorces his wife must give her a certificate of divorce.' But I tell you that anyone who divorces his wife, except for sexual immorality, makes her the victim of adultery, and anyone who marries a divorced woman commits adultery" (Mt 5:31-32). The accepted standard of righteousness on this subject was merely adhering to due process.[17] A man could divorce his wife for almost any reason as long as he "gives her a certificate of divorce" (v. 31). This certificate released her from obligations to her former husband and testified to her freedom to remarry.[18] But Jesus restricts divorce to one reason, adultery.[19] Jesus clearly views the marriage bond as inviolable. What interests me is what this says about human nature. Jesus expects us to be able to make a lifelong commitment to one person in marriage. How is it possible to reach out into the future and promise all our tomorrows to someone? We would need to get in touch with a truth about ourselves that will never change. According to Jesus, then, we are meant to be the sort of beings whose character and loves do not change, but, like God's character and loves, remain constant.

---

[15]Ibid., p. 246.

[16]According to Betz, "avoidance of adultery is a special application of the love-command, 'Love your neighbor as yourself' " (*Sermon on the Mount*, p. 239).

[17]This is the liberal view advocated by the rabbi Hillel. The more restrictive view, similar to Jesus' teaching, was held by Shammai. Apparently Jesus objects to the liberal view, which Betz claims eventually became dominant in rabbinic Judaism (see Betz, *The Sermon on the Mount*, p. 247).

[18]See Deut 24:1-2. This law permits a lawfully divorced woman to remarry, but she cannot return to her first husband under any condition. Jesus extends the prohibition to any divorced woman. For this issue, see Luz, *Matthew 1–7*, pp. 251-52.

[19]Mark 10:1-12 records a fuller statement of Jesus' teaching on divorce. There Jesus does not seem to leave any way out of marriage, for "what God has joined together, let no one separate" (v. 9).

Fourth, according to common opinion, good people keep their oaths. But Jesus goes to the foundation of promise keeping and truth telling:

> Again, you have heard that it was said to the people long ago, "Do not break your oath, but fulfill to the Lord the vows you have made." But I tell you, do not swear an oath at all: either by heaven, for it is God's throne; or by the earth, for it is his footstool; or by Jerusalem, for it is the city of the Great King. And do not swear by your head, for you cannot make even one hair white or black. All you need to say is simply "Yes" or "No"; anything beyond this comes from the evil one. (Mt 5:33-37)

In an oath you put yourself or something of great value in jeopardy to give added weight to your promises. This necessity already signals the presence of mistrust. As Betz observes, friends do not need oaths. Oaths are for enemies.[20] So Jesus tells his disciples not to swear at all. Although many moralists in antiquity criticized the excessive use of oaths and lamented their necessity, it seems likely that Jesus was the first to prohibit completely their use.[21] Jesus envisions individuals whose integrity is so beyond question that they feel no need to call on anything to vouch for their trustworthiness. He anticipates a community within which there is complete trust.[22]

Fifth, common opinion allows revenge according to the principle of an eye for an eye, but Jesus rejects altogether the spirit of revenge:

> You have heard that it was said, "Eye for eye, and tooth for tooth." But I tell you, do not resist [or retaliate] an evil person. If anyone slaps you on the right cheek, turn to them the other cheek also. And if anyone wants to sue you and take your shirt, hand over your coat as well. If anyone forces you to go one mile, go with them two miles. Give to the one who asks you, and do not turn away from the one who wants to borrow from you. (Mt 5:38-42)[23]

---

[20]Betz, *Sermon on the Mount*, p. 260.

[21]Luz, *Matthew 1-7*, p. 262.

[22]Jesus' teaching is paralleled in some Greek and Roman moralists. See Johannes Schneider, "ὀμνύω," in *Theological Dictionary of the New Testament*, ed. Gerhard Friedrich, trans. Geoffrey W. Bromiley (Grand Rapids: Eerdmans, 1972), 5.79-80, for references.

[23]Betz insists that, given the context, "retaliate" is a better translation of *anthistēmi* than "resist" (*Sermon on the Mount*, p. 280). The examples Jesus uses exemplify nonretaliation very well. These actions done in response to aggression do not show passive but active behavior, perhaps designed to give the aggressor opportunity to change. Jesus' teaching of nonretaliation is not utterly foreign to the moralists of his day. Many ancient philosophers questioned the practice of retaliation. For an extensive survey, see Betz, *Sermon on the Mount*, pp. 86-89.

According to the tradition Jesus critiques, vengeful people can maintain their good character as long as they limit their revenge to "eye for eye." But Jesus forbids all revenge. Instead, he commands his disciples to "turn the other cheek," and walk the "extra mile" (vv. 39-41). Jesus expects us not to feel anger or seek revenge when we are wronged; rather, his disciples should feel compassion for people who do us wrong and seek to save them from evil even at the cost of further suffering for ourselves. Just as a courageous person risks life to save a child from a burning house, Jesus' disciples will risk further injury to free their persecutors from the evil that enslaves them.[24]

Sixth, Jesus contradicts the common opinion that a good person must love their neighbor but is free to hate their enemy:

> You have heard that it was said, "Love your neighbor and hate your enemy." But I tell you, love your enemies and pray for those who persecute you, that you may be children of your Father in heaven. . . . If you love those who love you, what reward will you get? Are not even the tax collectors doing that? And if you greet only your own people, what are you doing more than others? Do not even pagans do that? Be perfect, therefore, as your heavenly Father is perfect. (Mt 5:43-48)[25]

It is as natural as breathing to hate your enemies, but Jesus tells us instead to "love your enemies." How can you love your enemies? Why love your enemies? What kind of person has the power to love enemies? Let us take these questions in reverse order.

What sort of person can feel compassion for their persecutors and seek their redemption? Jesus answers, "children of your Father in heaven." This is what God does, and human beings are created to image God's character.

---

[24]I think Luz is correct that Jesus is not advocating nonresistance as a strategy, as "shrewd advice" for winning over your enemies (*Matthew 1-7*, p. 274). As a "strategy" it often fails spectacularly. But disciples are also called to redemptive and vicarious suffering for others as they follow in the steps of Jesus.

[25]Although the idea of loving your enemies along with your neighbors would have sounded strange and unnatural to Jesus' contemporaries, Greek and Roman moralists taught that we should treat our enemies humanely "as an act of magnanimity or mercy, virtues becoming to the wise man and the good ruler" (Betz, *Sermon on the Mount*, p. 311). It is important to reject interpretations of these words that see Jesus as "shrewd." Luz's words are apropos: "It was not Jesus' intention to improve the world situation. From his perspective acts of love toward one's enemies are an expression of God's unconditional yes to people for their own sake. They are necessary in a fundamental sense, and they stand beside and *before* all realistic strategies of 'intelligent' love" (*Matthew 1-7*, p. 294).

Why love your enemies? Because love is rooted in truth, and hate arises from falsehood and fear. Your enemy is captive to fear and falsehood. When we see this we cannot help but have compassion for their suffering. We hate most that which threatens what we love most. If we love God above other things, we will be freed from hatred because nothing threatens God. For, if nothing can separate us from God's love and care, nothing can threaten us. This answers the third question also. We can love our enemies even when they persecute us because we know they cannot take our *Abba* away from us.

What, then, does it mean to be a human being? It means being a created child of God, one whose very being consists in imaging God's nature and character. Our true identity is established in relationship to God. We can enact our true selves only by imitating our Father in heaven. Like the eternal Son of God, we receive ourselves from the Father and we can act as ourselves only by returning ourselves to our *Abba*, Father. As I want to show in the next chapters, being God's child is the highest dignity possible for us, and receiving, returning and sharing God's love are acts of perfect freedom.

13

THE EMERGENCE OF
GOD-CENTERED IDENTITY

The great philosopher Immanuel Kant summed up his life's work as a quest for answers to three questions: "1. What can I know? 2. What ought I to do? 3. What may I hope?"[1] The first question concerns need for truth and the limits of our knowledge. The second deals with our moral duties, and the third asks about the conditions under which we may achieve ultimate happiness. To live well we must have satisfactory answers to these important questions. And there is another question that is just as urgent and perhaps even more foundational: Who am I? As we have seen in our study so far, the way we understand the self determines our actions. We cannot know what to do until we know who we are.

In chapters eleven and twelve we examined the picture of humanity painted in the teachings of Jesus and the New Testament. Jesus teaches that God created human beings to be dear children and to relate to God as their *Abba*. God's children desire God's glory and live by God's Word. They trust and obey in all things. They love God infinitely more than anything else. And they love all things, including themselves, within their love for God. In the power of the Holy Spirit they live and love in view of their destiny of becoming like Jesus Christ by sharing in his death and resurrection. In this chapter I will begin to address the final issue to be treated in this book: how

---

[1]Immanuel Kant, *Critique of Pure Reason*, trans. Norman Kemp Smith (New York: Palgrave, 1933), p. 635.

does the Christian view of humanity preserve human dignity and freedom? The first step toward answering this question is to return to the issue of the human self first broached in chapter six.

THE SELF AND FREEDOM

Every theory of freedom includes an understanding of the self. In chapter six I introduced Mortimer Adler's three types of freedom: circumstantial freedom of self-realization, acquired freedom of self-perfection and natural freedom of self-determination. Each type presents freedom as a power through which the self does something from itself and for itself; they differ from each other only in their understandings of the nature of the self and its acts. A self is circumstantially free when circumstances permit it to realize its desires. A self possesses acquired freedom when it attains the wisdom or virtue to will only good. A self acts from natural freedom when it alone determines what it chooses, does and becomes.

Freedom, then, has to do with the character of an agent's action. An agent (the self) is free when it can express itself in unhindered action. Adler's general concept of freedom, which applies to all three types, makes this clear: "A man is free who has in himself the ability or power whereby he can make what he does his own action and what he achieves his own property."[2] The self, as Adler puts it, is the "principle of freedom," that is, "my freedom must involve that which proceeds *from me* and that which achieves something *for me*. Whatever in my life merely happens to me or in me, but proceeds entirely from another, represents a compulsion I suffer rather than a freedom I enjoy."[3]

In chapter six I argued that in the competitive view of freedom and dignity I am criticizing the human self that acts as if it had no origin and no nature; rather, it acts as if it were the ever-changing sum of its fleeting desires. In that chapter I described this modern self as "empty desire." Its freedom is not to be found in following any predetermined course but in fulfilling its momentary desires. God and other people are the "other" to this self. They are competitors to be resisted or consumed, to be treated as

---

[2]Mortimer Adler, *The Idea of Freedom: A Dialectical Examination of the Conceptions of Freedom* (Garden City, NY: Doubleday, 1958), 1:614.
[3]Ibid., p. 610.

limits or means. Christian teaching, however, understands the self and the "other" in a very different way.

Whereas the modern self takes its existence for granted, Christianity asserts that we are not self-sufficient and self-defining beings that relate to things outside ourselves only at our pleasure. Our origin lies hidden in the love of God who gives us life continually because God wants us to know love and love in return. Living in awareness of truth requires us to acknowledge that we owe our being, with all its powers and possibilities, to God. The self that knows itself truly lives in joy and gratitude, for joy is the natural response to good, and gratitude is the fitting response to the giver of the good. Even this one insight renders it implausible that our Creator could also be our competitor. It also opens the possibility that our relationships with other people can become noncompetitive.

Whereas the modern view considers the self pure will without natural direction or ends, Christianity sees the self as having a nature and an end. We were created by God to enjoy certain goods, to pursue certain activities, to love certain things and become something in particular. Some activities and ends work against our nature and cause self-alienation and suffering. We were not created to love only ourselves; we were created to know and love God. We were created in the image of God, and our nature can be fulfilled only by becoming like God as his dear children.

Our view of freedom will be coordinated with our view of the self. If we identity the self with our momentary desires, we will identify freedom with favorable circumstances. If we consider the self the mysterious self-creative will at the core of our being, freedom will be understood as the natural power of self-determination. But if we think of the self as the created image of God revealed in Jesus Christ, we will think of freedom quite differently. In every view of freedom the self acts freely when it puts itself into action. In Christianity, the self is defined as a certain kind of relation to God, as God's image. This image is not an accidental relation that the self may or may not possess; it is its essence. And our lack of awareness of our true identity does not change the fact. But to *experience* true freedom the self must transform this objective God relation into its own subjective act.[4] The self must actually

---

[4]Or, to put it another way, it must relate itself to itself according to this relation to God. It duplicates its relation to God in its self-relation.

image God. As Kierkegaard express it, "in relating itself to itself and in willing to be itself, the self rests transparently in the power that established it."[5] We can enact ourselves freely only by willing God's will for ourselves and in this way imaging God's character. Refusal of this act is the self's refusal to be itself, that is, its refusal to be free. It is to "despair" of being free.[6]

THE TRUE SELF AND THE "OTHER"

Articulating an understanding of human freedom and differentiating it from other views requires us to clarify the way each distinguishes the self from the "other." Those thinkers who consider circumstantial freedom of self-realization the only true freedom view the self as the subject of sentences such as "*I* want to rest now" or "*I* plan to drive to Texas next week" or "*I* wish *I* were able to fly." The self is easily identifiable. There is no mysterious "true self" buried underneath the false self of the ego. The "other" is anything external to the self that hinders it from realizing its desires. For Christianity, however, the true self cannot be identified with the *I* of our ever-changing self-awareness, the sum of our momentary desires and thoughts. Not all of the desires and thoughts of the *I* arise from the true self. Some arise from the "other" in us.

For Christianity, the "other" is not a set of external roadblocks to realizing our desires. It is not God, other people, the government or a lack of money. It is an internal power that enslaves us through deception, compulsion and habit. To put it another way, it is our lack of power to hold the good and true in our minds so that we love them exclusively and pattern our lives after them wholly. In either case, we desire things that are not good and believe things that are not true. The *I* that believes untrue things and loves false goods is not the true but a false self. These misdirected desires and misinformed beliefs incite us to destructive actions that demonstrate our self-alienation.

The old and new selves. In his letters, Paul articulates a contrast between Adam and Christ, between the old, fallen humanity and the new condition brought by Jesus Christ:

---

[5]Søren Kierkegaard, *Sickness Unto Death*, ed. and trans. Howard V. and Edna H. Hong (Princeton, NJ: Princeton University Press, 1980), p. 14.
[6]Ibid., pp. 13-14.

For we know that our *old self [palaios anthrōpos]* was crucified with him so that the body of sin might be done away with, that we should no longer be slaves to sin—because anyone who has died has been freed from sin. (Rom 6:6-7 NIV 1984)

You were taught, with regard to your former way of life, to put off your *old self*, which is being corrupted by its deceitful desires; to be made new in the attitude of your minds. (Eph 4:22-23)

As for you, you were dead in your transgressions and sins, in which you used to live when you followed the ways of this world and of the ruler of the kingdom of the air, the spirit who is now at work in those who are disobedient. All of us also lived among them at one time, gratifying the cravings of our *sinful nature [sarkos]* and following its desires and thoughts. (Eph 2:1-3 NIV 1984)

Do not lie to each other, since you have taken off your *old self* with its practices and have put on the *new self*, which is being renewed in knowledge in the image of its Creator. (Col 3:9-10)

I have been using the terms *false self* and *true self*. Paul here uses the words *old self* and *new self*, which I have emphasized in these Scripture texts. He speaks in temporal terms and points to something that has happened and continues to happen to believers. It is a transition from the old age of Adam to a new age of Christ in which we now live by faith. The power of the new age works effectively to re-create and reorient the lives of believers. For Paul, the "old" and "new" selves are not two ontologically different natures but the one person set in two different relationships to God.[7] One is past, though still able to trouble the present; the other is future, though powerfully active in the present. The believer feels the "eschatological tension" between the two.[8] I do not think my shift in terms from *old-new* to *false-true* differs in substance from Paul's view. His temporal way of speaking underlines the fact that the transition from the old to the new self occurs deci-

---

[7]Douglas J. Moo, *The Epistle to the Romans* (Grand Rapids: Eerdmans, 1996), p. 373. John R. W. Stott said of the old man: "What was crucified with Christ was not a part of me called my old nature, but the whole of me as I was before I was converted" (*Men Made New: An Exposition of Romans 5-8* [London: InterVarsity Press, 1996], p. 45). Robert Jewett translates *palaios anthrōpos* (Rom 6:6), which in the classical period meant "the aged person," as "obsolete self" (*Romans: A Commentary* [Minneapolis, Fortress Press, 2007], p. 402).

[8]Moo, *Romans*, p. 375.

sively in the historical events of the death and resurrection of Jesus Christ. To mark the character of the old self as "false" and the character of the new as "true" does not deny their temporal order. For Paul, the new self is not merely one of many possible selves as if *new* meant "currently fashionable." The new is also the true self, which conforms to the "image of its Creator" (Col 3:10). Without the redemptive work of Christ and the renewing and empowering work of the Spirit, the human person cannot think, act or feel in conformity to the image of God, which is our created being. For Paul, this state of self-alienation is the old self, an identity that has been and should be left behind. The new self is the very same person who, because of the work of Jesus Christ and the Holy Spirit, now acts and feels and thinks consistently their true being. We can know our true selves only by looking at Jesus Christ.

Adam and Christ. In the middle section of Romans (chaps. 5–8) we find the most profound discussion of sin and redemption in the New Testament and in all theological literature.[9] In chapter 5, Paul compares and contrasts Adam and Christ, who are archetypes of the old and new selves. Sin, condemnation and death came to everyone because of Adam (Rom 5:12), but righteousness, grace and life have been given to all through Christ (Rom 5:15). Sin and death are "personified" as powers that reign over us in Adam.[10] As Douglas Moo puts it, "No one . . . escapes the reign of death because no one escapes the power of sin."[11] In chapter 6, Paul argues that this new righteousness can and must take concrete form in the lives of believers. We cannot leave it to Christ to be righteous while we use God's grace as an excuse to continue in sin (Rom 6:1). Paul reminds the Roman Christians that their baptism united them to Christ, to his death and resurrection. This union is not a metaphor for a moral reformation; it goes to the foundation of our being. We now participate in the life, righteousness and very identity of Christ. Christ has freed us from the "tyranny or

---

[9]See Gordon D. Fee, *Pauline Christology: An Exegetical-Theological Study* (Peabody, MA: Hendrickson, 2007), pp. 513-29, for a study of the Adam-Christ comparison and contrast in Paul's letters.

[10]Moo, *Romans*, p. 319.

[11]Ibid., p. 323. Ernst Käsemann argues that Paul is speaking cosmologically: "Paul is not speaking primarily of act and punishment but of ruling powers which implicate all people individually and everywhere determine reality as destiny" (*Commentary on Romans*, trans. and ed. Geoffrey Bromiley [Grand Rapids: Eerdmans, 1980], p. 150).

lordship" of sin; hence we need not and must not serve it any longer.[12]
Since Christ is our true being (Rom 5–7), Paul urges us to act, think and
feel as Christ does. Not, however, until Romans 8 does he tell us where we
get the power to do this.

The inner "other." In Romans 7, Paul explains why the power to act, think
and feel as Christ cannot come from the law.[13] God's holy law tells us what
we ought to be, but it cannot give us the power to become this good person.
To the contrary, when the law commands us not to covet what others have,
it actually makes us conscious of the envy that was there all along (Rom
7:7-8). Indeed, our sin becomes worse because we now add pride to envy
and continue to envy simply because we were told not to envy. Even our
most strenuous efforts to obey the law are doomed from the beginning. The
presupposition of these efforts is the pride-swollen notion that we can
overcome sin and become like Christ without God's help.

Paul is disheartened to find the "other" living within him (Rom 7:14-17).
He resolves to do the right thing but finds himself doing wrong: "For in my
inner being I delight in God's law; but I see another law at work in me,
waging war against the law of my mind and making me a prisoner of the law
of sin at work within me" (Rom 7:22-23). Moo comments:

> No, Paul reasons, there must be another "actor" in the drama. Another
> factor that interferes with his performance of what he wants to do. This
> other factor is indwelling sin. Sin is not a power that operates "outside"
> the person, making him do its bidding; sin is something resident in the
> very being, "dwelling" *[oikousa]* within the person, ruling over him or her
> like a master over a slave (v. 14b).[14]

---

[12]Moo, *Romans*, p. 350.

[13]See ibid., pp. 443-50, for arguments for and against the ideas that the experience of the "I" of
Rom 7:14-25 is preconversion and Jewish. Moo advances the opinion that Paul is discussing
his pre-Christian experience under the law as it looks now from his present Christian position. Jewett asserts that these verses depict "Paul's preconversion zealotism" (*Romans*, p.
455). It seems to me that preconversion views place the power of sin and death too handily in
the chronological past. For Paul, these powers are indeed of the past age and have no le-
gitimacy or future in Christ, but they are not simply left in the chronological past without
influence on the present. The warnings of Rom 6 make that clear. Paul makes clear in Rom
7 that the law was *and is* "holy, righteous and good" (v. 12). Viewing ourselves directly and
not as we exist in Christ, which can be perceived only in faith, our present (chronological)
existence is still troubled by sin, overshadowed by death and exposed by the law.

[14]Moo, *Romans*, p. 458.

Complete devotion to God is *one* of our desires; but it is not our *sole* desire. At the root of our being we hear a yes to God, but every move out of our inner being into action falls under that *other* power that perverts our inner yes into a no (Rom 7:18).

Paul understands sin as the "other" that robs us of freedom, blinds us to truth and alienates us from ourselves. Sin is not merely a forbidden act but a condition of our entire being. In analogy with the body, that inner condition can be called "death" or "slavery" or "blindness" or "corruption." Just as these physical conditions are not things in themselves, sin is not an evil substance that infects us. This *other* is so close to us that we cooperate with it and often mistake it for our very selves. But sin is not our true nature, and the desires and thoughts it inspires do not reveal our true selves. This *other*, which makes me do "what I hate" (Rom 7:15), Paul says, is "sin living in me" (Rom 7:17). It is a condition that keeps us from enjoying the fullness of what we were created to be. In this state, God's dear child is sick and in need of healing; she is blind and in need of enlightening. At the end of chapter 7 Paul asks for help: Who will rescue us from "this body of death," this condition of division within ourselves (Rom 7:24 NIV 1984)?[15] Paul answers immediately, "Thanks be to God, who delivers me through Jesus Christ our Lord!" (Rom 7:25). In Romans 8, Paul shows how God delivers us: God sent his Son "in the likeness of sinful flesh to be a sin offering" (Rom 8:3). The risen Christ comes to live in us through the Spirit that makes us "children of God" and enables us to "cry Abba, Father" (Rom 8:14-15). Because the Spirit unites us with Christ, his very identity becomes ours; we share in his death and resurrection. His righteousness becomes ours. His Father becomes ours. His Spirit becomes ours. He is our true self.

---

[15]The Stoic Epictetus (A.D. 55-c. 135) describes the human condition in a way similar to Paul; however, he sees the solution to the problem within the self rather than in God's saving action: "Every error [*hamartēma*, translated "sin" in Philo and the New Testament] comprehends a contradiction; for since he who errs does not wish to err, but to be right, it is clear that he is not doing what he wishes. For what does the thief wish to do? That which is for his own interest. If the theft is not for his own interest, he does not do that which he wishes.... He, then, is strong in argument and has the faculty of exhorting and confuting, who is able to show to each man the contradiction through which he errs and clearly to prove how he does not do that which he wishes and does that which he does not wish. For if any one shall show this, a man will himself withdraw from that which he does" (*Discourses* 2.26.4-5, in *Lucretius, Epictetus, Marcus Aurelius*, vol. 12, *Great Books of the Western World*, trans. George Long [Chicago: University of Chicago, 1952], p. 174).

Let me summarize. According to the Christian faith, the true human self returns to itself when it is united to Christ by the power of the Holy Spirit and liberated from sin that enslaves and corrupts. It is the self in which the desire to love God above all things has become the heart's *sole* desire. We cannot look within our consciousness to see this self. In this present life our existence is still divided and the "other" still troubles us. Our true self will become identical to our concrete existence only in the future that God will bring about. At present we can see it only by looking at Jesus Christ, who is our true being. But we live in hope, trusting that "we shall be like him, for we shall see him as he is" (1 Jn 3:2). Hence creation itself joins us as we wait eagerly for our adoption as "children of God" (Rom 8:18-23).

The Human and Divine Selves

In chapter eight we considered the divine self we come to know in Jesus Christ. God does not first exist as a solitary self who secondarily seeks relationships to enhance existence. God is a Trinity of persons, each of whom lives in the other eternally. The church fathers loved to say that the Father, Son and Spirit are three suns that shine from one center with one light. There is no self-centeredness in God. In love, each divine person freely centers on the other persons. There is no need or emptiness in the divine life. In Karl Barth's apt description, "God is the One who loves in freedom."[16] God's love overflows freely into the world in creation and incarnation, and returns to him freely in reconciliation and redemption.

According to the teachings of Jesus and the writers of the New Testament, human beings were intended to be living images of God. This teaching links knowledge of true humanity with knowledge of God. Hence, just as we cannot grasp God simply by thinking about a concept of the divine, we cannot define the true human self through direct knowledge of ourselves. We know God by considering God's revealed actions and attributes, and participating in the life bestowed by the Spirit. In a similar way, we can describe the true human self by listing its God-imaging attributes and actions, virtues and dispositions, but we can experience it only through the Spirit by participating in its life.

---

[16]Karl Barth, *Church Dogmatics*, vol. 2, pt. 1, ed. G. W. Bromiley and T. F. Torrance, trans. T. H. L. Parker et al. (Edinburgh: T & T Clark, 1957), p. 257.

Human beings, as images of God, are defined by the overflowing, other-directed nature of their being. We cannot become our true selves except by loving God with our whole heart and loving others. God loved us before we existed; we were dear to God when we could only envy God. And when we come to know through the Spirit how much God loves, we are set free to love God in return. God's love then flows from us to others. Hence, our first genuinely free act is accepting God's love for us. In accepting ourselves as a divine gift, we recognize and embrace the deepest truth about ourselves. We realize that being loved by God defines us as persons. This relation, it now becomes clear, is an inherent characteristic of our identity without which we would not exist as persons.[17]

Love gives itself freely. We cannot give ourselves in this way, however, until we have an authentic self to give and the freedom to let it go. Because of God's unconditional love for us, however, we can overflow in love following the divine pattern. God's love frees us to love in freedom. We no longer need to understand our self as an empty space we are desperate to fill. The one and only thing we need is supplied in superabundance: the love and fellowship of God.

Conclusion

What is the true self? Who am I? Who are you? We cannot answer these questions definitively by referring to our parents, our interests or our professions. These characteristics and relations might have been different and some may yet become different. The deepest and truest answers are: I am God's beloved. You are God's beloved. This relation never has and never will change. God is the "One who loves in freedom," and the true human self is the one liberated by God's love to love in freedom. As we shall see, human

---

[17]For an encyclopedic study of theological anthropology that generally tracks with the perspective I have developed here on the nature and identity of humanity, see David H. Kelsey, *Eccentric Existence: A Theological Anthropology*, 2 vols. (Louisville, KY: Westminster John Knox Press, 2009). In his 1051-page study, Kelsey reflects on humanity from three different angles: (1) Created: Living on Borrowed Breath, (2) Consummated: Living on Borrowed Time and (3) Reconciled: Living by Another's Death. Kelsey also expresses the true identity of humanity in terms of imaging God in union with Jesus Christ and in the power of the Spirit. He says, "The larger proposal urged here is that the three lines of thought about who human beings are as eccentric existence converge on the summary remark that human beings flourish as finite living mysteries in existential hows that image the image of the triune living mystery, Jesus of Nazareth" (2:1045).

beings can achieve no greater freedom and attain no higher dignity than the state in which every action of *this* self has become its own action, and every achievement its own property.

14

THE FREEDOM OF THE
CHILDREN OF GOD

The name Sisyphus has become synonymous with futility. In Greek mythology Sisyphus was condemned to eternally fruitless labor, having again and again to push a giant boulder to the top of a mountain only to have it crash down again.[1] Albert Camus, in his book *The Myth of Sisyphus* (1942), takes Sisyphus as a metaphor for the human condition. All our labor finally accomplishes nothing and is annihilated by death. And there is no God to remember our struggles. Camus attempts, nevertheless, to find something positive in Sisyphus's condition—which is the human condition—and advises us to assert our freedom to revolt against the meaninglessness of human existence by creating meaning and joy even in our ultimately futile labor. Whether Camus and other atheists can succeed in this fiction is a moot point. All agree that, objectively speaking, the human condition is meaningless and all our labor futile. But Christianity offers something very different to Sisyphus. It offers escape from futility, not through freedom to assert subjective meaning where there is no objective meaning but through freedom to become in reality what we were created to be, children of God.

In this chapter I want to explain why the Christian understanding of God and humanity leads to genuine freedom. We can accomplish this goal by showing how the Christian view of freedom fits Adler's general

[1]Herbert Jennings Rose, "Sisyphus," in *The Oxford Classical Dictionary*, ed. N. G. L. Hammond and H. H. Scullard, 2nd ed. (Oxford: Oxford University Press, 1970), p. 994.

definition: the ability or power whereby we can make what we do our own action and what we achieve our own property.[2] This definition singles out only the minimum qualifications for freedom. But I wish to show that the Christian view of freedom qualifies not only as authentic freedom but attains the goals of all three of Adler's basic types and thus fulfills the concept perfectly.

FREEDOM PERFECTED

I pointed out in earlier chapters that every concept of freedom involves notions of self, other, power, exemption and action. To defend a particular concept of freedom one must show how the *self* possesses the *power* to act *exempt* from the "*other*" so that its acts derive from itself and the properties it achieves are its own. We have already begun this project by clarifying the Christian understanding of the self. The self is not the sum of our momentary desires and wishes as is thought by those who think of freedom as circumstantial self-realization. Christianity explicitly denies us this freedom. Paul says, "Live by the Spirit, and you will not gratify the desires of the sinful nature. . . . [Y]ou do not do what you want" (Gal 5:16-17 NIV 1984). The self is not a pure will that determines itself to be whatever it wishes, as is held by those who consider freedom to be the natural power of self-determination. Again, Christianity denies that we have such power. The self is not the self-perfecting self of those who view the freedom of acquired self-perfection as a state one can achieve apart from divine grace. As we saw in my treatment of Romans 7, Paul denies that we can achieve perfect goodness by our own efforts. According to Paul, our true self is Christ living in us and enabling us to image God by loving as we have been loved (2 Cor 5:14-15; Gal 2:20; Phil 1:21).

Freedom as the power of a new life. According to the Scriptures, we are dearly loved children, created in the image of God to reflect God's character by loving. This is our true self, our deepest identity, our ultimate destiny. *Hence we can act freely only when we exercise the power to live as God's created image and arrive at a state in which we possess only our own properties, that is, properties that image God.* Freedom understood in a Christian

---

[2]Paraphrase of Mortimer Adler, *The Idea of Freedom: A Dialectical Examination of the Conceptions of Freedom* (Garden City, NY: Doubleday, 1958), 1:614.

way, then, is the power to live as we were created to live and to be what we were meant to be. It is the state of willing and acting as God's dear children. As we exercise this power, nothing in our acts or self derives from the "other," that is, from sin and death. Every desire, act and property of the self proceeds from the self and is possessed by the self. Whereas the Stoics taught that we can attain freedom by asserting our natural power of reason to dominate the body and its irrational passions, the New Testament teaches that "even in the retreat into inwardness man is not free."[3] We can attain genuine freedom, freedom from the "other" of sin and death, only through God's grace made actual in Jesus Christ and communicated to us in the power of the Holy Spirit.

This understanding of freedom finds clear expression in the writings of John and Paul. In the Gospel of John, Jesus teaches that "everyone who sins is a slave to sin. . . . So if the Son sets you free, you will be free indeed" (Jn 8:34, 36). In Romans 6, Paul describes sin as a dominating power that compels us to "surrender to . . . the concupiscent hunger of self-centered earthly and carnal life."[4] Paul insists, however, that we have been "freed" from sin (Rom 6:7, 18, 20, 22) and need not submit to its mastery. In Romans 8, he proclaims that we have been freed from "sin and death" through the work of Christ and the Spirit (Rom 8:2). We cannot achieve this freedom on our own, and this inability becomes clear in Paul's discussion of the law. The law itself is not the "other" that keeps us from attaining freedom; hence Paul does not speak of being "free" from the law as such. Instead he argues that Christ and the Spirit free us from the impossible requirement that we achieve our freedom from sin and death by our own power.[5] In this respect we are not "under the law but under grace" (Rom 6:15; cf. Gal. 5:18). What Paul speaks of is "freedom from an existence which in sin leads through the Law to death."[6] As Wolfhart Pannenberg puts it,

---

[3]Heinrich Schlier, "ἐλεύθερος," in *Theological Dictionary of the New Testament*, ed. Gerhard Friedrich, trans. Geoffrey W. Bromiley (Grand Rapids: Eerdmans,1972), 2:496.

[4]Ibid., p. 497.

[5]Jürgen Blunck, "Freedom," in *New International Dictionary of New Testament Theology*, ed. Colin Brown (Grand Rapids: Zondervan, 1975), pp. 715-21. According to the Blunck, Paul teaches that the power to liberate oneself from sin is not "within the realm of his own capacities."

[6]Schlier, "ἐλεύθερος," p. 496. See also, Douglas J. Moo, *The Epistle to the Romans* (Grand Rapids: Eerdmans, 1996), p. 402.

In Paul, as in John, the Spirit of Christ is conceived of as a liberating power. . . . But it is not primarily a liberation from any oppressive social system that is needed so that a natural freedom of man can be exercised fully without crippling impediments. *The human heart itself is considered the impediment.*[7]

In Romans 8, Paul speaks of the *glorious freedom* of the children of God. Creation itself groans while it waits to be freed from its "bondage to decay and brought into the freedom and glory of the children of God" (Rom 8:19-21). Paul also describes this glorious state as "adoption," "salvation" and "redemption" (Rom 8:22-25). As Paul's identification of freedom with these anticipated blessings makes clear, the freedom offered to us in Christ is not a natural possession or our own accomplishment.[8] True freedom is an eschatological blessing synonymous with salvation, redemption and eternal life. In the words of Hans Dieter Betz, Paul's "doctrine of salvation is very clearly and consciously formulated as a doctrine of freedom."[9] The freedom Christ makes possible embodies the perfect realization of human nature, the unambiguous manifestation of the true self, and the revelation of our destiny as children of God (Rom 8:19).[10]

---

[7]Wolfhart Pannenberg, "Human Nature and the Individual," in *Human Nature, Election, and History* (Philadelphia: Westminster Press, 1977), p. 19, emphasis added.

[8]See the following scholars for support for the reading of Paul I am proposing: Robert T. Osborn, *Freedom in Modern Theology* (Philadelphia: Westminster, 1963), p. 12: "Freedom in the New Testament is not a self-determination but a determination of the self." Ernst Fuchs, "Freiheit," in *Die Religion in Geschichte und Gegenwart*, 3rd ed. (Tübingen: J. C. Mohr, 1958), 2:1102, where he explains that freedom "now means no longer that I do what I will, but rather that I do what God does," quoted in Robert T. Osborn, *Freedom in Modern Theology* (Philadelphia: Westminster, 1963), p. 12. See also entry on "Freedom," in *Encyclopedia of Theology: The Concise Sacramentum Mundi*, ed. Karl Rahner (New York: Crossroad, 1975), pp. 533-44: "The free man is the man at one with God. Only if he abandons himself to God does he receive himself back as his own personal possession."

[9]Hans Dieter Betz, *Paul's Concept of Freedom in the Context of Hellenistic Discussions About Possibilities of Human Freedom*, Protocol Series of the Colloquies of the Center for Hermeneutical Studies in Hellenism and Modern Culture 26 (Berkeley, CA: Center for Hermeneutical Studies in Hellenism and Modern Culture, 1977), p. 7. For a recent study of Paul's teaching about freedom in its Hellenistic context, see Lincoln E. Galloway, *Freedom in the Gospel: Paul's Exemplum in 1 Cor 9 in Conversation with the Discourses of Epictetus and Philo* (Leuven: Peeters, 2004).

[10]Karl Hermann Schelkle, "New Testament Theology: Pauline Theology," in *Encyclopedia of Theology: The Concise Sacramentum Mundi*, ed. Karl Rahner (New York: Crossroad, 1975), pp. 1072-80. According to the author, "The fullness of freedom is a gift reserved for the end. It is liberation from the slavery of the perishable to the freedom of the glory of the children of God (Rom. 8:21)." According to Schelkle, Paul's teaching on freedom is to be understood within

How does this happen? How does the true self realize perfect freedom? Clearly we cannot do this alone. According to New Testament teaching, we are rescued from sin and death by the grace of God in Jesus Christ. The Spirit works for us and in us to free us from the "other" and change us from God's enemies into his dear children. The Spirit does not act impersonally and automatically in this transformation. We are not *coerced* into freedom against our wills. In the power of his Spirit, God moves us and liberates us to will his will through deep spiritual persuasion or enlightenment, Spirit to spirit (Rom 8:16). The Spirit pours God's love into our hearts (Rom 5:5) and strengthens "your inner being" so that "Christ may dwell in your hearts through faith" (Eph 3:16-17).[11] God's is the freedom that frees!

Freedom as a gift. How can genuine freedom be *given* to us? Can freedom be something done to us and not something we do? Adler's general definition of freedom requires that the actions and properties of the self arise from the self and remain in its possession. But it seems that the Christian view of freedom, as presented here, does not conform to this definition. Though it views freedom as a genuine property of the self, it does not see it as generated by the self alone.

In answer to this objection we should first observe that it could be leveled at every other view of freedom. Whatever its view of freedom's nature, none accounts for our original possession of freedom by arguing that it is an achievement of the self. They assume that freedom is given along with our existence, or that it is achieved with help from outside, or they give no explanation at all. It should be obvious that the demand implicit in this objection to the Christian view of freedom is unreasonable, for how could our original possession of freedom in any form result from our own efforts? Every achievement presupposes that we are already free. For freedom to be our own achievement, then, we would need to possess freedom already in order to achieve it, which would in-

---

the horizon of Hellenism, "where freedom was regarded as a precious possession and a prize to be sought after in philosophy, ethics and religion. . . . It was a point at which the world and the gospel met and parted. In the former, in the Stoa, for instance, freedom is won by the wise man's own effort. In the latter, it is the gift of the liberating grace of God" (p. 1078).

[11]Schlier observes: "In the Spirit of the freedom of Jesus Christ, there arises our freedom" ("ἐλεύθερος," p. 499).

volve us in an infinite series of ever more fundamental levels of freedom.[12]

Christian teaching does not take our original possession of freedom for granted; it gives an account of how we received it. God created us in love, bestowing life and all the powers of our nature, which include "natural" freedom and "circumstantial" freedom. Even these two common freedoms become our possessions as gifts, and yet they are admittedly genuine properties of the self. Hence it should not count against its authentic character that the Christian version of *acquired* freedom is also a gift. Just as we can exercise natural freedom and circumstantial freedom only after we exist, we can exercise perfected freedom of which the New Testament speaks only after we have been freed from sin and death. Paul seems to have this truth in mind when he speaks of salvation in Christ as a "new creation" (2 Cor 5:17; Gal 6:15).

Freedom here and now. Some readers may be wondering how this future state of perfect freedom is relevant to our present circumstances. It may seem that I have made freedom into a distant hope unlike anything we currently experience. You are entirely within your rights to ask, "But do we have genuine freedom here and now?" Allow me to put aside for the present issues of natural and circumstantial freedom, and focus on whether we can exercise in this life anything like the perfect freedom of which the New Testament speaks.

We do not yet possess perfect freedom in the strict sense since it becomes fully actualized only with the resurrection of the dead into eternal life. But the power that will liberate the children of God into perfect freedom is already at work. First, through the power of the Spirit God has already made perfect freedom a reality for the representative human, Jesus Christ. He is the true image of God and the archetype of our true self. He has revealed and

---

[12]Only God is the ground of his own freedom. For my understanding of divine freedom, see my *Great Is the Lord: Theology for the Praise of God* (Grand Rapids: Eerdmans, 2008), pp. 222-54. Thinking of freedom as an achievement of freedom might make sense if we used the word *freedom* in two different senses. For example, if we were endowed with the natural freedom of self-determination perhaps we could decide freely to work toward greater circumstantial freedom of self-realization. But even this example fails. Unless we were given some circumstantial freedom, we would have no capacity to work for more. We need not only an original freedom to *will* something, we must be endowed with the power to *do* something. Without an originally given freedom we can achieve nothing. Why should we take seriously an objection to the Christian view of freedom that implies either that we have the power to create ourselves from nothing or that there is no such thing as human freedom?

realized every possibility of our created nature. Jesus Christ is the living truth. Knowledge of this truth puts us in touch with our true selves and shows that perfect freedom is possible for us. Just believing in the possibility of such freedom is liberating. This revelation of our true nature and destiny guides our actions and prayers and liberates us from illusions. But it is not enough. We still lack power to overcome the "other" of sin. The Holy Spirit is the power that even now helps us believe, strengthens our wills, purifies our prayers and enables us to receive God's love into our hearts. The Spirit bears fruit here and now: "love, joy, peace, patience, kindness, goodness, faithfulness, gentleness and self-control" (Gal 5:22-23 NIV 1984).

The freedom we now experience, though imperfect and fragmentary, participates nevertheless in the character of true freedom. We are being changed into the person Jesus describes in the Sermon on the Mount. We find ourselves loving righteousness and hating evil. We catch ourselves thinking about, longing for and praising God. We are surprised to find ourselves loving our enemies and breaking free from the bonds of lust and greed. Our freedom is not yet a secure possession, for we cannot yet directly and consciously will and do God's will in all circumstances. Paul makes this painfully clear in Romans 7. When we take ourselves into our own hands to will and do the good by our own power, we have already failed. But if we look not at ourselves but at Jesus Christ, confess our sins and rely on the Spirit's empowering power, we will experience his power liberating us to will and do his will. We do not experience this power as an alien force (the "other") but encounter it as "Another," a helper who frees us to enact our true selves. Though the Spirit liberates our will, we really do the willing. Our new willing of God's will is a genuine property of our true selves and is thus an act of genuine freedom.

Christian freedom as the perfection of freedoms. How does Christian freedom relate to Adler's three basic types of freedom: *circumstantial* freedom of self-realization, which is freedom from external constraints; *natural* freedom of self-determination, which is freedom from coercion of the will by an alien force; and *acquired* freedom of self-perfection, which is freedom from internal blindness that keeps us from always willing the good? Does Christian freedom bring about *circumstances* that allow the self to realize itself so that it acts from itself and whatever it becomes is a property of itself? Yes, it does. In the state God brings about through the work of Christ and the Spirit, the self is freed from sin, death and blindness. It no longer wants anything evil. In the clear light of truth, it wills only good things. There is no "other" hindering it from achieving its wants. Hence the ideal of perfect self-realization, impossible in the circumstances of this life, will be achieved.

Does the freedom offered by Christ enable the self to *determine* itself so that it acts from the self and whatever it becomes is a property of the self? Indeed it does. In the perfect freedom given by the Spirit, the self determines itself to be what it truly is, God's dear child and the image of God. The true self wills to be nothing other than itself. To recall again Kierkegaard's definition of the self free from despair, the self "in relating itself to itself and in willing to be itself, the self rests transparently in the power that established it."[13] It has no alien properties. To put it another way, in that freedom we are what we would create ourselves to be if we had the power to create ourselves from nothing. This freedom far surpasses the power attributed to the self by those who defend the *natural* freedom of self-determination. Even the most radical advocates of free will recognize that in this life we will always possess properties that we did not choose.

Does the Christian version of freedom envision a state of the self in which it acquires *self-perfection* so that it acts from itself and whatever it becomes is a property of itself? As I have said many times in this book, acquired freedom of self-perfection resembles Christian freedom more than the other two types resemble it. It recognizes the need to discover the true self rather than identifying the self with our momentary desires and wishes. It is aware of the necessity for the self to know and will truth and goodness. However, some advocates of this view think that insofar as it can be attained, this state must result solely from our own work. In contrast, for Christianity this state cannot be attained without divine help. The fullness of Christian freedom, then, is a state in which the self (helped by the Spirit) has come to will what God wills without wavering and so has become perfect. Its act of willing perfectly the good is its own act and its perfect character is its own property.

---

[13]Søren Kierkegaard, *Sickness Unto Death*, ed. and trans. Howard V. and Edna H. Hong (Princeton, NJ: Princeton University Press, 1980), p. 14.

Does my conception of perfect freedom imply that our ordinary experience of circumstantial and natural freedom is illusory? It does not imply this, but it requires that we assess these freedoms from the higher perspective of perfect freedom. From this vantage point we can see that these two freedoms are imperfect forms that only dimly resemble perfect freedom. Even if circumstances permit us to act for our self-realization, that is, to do what we want, we are not genuinely free in those acts unless we want the right thing. You cannot be free in willing evil because the desire for evil keeps us from realizing our true selves. Those captive to evil desires are slaves, not masters. Under the conditions of our existence ordinary acts of circumstantial freedom are mixed, containing elements of freedom and elements of slavery. Insofar as these acts realize the true self they can be considered free, but insofar as they express the "old" sinful self they lack genuine freedom.

The idea of self-determination, as it is understood in the most common versions of natural freedom or free will, suffers from the same imperfections that plague the concept of circumstantial freedom. We have been created with certain God-given properties, needs and ends. Of course, we can imagine ourselves being something else. We can wish we were God and attempt to play that role. But we cannot succeed. We create only a false and imaginary self. And in willing evil, we fall victim to self-deception and futility. This state hardly qualifies as free by the standards of perfect freedom. Nevertheless, acts of self-determination may involve some truth as well as much falsehood. Insofar as we determine ourselves to be what we are truly meant to be, God's living images, we act freely. But separated from divine grace, our self-determinations involve much delusion and hence much slavery.[14]

Christianity presents itself as the way to true and perfect freedom, as liberation from the powers of sin and death. It is not satisfied with lesser freedoms. Circumstantial freedom to do as you wish or natural freedom of the will fall far short of the supernatural freedom God has promised his

---

[14]Hence, to use Karl Rahner's terminology, freedom is an analogous concept and its various forms manifest levels of analogy to the real thing, which only God possesses by nature. For my study of Rahner's thought on this topic, see Ron Highfield, "The Freedom to Say 'No'? Karl Rahner's Doctrine of Sin," *Theological Studies* 56 (1995): 485-505.

dear children. The Christian hope envisions a state in which we attain freedom to become fully our true selves. We were created to image the character of God and to reflect his glory to all creation. Through Christ and in the Spirit, God empowers us to overcome the "other" so that we become truly free, that is, we become in our actions and existence what we are in our true being.

15

GOD'S LOVE AS THE GROUND AND MEASURE OF HUMAN DIGNITY

Friedrich Nietzsche's views on human dignity stand radically opposed to those of Immanuel Kant. Kant rooted human dignity in the independent, inherent and universal power of autonomy and asserted that even God had to respect it. Nietzsche hated Christianity and thought Kant's views secretly depended on Christianity. Attempting to return to pre-Christian notions of dignity, Nietzsche denies the inherent and universal presence of dignity in human beings, asserting, rather, that dignity must be earned and can be acquired only by people who make themselves worthy by their own bold action. For Nietzsche, dignity is not a moral concept implying universal respect for others but an esthetic one and is acquired by making oneself pleasing to oneself.[1] In this chapter I want to develop a view of human dignity that neither Kant nor Nietzsche would accept: that God's love for us is the fundamental ground of our worth.

In chapter fourteen we saw that true and perfect human freedom can be realized only with help from divine grace. But we have not yet addressed the issue of the dignity of this situation. Does this state represent the highest possible human dignity or does our dependence on divine grace forever compromise our dignity? In chapter six I pointed out that the common way

---

[1]See the interesting paper by C. J. Murdoch, "Kant's Antipode: Nietzsche's Transvaluation of Human Dignity and Its 'Implications' for Biotechnology Policy," FreeLibrary, 2007. This paper was originally published in the *Health Law Review* (Spring 2007).

of thinking about human dignity leads ultimately to despair, to perpetual restlessness and insatiable ambition. We ordinarily think of our dignity as indexed to our dependence on something outside ourselves. More dependence means less dignity and more dignity requires less dependence. Unlimited dignity would require total independence. Since we can never achieve total independence we must settle for a lesser dignity.

I want to challenge this comparative way of understanding our worth and craft another view of dignity. I will argue that dignity in its most basic form is a relation of being loved by another. And God is the only "Other" whose love can establish our dignity beyond dispute. I wish to show that the Christian understanding of human dignity attains the highest dignity possible for us. But I want to go even beyond this already lofty claim to affirm that Christianity offers us the highest dignity conceivable.

DIGNITY IN THE CHURCH FATHERS AND MEDIEVAL THEOLOGY

The church fathers and medieval theologians reflect extensively on the dignity and misery of humanity. In what follows we notice three distinct but related ways Christian thinkers have understood human dignity: as excellence of nature, moral excellence and belovedness. The excellent qualities of human beings set them above all other earthly creatures. Such excellence bestows power and authority to rule other creatures. In a fallen world, however, humanity does not live up to its noble birth. It misuses its excellent qualities to engage in degrading behavior. But with the aid of divine grace human beings can regain some moral excellence in their lives. Human beings cannot take credit for their excellent qualities and actions; rather, these are gracious gifts of God their Creator. Humanity's status of greater dignity in relation to other creatures derives from the love and favor with which God relates to them. Hence the relationship of being loved and favored by God is the more fundamental basis of human dignity. Excellence of nature, though in a sense inherent in humanity, is measured in comparison with other creatures. Belovedness, in contrast, is not a quality inherent in humanity but a relationship with God, eccentric to our being. We will begin our survey of Christian thought on human dignity with Augustine of Hippo.

In books one through five of his *Confessions*, Augustine details by means of his autobiography the misery of humanity in rebellion to God. Apart from divine grace, lust, envy and pride enslave us and drive us to despair. And why does Augustine write about the follies of his youth? "It is that I and any of my readers may reflect on the great depth from which we cry to you."[2] He laments, "But I in my misery seethed and followed the driving force of my impulses, abandoning you."[3] He says of his lost state:

I was tossed about and split, scattered and boiled dry in my fornications. And you were silent. How slow I was to find my joy! At that time you said nothing, and I traveled much further away from you into more sterile things productive of unhappiness, proud in my self-pity, incapable of rest in my exhaustion.[4]

After his conversion, which he describes in book eight, Augustine enjoys delivery from the miserable state he described earlier and experiences restoration of a measure of dignity to his affections and actions:

Suddenly it had become sweet to me to be without the sweets of folly. What I once feared to lose was now a delight to dismiss. You turned them out and entered to take their place, pleasanter than any pleasure but not to flesh and blood, brighter than all light yet more inward than any secret recess, higher than any honour but not to those who think themselves sublime. Already my mind was free of "the biting cares" of place-seeking, of desire for gain, of wallowing in self-indulgence, of scratching the itch of lust. And I was now talking with you, Lord my God, my radiance, my wealth and my salvation.[5]

Having described the misery humanity experiences apart from God's grace and the renewed dignity of moral excellence bestowed by grace, Augustine feels free to express his wonder at the natural greatness of humanity. In book ten he addresses the question of how and where to seek for God. God cannot be identified with any of the natural forces we experience through the five senses. What is God? Look at the external world; ask sea,

---

[2]Augustine, *Confessions* 2.5, in *The Confessions of Saint Augustine*, trans. Henry Chadwick (New York: Oxford University Press, 1991), p. 26.
[3]Ibid., 2.4, p. 25.
[4]Ibid., 2.2, pp. 24-25.
[5]Ibid., 9.1, p. 155. Clement of Alexandria also discusses this type of dignity. If we allow Christ to train us in "moral excellence" we can gain a "superior dignity" (*The Instructor* 1.12, in *Fathers of the Second Century*, vol. 2, Ante-Nicene Fathers, ed. Alexander Roberts and James Donaldson [Grand Rapids: Eerdmans, 1979], p. 235).

air, mountains, sun, moon and stars. They all say, "we are not the God you seek. . . . [H]e made us."[6] Next, look inside your own mind and you will find something greater than the external world: "This power of the memory is great, very great, my God. It is a vast and infinite profundity. Who has plumbed its bottom? This power is that of my mind and is a natural endowment, but I myself cannot grasp the totality of what I am."[7] Augustine continues to enumerate the innumerable images, skills and concepts within the mind. There he also meets himself, memories of his actions, feelings and thoughts. These reflections leave him awestruck: "Great is the power of memory, an awe-inspiring mystery, my God, a power of profound and infinite multiplicity. And this is mind, this is I myself. What then am I, my God? What is my nature?"[8] But God is not found in the mind, great though it is. God is the Lord and light of the mind, its Creator and Sustainer. Augustine finds his own nature greater than he can grasp. How much greater is God!

In his commentary on Genesis 1:26, concerning the creation of humanity in the "image and likeness of God," Augustine finds humanity's highest dignity in the reasoning function of the soul, which corresponds to "the excellence of nature" I mentioned earlier. Reason enables human beings to rule over the earth as God rules over all things and enables humanity to contemplate God.[9] In his highly influential treatise on the Trinity, especially in books 9-10, Augustine explores the human mind, which he believes is constructed in the image of the Trinity. At the beginning of this study he says, "Where, then, is the trinity? Let us attend as much as we can, and let us invoke the everlasting light, that He may illuminate our darkness, and that we may see in ourselves, as much as we are permitted, the image of God."[10]

In Augustine's thought on human nature we can see all three types of dignity listed previously. Excellence of nature and excellence of moral char-

---

[6]Augustine, *Confessions* 10.9, p. 183.

[7]Ibid., 10.15, p. 187.

[8]Ibid., 10.26, p. 194.

[9]Augustine, *Two Books on Genesis Against the Manichees* 17, and *On the Literal Interpretation of Genesis: An Unfinished Book* 16, in Fathers of the Church 84, trans. and ed. Roland J. Teske (Washington, D.C.: Catholic University of America Press, 1991), pp. 74-76, 182-88.

[10]Augustine, *On the Trinity* 9.2, in *St. Augustine: On the Holy Trinity, Doctrinal Treatises, Moral Treatises*, vol. 3, Nicene and Post-Nicene Fathers, 1st ser., ed. Philip Schaff (Grand Rapids: Eerdmans, 1979), p. 127.

acter (or its lack) are the central focus; however, the dignity of belovedness is always assumed as the foundation of the other two. Being created as the image of God is a great blessing bestowed by our gracious Creator, and only in love and grace may we receive the power needed to return to the moral excellence in which we were created. Did God not love us, we would not possess the other marks of dignity. As we shall see, this same pattern holds in the following writers.

Though Augustine was the most influential theologian in the West, others also wrote on the dignity of humanity. Gregory of Nyssa (c. 330-c. 395) wrote *On the Creation of Man*, in which he extolled the excellences of humanity. According to Gregory, it is clear that God made humankind for the exercise of kingly rule; for "the soul immediately shows its royal and exalted character, far removed as it is from the lowliness of private station, in that it owns no lord, and is self-governed, swayed autocratically by its own will; for to whom else does this belong than to a king?"[11] The greatness of humanity consists not in being an image of the world but "in his being in the image of the nature of the creator."[12] Since God is the good beyond all good we can conceive, Gregory argues that being in the image of God indicates we are created to participate in all the best things:

> Thus there is in us the principle of all excellence, all virtue and wisdom, and every higher thing that we conceive: but pre-eminent among all is the fact that we are free from necessity, and not in bondage to any natural power, but have decision in our own power as we please; for virtue is a voluntary thing, subject to no dominion: that which is the result of compulsion and cannot be virtue.[13]

The apologetic writer Lactantius (c. 250-c. 325) wrote *On the Workmanship of God or the Formation of Man* as an attempt to prove the existence of God by showing the greatness of his human creation. Critics charge that the weakness and vulnerability of humanity in comparison to the other animals counts against divine providence. Lactantius replies that God gave

---

[11]Gregory of Nyssa, *On the Making of Man* 4.1, in *Gregory of Nyssa: Dogmatic Treatises, Etc.*, vol. 5, Nicene and Post-Nicene Fathers, 2nd ser., ed. Philip Schaff and Henry Wace (Grand Rapids: Eerdmans, 1979), p. 391.

[12]Ibid., 16.1, p. 404.

[13]Ibid., 16.11, p. 405.

humankind reason and wisdom, excellences that show "that we are descended from Him, because he himself is intelligence."[14] Reason gives humanity the power to rule the animals and provide for itself far better than the animals. The beauty of his body is enhanced by the absence of fur and sharp teeth and claws. In his *Divine Institutes*, Lactantius argues that humankind's dignity and God's wisdom are demonstrated in that the world was made by God not for himself but for living beings. And all "other living beings were given for the sake of man."[15]

One other patristic writer deserves mention, Nemesius of Emesa (fl c. 390), who wrote *On Human Nature*. He writes, "When we consider these facts about man, how can we exaggerate the dignity of his place in the creation?" Humanity incorporates every dimension of the created world in its being and "is rightly called 'the world in little' *[micros kosmos]*." All other creatures were made for the sake of humanity. God made human beings in his image and likeness and became incarnate for their sake. Humankind's greatness is inexpressible:

> Who, then, can fully express the pre-eminence of so singular a creature? Man crosses the mighty deep, contemplates the range of the heavens, notes the motion, position, and size of the stars, and reaps a harvest both from land and sea, scorning the rage of wild beasts and the might of whales. He learns all kinds of knowledge, gains skill in arts, and pursues scientific inquiry. By writing, he addresses himself to whom he will, however far away, unhindered by bodily location. He foretells the future, rules everything, subdues everything, enjoys everything. He converses with angels and with God himself. He gives orders to creation. Devils are subject to him. He explores the nature of every kind of being. He busies himself with the knowing of God, and is God's house and temple. And all these privileges he is able to purchase at the cost of virtue and godliness.[16]

---

[14]Lactantius, *On the Workmanship of God* 2, in *Fathers of the Third and Fourth Centuries*, vol. 7, Ante-Nicene Fathers, ed. Alexander Roberts and James Donaldson (Grand Rapids: Eerdmans, 1979), p. 282.

[15]Lactantius, *Divine Institutes* 7.3, in *Fathers of the Third and Fourth Centuries*, vol. 7, Ante-Nicene Fathers, ed. Alexander Roberts and James Donaldson (Grand Rapids: Eerdmans, 1979), p. 198.

[16]Nemesius of Emesa, *On Human Nature*, in *Cyril of Jerusalem and Nemesius of Emesa*, vol. 4, Library of Christian Classics, ed. William Telfer (Philadelphia: Westminster Press, 1955), pp. 254-55.

Theologians of the Middle Ages inherited the ideas of Augustine, Gregory, Nemesius and others. Following Augustine and other patristic writers, Peter Lombard (1100-1160), author of *The Sentences,* the Middle Ages' most used textbook of theology, explains the creation of humanity in the image and likeness of God. Commenting on Genesis 1:26 ("Let us make mankind . . ."), Lombard argues, "this is said in the person of the Father to the Son and Holy Spirit, not, as some hold, to the angels, because the image or likeness of God and the angels is not one and the same."[17] According to Lombard the human mind, not the body, is the "image and likeness" of God. Following the tradition, Lombard distinguishes the "image" from the "likeness," giving three acceptable opinions of the difference:

> And so man was made in the image and likeness of God in respect to his mind, by which he excels irrational creatures; [1] in his image, however, according to memory, intelligence, and love; in his likeness according to innocence and justice, which are naturally in the rational mind—Or [2] image is considered in the knowledge of the truth, his likeness in the love of virtue; or [3] image in all other things, likeness in the essence, because it is immortal and indivisible.[18]

Theologians after Lombard became interested in the issue of the relationship of human dignity to that of angels. Are human beings of less dignity or more? Bonaventure (c. 1217-1274), for example, admits that according to their inherent nature angels are probably of greater dignity than human beings, since angels are of greater similarity to God. Human beings possess a material body as well as an immaterial soul, while angels are pure mind. However, through God's grace humankind may be "elevated even to the capacity of the Angel and in some way beyond."[19] According to Trinkaus, later medieval thinkers tend to place human dignity unambiguously below the angels.[20]

Living at the boundary between the Middle Ages and the Renaissance, Petrarch (1304-1374) wrote about the dignity of the human condition. Re-

---

[17]Peter Lombard, *The Sentences: Book 2 On Creation,* 2.16.2, trans. Giulio Silano (Toronto: Pontifical Institute of Mediaeval Studies, 2008), pp. 68-69.

[18]Ibid., 2.16.5, p. 70.

[19]Bonaventura, *Commentary on the Sentences* 2.1, quoted in Charles Trinkaus, *In Our Image and Likeness: Humanity and Divinity in Italian Humanist Thought* (Notre Dame, IN: University of Notre Dame Press, 1995), 1:189.

[20]Trinkaus, *Our Image and Likeness,* 1:189-90.

maining solidly within the Christian tradition on the subject, he anticipates
later humanists' positive estimation of human nature and condition:

> And what surpasses all dignity, not only human but angelic, humanity
> itself is so conjoined to divinity that He who was God is become man . . .
> so that He makes man God. . . . But what, I pray, can man, I do not say
> hope, but choose, but think that is higher than that he should become
> God? Behold, now he is God. What now remains, I ask, toward which
> your prayers aspire? Nothing greater is left to be found or even imagined.
> . . . He assumed nothing other, although he was able, than a human body
> and a human soul, nor did He wish to be ascribed to the angelic species
> but the human so that you might know and rejoice at how much your
> Lord loved you.[21]

As I indicated at the beginning of this section, traditional Christian
thinkers understood human dignity as excellence of nature or moral excellence or belovedness. As this summary shows, humanity's excellence of
being, though it can inspire awe, as we saw in Augustine, is finite. We can
conceive of more excellent beings. The issue of moral excellence (or its lack)
offers most writers merely an opportunity to lament the sin, misery and
degeneracy of fallen humanity. Dignity of this sort is in short supply.
However, the dignity of belovedness offers some exciting possibilities, assumed in earlier writers, hinted at in Bonaventure and expressed clearly in
Petrarch. Being loved by God bestows a dignity on us that far surpasses the
excellence of our nature or of our moral performance.[22] It is potentially infinite. I will develop this possibility in the next section.

---

[21]Petrarch, quoted in ibid., p. 191.
[22]Christoph Schwöbel argues that the church should "criticize all views of what it means to be
human . . . which define human dignity on the basis of observable attributes based on the
capacities of human nature that humans may possess to a greater or lesser degree" ("Recovering Human Dignity," in God and Human Dignity, ed. R. Kendall Soulen and Linda Woodhead [Grand Rapids: Eerdmans, 2006], p. 57). While I share Schwöbel's concern with defending the human dignity of the aged, the preborn and other "unproductive" people, it is also
important to recognize the dignity of human nature itself and of moral character. The
church fathers and medieval theologians include excellence of nature and moral excellence
among the marks of human dignity for important reasons. Consider for example how
human dignity is distinguished from that of "lower" animals. Perhaps God loves all living
things. Does this mean that squirrels possess dignity equal to humans? Human beings possess qualities that mark them as superior to other animals, and these superior qualities are
at least signs of a higher dignity before God.

DIGNITY WITHOUT LIMITS

Pride and shame. Before we look at the genuine thing, let us consider counterfeit dignity. In chapter six we noticed that we tend to ground our dignity in certain qualities we possess or wish we possessed, the most important being independence. The greater our power or wealth the more independence we boast, and hence the more dignity we think we possess. In this brief section I want to mention two types of counterfeit dignity: pride and shame. Despite coming to opposite conclusions, both result from attempting to judge one's own worth from within oneself. However, attaining an objective view of one's dignity from within oneself is as impossible as lifting oneself by the collar or examining one's own retina without a mirror. Pride arises out of an insecure wish to be significant given fantastic form by imagination. In relation to others, wish becomes assertion in search of confirmation. Pride desires to experience admiration or envy from others so that it can relish its own worth. It feels entitled to be noticed, admired and feared, and it becomes indignant when it fails to receive the deference it expects. As we shall see in the next section, pride possesses elements in common with genuine dignity; it vaguely senses the relative nature of dignity, that is, it feels that our worth is somehow dependent on other people's evaluation of us.

The proud imagine they possess admirable properties in abundance. To conceited eyes, trifling accomplishments cast mountainous shadows. If other people do not seem to be conscious of these qualities and achievements, they feel compelled to make them aware. Of course, proud people never possess these traits to the degree they imagine. The book of Proverbs observes, "Pride goes before destruction, / a haughty spirit before a fall" (Prov 16:18). The fall inevitably comes because pride breeds falsehood, and falsehood sooner or later will be dashed against the rock of truth. Proud people's exaggeration of their excellence is derived from belief that their dignity must be rooted in inherent qualities. But since the proud cannot assess the value of their inherent qualities apart from comparison with others, they can experience dignity only by feeling comparative merit over others. One whose dignity is determined by its level of superiority over others can never be satisfied as long as there is someone whose dignity is greater.

Just as pride is an unreliable indicator of dignity, shame is a defective sign of unworthiness. Shame is a feeling of unworthiness not before our own consciences, which is guilt, but with reference to others. On the surface it seems opposed to pride. In shame we imagine that others despise us. Rather than wanting to fill their minds with thoughts about us, we want to escape being noticed by others. In shame we feel that everyone is laughing at us, as if our very existence were a mistake, a living joke. Shame agrees with pride that our worth must be grounded in our inherent qualities. We are ashamed when we look at ourselves because do not see the qualities others admire. Shame and pride also concur that the thoughts of others reveal the truth about us. Hence, pride glories in the thoughts it imagines others have about us and shame turns away from judging eyes. Finally, both shame and pride think of dignity in comparative terms. Pride relishes its preeminence while shame suffers the ache of inferiority. What, then, is dignity, and on what foundation must it be grounded?

Dignity and love. It is important to remember that dignity is the measure of our worth and is therefore a relative term. Worth is a kind of relation. Something is "worth" something because it is worth something to someone as a means or as an end. We can prize gold because of its purchasing power or for its beauty, as a means or as an end. It should be clear that a means is always subordinate to its end. Hammers are valuable because houses are more valuable. If we think of human dignity as the measure of a person's power to do us good or ill, we will treat people as means. In contrast, by valuing people as ends we find dignity in them for what they are, not merely in what they can do for us. Plainly, we are given a higher dignity if we are valued as ends than if we are valued as means to other ends. But to be valued as an end is to be loved. Hence the highest dignity we can bestow on another person is love, and the purer this love is from selfishness, the greater the dignity we give to the object of our love.

But human love cannot serve as a secure foundation for human dignity, for human love is unreliable and far from universal. We cannot be satisfied with dignity that rises and falls with others' feelings about us.[23] Doing

---

[23]Unless we understand dignity as conferred by God, argues Christoph Schwöbel, "dignity becomes something that is conferred or withheld by other finite entities. . . . If it is constituted in this way, however, it can also be denied and destroyed in this way" ("Recovering Human Dignity," p. 53).

justice to the concept of human dignity requires that it be something that compels recognition rather than a subjective value that can be arbitrarily bestowed or withheld. Dignity must be, in a sense not yet defined, inherent in human beings. But the concept of "inherent" dignity—Kant's idea that humans have "worth" apart from relationships in which they are valued—is plagued with conceptual problems. Dignity or worth is a relationship, and you cannot possess a relationship alone. Webster correctly observes, "To be a creature, therefore, is not simply to be a self-standing product of an initial cause; it is to be and to live—without restriction—*ab extra*" [i.e., from outside].[24] Human dignity, I conclude, needs a foundation that is unchanging, universal *and relational*. This threefold foundation can be secured only in God's love for us.[25]

Human dignity as a relation to God. God's very being is relational, for God *is* Father, Son and Spirit. The love among the three is eternal, constant and total. By loving the others each bestows on them infinite dignity. God's dignity, therefore, is both inherent and relational. It is inherent because it is an essential aspect of God's eternal nature. The love among the Trinity is a feature of what it means to be God. It is relational because God has been esteemed worthy from all eternity. God (as Trinity) is the foundation and origin for God's own dignity and for the dignity of all other beings. God does not love his dear children because of their inherent dignity or moral excellence. He *bestows* dignity on them by loving them, the dignity of belovedness. As John Webster expresses it, "The 'true honour' of creatures—life in the divine image and likeness—is not so much an unchanging property of humankind but the history of a relation between God the creator and his creatures."[26] Or more compactly, Webster asserts, "Creaturely dignity is an ontological and moral relation to God."[27] Wolfhart Pan-

---

[24]John Webster, "The Dignity of Creatures," in *The God of Love and Human Dignity: Essays in Honour of George M. Newlands*, ed. Paul Middleton (New York: T & T Clark, 2007), p. 22.

[25]"Only God the creator can crown with glory and honour; creatures are not competent to ascribe dignity to themselves or to other creatures. . . . And because it is rooted in God's free favour alone, creaturely dignity is secure" (ibid., p. 24). In this fine essay, though he expresses himself in different terms, Webster clearly works with what I call the relational view of dignity or belovedness. He speaks of dignity in terms of divine "blessing" (p. 21), "loving act of God" (p. 22), "gift of God" (p. 23), "divine gift" (p. 23), God's "acknowledging and approving" (p. 24), God's "free favour" (p. 24), "fellowship" with God (p. 25) and a "relation" to God (p. 25).

[26]Ibid., p. 25.

[27]Ibid., p. 30.

nenberg also argues that unconditional divine love is the ground for human dignity: "God does not love men because of the intrinsic value of some individuals or because of their achievements [excellence of nature or excellence of moral character]. Rather, infinite value is attributed to people because of the eternal love of God for them."[28]

Does our dignity relation to God impose obligations on human beings to recognize each other's dignity? Most certainly it does. Consider the parallel between our existence and our dignity. We exist because God loves us and wills our existence. Existence too is a relation to our Creator. Yet because we exist for God, we exist also for each other as an objective fact. Other people do not exist because we want them to exist. In the same way, even though our dignity is a relation to God, it is also a reality for all human beings. God's love for his dear children creates a real dignity relation. We must recognize human dignity as relationally inherent in our fellow human beings; that is, each and every human being exists and possesses a dignity bestowed by God. They are worthy of our love because God makes them worthy of God's love. Our neighbor's worth precedes our love for them because God's love for them precedes their worth. We love God because God first loved us, and we love our neighbors because God first loved our neighbors.

Dignity and envy. We have established that our dignity derives from God's love for us. Now we can ask about the quality of this dignity. If dignity is a relation of being loved, and God's love for us is the only constant and universal love, then our God-bestowed dignity is the highest dignity possible for us. Further, since God is the greatest possible being and his love is the greatest possible love, the dignity it bestows is the greatest possible dignity. Paul prays that we "may have power . . . to grasp how wide and long and high and deep is the love of Christ, and to know this love that surpasses knowledge—that you may be filled to the measure of all the fullness of God" (Eph 3:18-19). John directly connects God's great love of us to our dignity: "See what great love the Father has lavished on us, that we should be called children of God! And that is what we are!" (1 Jn 3:1). In love, God makes us what he calls us. Because he treats us as worthy, we are worthy. Clearly John thinks there is no greater dignity possible for us than to be given the status of God's dear children.

---

[28]Wolfhart Pannenberg, "Human Nature and the Individual," in *Human Nature, Election, and History* (Philadelphia: Westminster Press, 1977), pp. 16-17.

Being loved by God bestows on us the highest dignity possible for creatures. But is our dignity as high as we can imagine or conceive? Here we face again the troubling issue with which this book began: is there a reason to envy God and resent God's superior status? Does God possess higher dignity than we do? If so, may we not envy that higher dignity even if it is not possible to attain it? Is our joy tempered by knowing that we are not the source of our own dignity? Are we thrust back into the vicious dilemma of having to choose between rebellion and subservience—or simply to slip into indifference?[29]

As we approach the crux of this chapter it is very important to keep in mind the three different ways human beings are said to possess dignity.[30] Clearly, God's nature and life are infinitely more excellent than the nature and the moral life of creatures. It is impossible to equal God in dignity of attributes or powers. As the word *excell*-ence indicates, excellence in nature or life is measured comparatively. And in comparison with God we are nothing. Hence, as long as we think of dignity as the quality of our nature or life, the possibility of envying God and wishing to attain divine status will plague our thoughts of God. But this issue does not arise when we think of our dignity as belovedness. Developing this third understanding of human dignity, I want to suggest perhaps the most revolutionary idea in this book: *God bestows on us the same dignity that God bestows on himself, for God loves us no less than God loves himself.* The Father loves us with the *very same* love with which God loves the beloved Son. No higher dignity can be imagined

---

[29]R. Kendall Soulen and Linda Woodhead hint at possible conflict between divine and human dignity in their rejection of such tension: "Rightly understood, divine and human dignity are not contraries in Christian thought, destined to wax and wane in inverse proportion to one another." They do not take this objection seriously, however, for their response is only six lines long (R. Kendall Soulen and Linda Woodhead, eds., "Introduction: Contextualizing Human Dignity," in *God and Human Dignity* [Grand Rapids: Eerdmans, 2006], p. 8).

[30]Fraser Watts distinguishes two senses of dignity; one is universal and given with our humanity, and the other can be acquired. Both of these are found in modern secular thought and in Christian thought. Theologically understood, the first corresponds to the dignity given in creation, and the second to a dignity for which we hope in God's future. However, Christianity sees both of these as gifts, an idea that is absent in secular thought. See "Human Dignity: Concepts and Experiences," in *God and Human Dignity*, ed. R. Kendall Soulen and Linda Woodhead [Grand Rapids: Eerdmans, 2006], pp. 249-56). Clearly, Watts's distinctions in dignity correspond to my three types. However, he sees the "giftedness" of dignity not as a (third) distinct type but as the personal origin of the two basic types. I would argue that as the "origin" of our natural and moral excellence, belovedness is our dignity in an even deeper sense than the other types.

or conceived. Hence, there are no grounds to envy God or resent God's status. But making this suggestion credible will require some explanation.

It is essential to keep clearly in mind that God's dignity does not rest entirely on God's comparative excellence of nature and life. Thinking of divine dignity exclusively as excellence would turn our attention toward God's superiority over us and God's ability to do us good or ill, and hence tempt us to treat God as a means to our ends. Or perhaps such a comparison would remind us of our lesser dignity and tempt us to envy God's status. But comparisons do not apply to the dignity of belovedness. Dignity is a relation of love in which one person bestows worth on others by loving them. Divine dignity is no less relational and must be understood in trinitarian terms. In the eternal love among the Father, Son and Spirit, each bestows infinite worth on the others. The Son's dignity is his loving relationship with the Father through the Spirit. The Father's dignity is the Son's love for the Father through the Spirit. God's dignity, then, is founded on God's love for God.

Our dignity is founded on God's love for us.[31] Hence our dignity and God's dignity have the same ground: the love of the Father, Son and Spirit. But someone may say, surely the Father does not love us *as much* as he loves the Son, or the Son as the Father. On the contrary, the central thrust of the Christian doctrines of the incarnation and atonement is precisely that the Father loves us exactly as much as the Father loves the Son. Becoming incarnate, he became one of us and took on our nature. This one man Jesus *is* God's eternal Son, and the Father loves him with an eternal love. Hence, the Father bestows on this human being the same dignity in time that the Father, Son and Spirit bestow on each other eternally.

The doctrine of the atonement makes clear that the divine dignity bestowed on Jesus is a possibility for all human beings. Paul places this truth at the center of his gospel: "But God demonstrates his own love for us in

---

[31]For a similar view, see Emil Brunner: "The dignity of human personality is not grounded in an abstract, general element in all men, namely reason, but individual personality as such is the object of this appreciation because it is deemed worthy of being called by God. Only the personal God can fundamentally establish truly personal existence and responsibility. . . . The love of the personal God does not create an abstract, impersonal humanity; it calls the individual to the most personal responsibility" (*Christianity and Civilization* [New York: Charles Scribner's, 1948], p. 94, quoted in Craig Gay, *The Way of the World* [Grand Rapids: Eerdmans, 1998], p. 176).

this: While we were still sinners, Christ died for us" (Rom 5:8). The Son of God "loved us and gave himself up for us as a fragrant offering and sacrifice to God" (Eph 5:1-2). In doing this, God counted us worthy and made us worthy of God's love. The principle of the atonement is this: what the one does all do, or what happens to the one happens to all, or what the one is all become. As Paul puts it, "Through the obedience of the one man many will be made righteous" (Rom 5:19). Christ's love becomes our love; his obedience, suffering, righteousness, holiness and *dignity* count as (and therefore *are*) ours. Listen again to Paul: "I have been crucified with Christ and I no longer live, but Christ lives in me. The life I now live in the body, I live by faith in the Son of God, who loved me and gave himself for me" (Gal 2:20). The Father treats each of us as if we were the Father's own dear Son, and that is why we are God's children.

Perhaps the most important link in this chain of argument is Paul's teaching that in our redeemed existence we live only "in Christ." The most extensive and profound reflection on this doctrine can be found in the book of Ephesians. Every act of God toward us and every blessing that comes to us touches us "in Christ." We were chosen "in him before the creation of the world" (Eph 1:4). We are adopted as God's children "through Jesus Christ" (Eph 1:5). We have redemption, the forgiveness of sins, holiness, hope, predestination and election in Christ. We were raised from the dead "with Christ" and have been "seated us with him in the heavenly realms in Christ Jesus" (Eph 2:6). We have been recreated "in Christ," so that God loves us with the same love with which the Father loves the Son. I am not saying that in our union with Christ the distinctions between Creator and creature and the divine Son and the human children of God are blurred. We do not become God's children through natural birth but by adoption through the power of the Spirit (Rom 8:14-15). Nor are we in Christ by nature. We are united with Christ by grace through faith. Paul explains that we were "included in Christ when you heard the message of truth, the gospel of your salvation. When you believed, you were marked in him with a seal, the promised Holy Spirit" (Eph 1:13-14). He says in Romans that we were "baptized into Christ" and have been "united with him" in his death and so will be "united with him in a resurrection like his" (Rom 6:3, 5).

We know that God loves us no less than God loves himself, because God does not love us for what we are. God's love for us is grounded in the Father's love for the Son. The Father does not love God's human children less because they are not God's equal in excellence of being or character. God loves us just like, and just as much as, the Father loves the Son. Even though we were by nature nothing, by deeds sinners and by affections enemies, God loved us. There is and can be no higher dignity. It is beyond our wildest imagination, transcending all our conceptual powers. It makes no sense, therefore, to envy God's freedom or long for his dignity. God's freedom is expressed in the perfect love the Father, Son and Spirit give to each other, and God's dignity is grounded in the love received by the three from each other. By loving us with the love of God, God bestows on us the highest dignity conceivable and frees us for the most perfect freedom possible.

16

THE RECONCILIATION OF
HEAVEN AND EARTH

Now we return to the original issue of the book for a comprehensive answer. Does the Christian way of viewing God and humanity overcome the idea that God is a threat to our genuine freedom and dignity? Does it give us reason to believe that we may place ourselves in God's care without fear of loss? Can we now love God with all our hearts and hold back nothing in praise of our Creator? Is the way clear for heaven and earth to come together in perfect unity?

COMPETITION TRANSCENDED

Competition requires the existence of two or more incomplete, separate persons wanting the same finite good. Obviously, the very nature of competition requires the existence of more than one center of need and desire. Competitors must be incomplete rather than whole and fully satisfied; only then would they have reason to compete. In addition, competition makes sense only where the good that rivals desire is finite, that is, it cannot be enjoyed to the full by all.

In this chapter I want to show that the Christian vision of redemption excludes the conditions that create competition. In the future resurrection life, our relationship with God and each other will no longer be characterized by separateness, unfulfilled desire and limited good. We will be united with God, completely satisfied by the infinite good that God is and fully present in one another's joys. How shall we conceive this victory and how will it be achieved?

The ultimate answer is found in Jesus Christ. In the person of Christ, God and humanity are so united that even the possibility of competition is overcome. According to the traditional teaching about Christ, Jesus Christ is one reality (or person), yet he is both divine and human. The existence of Christ shows that God and humanity are not intrinsically exclusive of one another; only the sin, evil, blindness and death that distort and wound humanity are excluded. True humanity is God's image, God's dear child. It contains no qualities that contradict the divine nature. By taking humanity into his person, the Son of God frees it from the "other" that troubles it. Its union with God is so perfect, its vision of God so clear, and its love so pure that its affirmation of God is at the same time perfect affirmation of its own being. In this state, harmony between humanity and God is as perfect as harmony among the persons of the Trinity.

As noted earlier, the conditions under which it makes sense to compete are incompleteness, separateness and scarcity. These conditions are overcome in Jesus Christ, for Jesus is fully human and fully divine. His divinity is eternally complete, and in his resurrection Christ brought his humanity to complete fulfillment. His humanity and deity are so united that the joy of one is included in the joy of the other; for they enjoy the same inexhaustible good, God.

But we may ask what has the perfect harmony of Jesus with God to do with us? First, we must be clear that Jesus' humanity is not only *like* our humanity, it is the *very same* humanity. In him our true humanity—humanity freed from the "other" and perfected—has become a living reality. The union of God and humanity is an accomplished fact. God did this without our participation, but there is something for us to do. As individuals we can allow ourselves to be united to Christ and through him be united to the Father. Through faith, the sacraments and the uniting and life-giving power of the Holy Spirit, we are incorporated into him. We share the same harmonious relationship to God that the Son of God possesses. But how can this be?

Even if we agree that our human nature has been united to God in Christ, will there not always be a distinction among human individuals and between each of us and the Son of God? And do not these continued distinctions create the possibility of competition? In answer to the first question, it is true that our union with God and each other will not erase the distinctions among persons or our distinction from God. Unlike some religious perspectives, Christianity does not teach the dissolution of personhood into an impersonal absolute. In answer to the second question, the distinction among persons does not by itself create the conditions for competition. Distinction among persons is a necessary condition for love. Why continued personal distinctions do not continue to foster competition will require some explanation.

In human love we experience bonds of affection in which we find our joy in seeing good things come to others. Jesus teaches that we should love our neighbor as ourselves. He did not say, "Love your neighbor as *you love* yourself." This would define self love independently of neighbor love and imply that you could love yourself truly without loving your neighbor. Rather, Jesus calls us to see our neighbor's good as our own. The ideal implicit even in human love is a union between persons that rules out competition without erasing distinction. But we do not experience perfect love in this life.

In chapter eight I probed the doctrine of the Trinity for a noncompetitive view of God. I pointed out that the Father, Son and Spirit receive their identity in their love for each other. The members of the Trinity love themselves only in their love for the others. Here I want to explore one more element in the traditional Christian doctrine of the Trinity for its relevance to this chapter. In trying to safeguard the unity and distinction of the Father, Son and Spirit, the church fathers and later theologians developed an idea hinted at in the Gospel of John. In answer to Philip's request to "show us the Father" (Jn 14:8), Jesus said, "Anyone who has seen me has seen the Father. . . . Don't you believe that I am in the Father, and that the Father is in me?" (Jn 14:9-10). Trinitarian thinkers saw something unusual in this text. In our ordinary experience of space, one thing cannot dwell inside another and *also* be contained by the other. In the divine life, however, this is possible. Father, Son and Spirit dwell in each other, a relationship the church fathers called *perichōrēsis*. This Greek word means literally "to dance around," but the idea is best captured by the term "mutual indwelling." Though distinct persons, they share the same nature—life, will, attributes and acts. In the words of the Puritan theologian William Perkins, "The communion of the persons, or rather union, is that by which each one is in the rest, and with the rest, by reason of the unity of the Godhead: and therefore each one doth possess, love and glorify another, and work the same thing."[1] The Trinity is the ideal community—perfect union without loss of personal identity.[2]

Now that we have seen what an ideal community is we can reflect on how this ideal is realized in Christ and thus overcomes the conditions that make competition possible. In the incarnation our humanity has been united to God in the most intimate way possible. This first phase of our salvation did not require our personal participation. We still need, however, to join ourselves freely and personally to the Son of God. By the grace of the Father, the love of Christ and the power of the Holy Spirit, our responding faith and love seals a personal bond between us and the Son of God. As persons we are called to indwell each other, to share the same perfect human nature realized fully in Christ—life, will, attributes and acts. In this way our relationship with Christ and each other becomes like the mutual indwelling of the Father, Son and Spirit.

By joining ourselves to Christ we also have fellowship with the Father through the Spirit. By being united to Christ, therefore, we have been brought into the perfect community of the blessed Trinity. The conditions for competition have been overcome! Like the Son of God, we have everything the Father has except fatherhood. The Father's identity as Father is not a thing to be envied; indeed, it's not a thing at all, for fatherhood is the Father's relation of love to the Son, and this love for the Son is the same love with which the Father loves us.

A LIFE OF FAITH, HOPE AND LOVE

We have seen a vision of our destiny, but one look at our world reminds us that we are not there yet. We do not yet enjoy uninterrupted fellowship in

---

[1]William Perkins, *A Golden Chaine or the Description of Theology* 5, quoted in Richard Muller, *Post-Reformation Reformed Dogmatics: The Rise and Development of Reformed Orthodoxy*, vol. 4, *The Triunity of God* (Grand Rapids: Baker Academic, 2003), p. 208.

[2]G. L. Prestige, *God in Patristic Thought*, 2nd ed. (London: SPCK, 1952), pp. 282-301. See also Dumitru Staniloae, *Revelation and Knowledge of the Triune God*, vol. 1, *The Experience of God*, trans. and ed. Ioan Ionita and Robert Barringer (Brookline, MA: Holy Cross Orthodox Press, 1994), pp. 248-78.

perfect community. We still suffer conditions that make competition possible. We still compete, even with the ones we love most. We are incomplete and separate, and good things come to us in finite portions. We long for salvation. As Paul expressed it, we "groan inwardly as we wait eagerly for our adoption as sons, the redemption of our bodies" (Rom 8:23 NIV 1984). How should we live now in this state of "not yet," in this time of waiting?

In the present, the Christian life is one of faith, hope and love (1 Cor 13:13). In faith we trust the One who loved us, gave himself for us and promised us he would return "and take you to be with me that you also may be where I am" (Jn 14:3). We cannot see the way with our own eyes or grasp the truth with our own minds. Faith is the means through which we receive the knowledge we need to live in freedom, that is, in view of our true identity and destiny. In hope, we sense the reality and inevitability of the future we have been promised. God "put his Spirit in our hearts as a deposit, guaranteeing what is to come" (2 Cor 1:22). Spirit-inspired hope gives us confidence and power to begin to live the future now.

In love God created us and sent Christ to redeem us, and in love God will bring us into the intimate fellowship of eternal life. Divine love encircles us on every side and enfolds us within its warmth. Even now, God pours divine love into our hearts by the Spirit; this love overflows first in love to God, then to friend and enemy. Even now, in the life inspired by the Spirit, the conditions that make competition possible and almost necessary begin to lose their grip. We no longer see ourselves as incomplete, for we feel our connection to the infinite source of our joy. Our union with Christ instills in us a sense of unity with others that replaces the former sense of separateness. We see clearly that the one and only good we really need is the infinite and inexhaustible God. And everyone can have their fill.

THE MODERN SELF REBORN

I began this book with the image of the modern self painted by Charles Taylor and Alasdair MacIntyre. According to these thinkers, our contemporaries tend to locate all values and goods within their own persons. They ground respect for others, hope for fullness and belief in their own dignity in the self, in its inward qualities, its ordinary life, and its ability to express itself and impress itself on the world. This modern self feels within itself the power and freedom to actualize all its potential. Hence many of our contemporaries feel little need for divine law to guide their actions, divine grace to empower their freedom or divine love to ground their worth. They may even feel hostility to the suggestion that they need God's guidance, grace and love.

Our analysis has shown, however, that the modern self is an illusion, a vain wish to be like God and to possess divine attributes and prerogatives. This illusion, attractive and flattering at first, can maintain its hold on us only as long as we are not aware of it. Once it is fully articulated, however, we can no longer believe it; for we are not gods. We cannot create ourselves, give ourselves dignity or free ourselves from the "other" that blocks our self-realization. We are mortal, blind and weak. Confusion, restlessness and division plague our existence. We do not know ourselves well enough to guarantee that our "free" actions will produce happiness or that we will approve the results of our actions after they become actual. Kierkegaard rightly observed:

> I will call to mind that even if I had my soul concentrated in one single wish and even if I had it concentrated therein so desperately that I could willingly throw away my eternal salvation for the fulfillment of this wish— that still no one can with certainty tell me in advance whether my wish, if it is fulfilled, would still not seem empty and meaningless to me.[3]

Speaking of the lesson taught by our mortality, Augustine laments, "What madness not to understand how to love human beings with awareness of the human condition!"[4]

As my argument unfolded, we saw that Christianity faces squarely the desperate nature of the human condition and deals with it at its roots. In our study of Romans 5–8 we saw sin, death and blindness are too powerful and too close for us to escape. But Jesus Christ, by entering into the human condition, creates the possibility for overcoming the "other" and realizing our true selves. We receive power to become God's children, are given dignity rooted in God's love for us and freedom empowered by God's Spirit. Our respect for others and our sense of our own dignity are grounded in

---

[3]Søren Kierkegaard, *Christian Discourses*, trans. Howard V. Hong and Edna H. Hong (Princeton, NJ: Princeton University Press, 1997), pp. 256-57.
[4]Augustine, *Confessions* 4.12, in *The Confessions of Saint Augustine*, trans. Henry Chadwick (New York: Oxford University Press, 1991), p. 59.

God's eternal love. Our hope for fullness rests in the confidence that God will bring to completion the work begun in us, that we shall become fully who we always have been in God's eyes, that we shall experience "the glorious freedom of the children of God" (Rom 8:21 NIV 1984).

PROMETHEUS UNBOUND

In chapter two we pondered the image of the defiant Prometheus chained to the mountainside, tortured by the arrogant and paranoid Zeus. We found ourselves sympathetic to the wronged god and admiring his unbroken spirit. But the rightness of our sympathy and the aptness of our admiration depend on the truth of Prometheus's estimation of Zeus and our kinship with Prometheus. We have learned, however, that the God revealed in Jesus Christ, the Father, Son and Spirit, bears no resemblance to Zeus. God's very life consists in self-giving. God's relationship to us is no less self-giving than the relations among the Father, Son and Spirit. In a great reversal of the roles of Zeus and Prometheus, God allowed God to be nailed to the cross for us rebels. We cannot envy this God, and there are no motives for defiance. God will not become our competitor.

The true human being revealed in Jesus is nothing like Prometheus. Prometheus and Milton's Satan understood the foundation of their dignity and freedom to reside in their unshakable will for absolute self-determination. The Promethean self defines itself apart from relationships with others. It is a lonely self whose relation to other selves can only be to dominate or be dominated by them. If it cannot dominate, it retreats inside itself to the last refuge of its "impenetrable Spirit" and its "unconquerable soul."

In Jesus, we learn that we were made to love others. We can exist as our true selves and exercise genuine freedom only by loving God and others. Our highest dignity is grounded in God's love for us. Through the eyes of Christ we see clearly that God is love and that our true humanity is love as well. Competition no longer makes sense. Self-giving love cannot compete with self-giving love. *Our love of freedom can find fulfillment only in the freedom of love.*

RELIGION PURIFIED

In chapter three I told the story of myself as a six-year-old child wishing I had been born God. In fear, I chose subservience instead of defiance. Using

Bernard of Clairvaux's staging of love for God, I called this way of relating to God "stage-two religion." In this state we love God for ourselves' sake. We deal with God because of what God can do *for* us or what God might do *to* us. Though we recognize that we need God, we still treat God as our competitor. But Bernard calls us higher. When we come to know God rightly we will love God "for God's sake"; that is, we will love God for the beauty and love that God has revealed in Jesus, not simply as a means to our ends. The great reconciliation accomplished in Christ calls for a religion purified of all selfishness and servility, a spiritual religion of love for God and neighbor.

Stage-three religion. Bernard's third stage of love can be achieved only when we become conscious of how much we have been loved by God. We realize that God created us out of love, freely giving us our lives and all good things. In contrast to our inattentiveness, God's love for us has been constant, patient and relentless. In Jesus, the omnipotent, omnipresent and omniscient God hides his glory and shows a servant's heart. In contrast to our pride, Jesus washed our feet, called us friends and laid down his life for us. Our envy and pride get exposed, and in his humble presence we stand without excuse. Thankfully, Jesus also extends God's forgiveness, and the Holy Spirit assures us of God's unconditional love for us. Our shame is removed by his accepting embrace, and our downcast eyes are lifted up by the sound of our names on his lips. And we are amazed.

Until we know we are loved unconditionally we cannot really love. God's unselfish love for us, made so clear in the self-giving of Christ, eventually touches our hearts and sparks our love for God. We no longer think of God merely as a *source* for other things or a *resource* in time of need. God is no longer a means to be used but an end to be enjoyed, a wonder to be praised rather than a power to be feared. We come at last to understand Augustine's words: "Late have I loved you, beauty so old and so new; late have I loved you."[5] We realize that only now do we love God—so long, so very long after God loved us. Only at this stage are we able to love our neighbors and treat them according to their genuine dignity. It is not enough to love our neighbors for our own sake, for that is merely to use them. Nor is it adequate to love our neighbors because they are loveable. They are not always loveable.

5Ibid., p. 201.

We must love our neighbor because God loves our neighbor, because if we love God we will love what God loves and find worthy what God values.

Stage-four religion. In the fourth stage of love, which Bernard finds the most difficult and rare, we learn to love ourselves for God's sake alone. We love ourselves rightly by loving God supremely and loving ourselves only *in* our love for God. We love ourselves for the same reason and in the same way we love our neighbors—by loving God. By responding to God's love for us by loving God in return, we validate and accept God's love for us. Kierkegaard puts the same thought in other words:

> Christianity teaches that love is a relationship between: man-God-man, that is, that God is the middle term. . . . For to love God is to love oneself in truth; to help another human being to love God is to love another man; to be helped by another to love God is to be loved.[6]

If we attempt to love ourselves directly, for example by seeking pleasure, we will lose ourselves in the objects of desire. If we try to love ourselves in the image we have of ourselves, we will inevitably be torn between pride and shame, for the shape of our self-image depends on the medium we use to reflect it. If the medium tells us we are worthy, our pride will inflate. If it tells us we are unworthy, we will suffer shame. In Jesus Christ can we see a true image of ourselves. Loving him enables us to love ourselves in him without pride or shame. We are so conscious of God's beauty and glory that we see ourselves through God's eyes only. We now understand what Gregory of Nazianzus meant when he said, "It is more important that we should remember God than that we should breathe. Indeed, if one may say so, we should do nothing else besides."[7] For God is the breath, life and light of the soul.

In this purified religion we come truly to image the self-giving God in the world and show the glory of God's love. We view our lives as reflections of divine glory and our actions merely as different ways to give ourselves to God in worship, praise and service. Empowered by God's love for us, we come to love God freely and ourselves unselfishly. Our new love for God

---

[6]Søren Kierkegaard, *Works of Love*, trans. Howard and Edna Hong (New York: HarperCollins, 2009), pp. 112-13.

[7]Gregory of Nazianzus, *Oration 27*, chap. 4, in *On God and Christ: The Five Theological Orations and Two Letters to Cledonius*, trans. Frederick Williams and Lionel Wickham (Crestwood, NY: St. Vladimir's Seminary Press, 2002), pp. 27-28.

actualizes our true self and participates in God's victory over the "other" that limits our freedom. Loving God and all things for God's sake expresses our highest dignity, for our dignity rests in God's love for us. Loving God in return acknowledges and validates that love, which dignifies us yet again. The circle of love and dignity never ends. It is the substance of eternal life. It is the essence of the "freedom and glory of the children of God" (Rom 8:21).

INDIFFERENCE TRANSFORMED

In chapter four we explored four ways of being indifferent to God: the esthete, the conformist, the celebrity and the agnostic. Each of these lifestyles focuses so intently on something else that it becomes insensitive to God. Esthetes seek only pleasure and maintain distance from anything that would evoke reflection on their despair. Conformists are so busy seeking success as measured by others that they never ask themselves how God might view their lives. Seeking to live only on the lips and in the thoughts of others, the celebrity possesses no identity in relation to God. Agnostics say whether God exists or not cannot be known, and, judging from their lack of concern about which is true, think it does not matter.

However, we have learned that an attitude of indifference to God is so out of place, so mismatched and so absurd that the indifferent person cannot possibly have formed an adequate concept of God or grasped the human condition. The reality of God or even the concept of God is so all-encompassing in scope and heavy with implications that no one can become aware of God or even grasp the meaning of the word *God* and remain unmoved. No one can seriously have engaged in self-examination or have even the slightest self-knowledge who can remain unmoved by the idea of God. To know God is either to seek God with all our hearts or to flee God's presence with all our might, to love God utterly or to hate God infinitely. To remain unmoved in God's presence is to be no self at all but a stone or worse than a stone, for in God's presence even the stones cry out to proclaim his glory.

In our study of indifference we learned that the indifferent soul pictures God as indifferent objectively and subjectively. The indifferent cannot think of a reason to seek God and cannot imagine that God would have a reason to seek them. What blindness to the human condition! What ignorance of the self! How could the blind remain indifferent to the physician who can restore sight or the starving to the benefactor who can supply food? Can the suffering remain indifferent to relief or the dying to life? Can the lonely and lost blithely ignore the clearly marked way home? What a different picture we see in Jesus Christ! Even when God did not matter to us, we mattered to God. Our indifference to God cannot make God indifferent to us. God enters the human sphere to seek the lost, heal the sick and raise the dead. The extent to which we matter to God is revealed in the passion of Christ in giving himself for us. God opens his heart in a way no human would or could do, to his enemies, to strangers and to the indifferent. And for those who see and believe, God's love creates love in them, love for God and all those whom God loves. And in their joy they know that nothing else matters.

CONCLUSION

At the beginning of this book I expressed concern that we may hold back part of ourselves from God because we fear that God is in some way our competitor, that we might lose something if we give ourselves to God and that God may not be wholly for us. I hope by now we can see that there is not the slightest ground for such fears. The very opposite is true. God is so much for us and we are made so much for God that only by returning ourselves to God utterly may we become truly ourselves and live life to the full. In loving God for God's sake alone we will find genuine freedom, and in allowing ourselves to be loved by God we will discover our true dignity.

Subject Index

Abraham (biblical figure), 128, 156
Adam (biblical figure), 44n5, 120, 152, 153,
    173-76
Adler, Mortimer
    definition of freedom by, 181-82, 185
    on self as principle of freedom, 148-49
    three types of freedom and, 91, 91n2,
        93-95, 99n27, 104, 171, 182, 187
adoption, divine
    Abba, Father, and, 160-61, 160n2, 163, 177
    atonement and, 205
    being in Christ and, 205
    celebration of, 159
    children of God and, 161-63
    God's glory and, 170
    human condition and, 212
    love and, 202
    perfection and, 163-69, 164n12
    waiting for, 211
adultery, Jesus' teaching on, 165-66, 166n16
Aemilius Paulus, 71-72n21
Aeschylus, 40-42, 48
agnosticism, 74, 74n28, 216
altruism, 36
ambition, 90, 99-101
Amos (prophet), 56
Anderson, Bernhard W., 78, 116
angels, 162, 162n8, 197
Anselm of Canterbury, 80, 81-82, 141
Apostles' Creed, 85, 128
Aquinas, Thomas, 80-82, 86, 137, 137n22,
    140-41
Arendt, Hannah, 103n1
Aristotle
    on ambition, 90
    on free will, 92
    on habit formation, 22
    on mythic picture of the gods, 79
    Nicomachean Ethics by, 33-34
    on ordinary life, 23
    on rhetoric, 132-33
    traditional understanding of self and,
        25-26n24
art, mimetic view of, 30n42
atheism, 28-29, 82-83, 83n21
atonement, 132, 204-5
Augustine
    conversion of, 193
    development of inwardness and, 19-20
    on the fall, 53-54

fragmented self and, 111
    on God's excellence, 80, 80n10
    on God's knowledge, 140n2
    on God's omnipotence, 85, 128
    on human condition, 192-95
    on human dignity, 192-95, 198
    image of God and, 81-82
    on lesson of mortality, 212
    on love, 214
    on love of praise, 71n20, 72
    on rhetoric, 133-34
    on self-knowledge, 149
    on Trinity, 194
Badcock, Gary D., 118-19n10
Barth, Karl
    on creation, 117
    critique of religion by, 51-52n5, 60-61
    on divine glory, 122
    on freedom, 93
    on God's love, 178
    on temptation of Christ, 156n10
behaviorism, 22n14
belief
    versus action, 11
    love and, 217
Bentham, Jeremy, 28
Berlin, Isaiah, 91n2, 95n14, 106n8
Bernard of Clairvaux
    on God as Creator, 116
    on love for God, 120-21
    on stages of relationship with God,
        51-52n5, 61-63, 93, 214-15
Betz, Hans Dieter, 164n13, 166n16, 167-68n23,
    184
Biel, Gabriel, 81
Blake, William, 44n6
Blunk, Jürgen, 183
Bonaventure, 197, 198
Bonhoeffer, Dietrich, 51, 51-52nn4-5
Brümmer, Vincent, 118-19n10
Brunner, Emil, 204n31
Buckley, Michael J., 82n18
Byron, Lord, 45
calling, 24-25
Camus, Albert, 181
celebrity, 70-73
Charter of Fundamental Rights of the
    European Union, 98-99
Christianity
    cross as emblem of, 115

freedom at heart of, 107
human condition and, 212
as life of faith, hope and love, 210-11
ordinary life and, 23-24
post-Christian culture and, 37-38
Trinity as fundamental doctrine of, 124-25
younger generation's perception of, 37n64
Cicero, 92
Clark, Chap, 17n1
Clement of Alexandria, 86, 193n5
Clement of Rome, 86
Cobb, John, 134
coercion, 136, 136n18, 137, 137n23
common good, 26
competition
for dignity, 46, 171
the fall and, 95-96
for freedom, 46, 95-96, 171-72
transcended, 207-10, 213
conformity, 67-70, 155, 216
creation
doctrine of, 116
evidence of God's benefits and, 62
God as Creator and, 116-17, 119
God's knowledge and, 140-41, 140n2
groaning of, 163, 184
human origins and, 109-10
redemption and, 131-32
second, 123
superhuman image of God and, 78
cross, 115. See also Jesus Christ; resurrection
Dawkins, Richard, 59n15
default religion
Bernard of Clairvaux's stages and, 61-63
Bible as critic of, 54-58
insider versus external critics of, 59n15
modern critics of, 59-61
paganism and, 49-50
self-centeredness and, 61-63
unoriginal sin and, 53-54
wishes that reveal the heart and, 50-51
defiance of God
as assertion of dignity, 84
God as pure power and, 48
image of God and, 12-13, 74
original sin and, 51-52
in Paradise Lost (Milton), 42-44
Prometheus and, 40-47
subservience and indifference and, 76
deism, 25-26n24, 26, 28, 135n21
dependence, of humans on God, 129-30, 191-92

Derrida, Jacques, 117-18
Descartes, René, 20-22, 20-21nn9-10, 81n17, 92, 102
desire
conflicting, 93
for control, 50-51
empty, 171
happiness and, 104-6
misdirected, 173
power and, 103
versus will, 88-89n29
despair, self and, 145-47, 145nn10-12, 146n14
d'Holbach, Baron, 28, 82
Diderot, Denis, 28-29, 35-37, 64
dignity
ambition and, 99-100
of angels versus humans, 197
atonement and, 204-5
autonomy-based, 98-99
as axis of moral space, 23, 27, 31, 37
of belovedness, 198, 201, 201n25, 203-4, 203n30, 206, 217
competitive, 171
counterfeit, 199
defiance of God and, 84
dependence and, 191-92
divine, 121-23, 125-26
divine versus human, 203, 203n29
envy and, 202-6
excellence and, 192-96, 198, 198n22, 203-4, 203n30, 206
freedom and, 84, 96, 99, 107-8, 110
God as competitor for, 46
God as ground for, 39n65, 124, 191, 200-202, 204, 204n31, 212-13, 216
from God versus finite entities, 200-202, 200n23
heights of in Christ, 113
of human condition, 197-98
human self-creation and, 97
in international declarations of rights, 98-99
intrinsic qualities and, 31
as inviolable, 107
limitless, 199-206
limits on, 102, 107-10
love and, 200-201
modern concept of, 96-100
Nietzsche versus Kant on, 191
patristic and medieval thinkers on, 97n18, 192-98, 193n5
pride and shame and, 199-200

reason and, 194
recognition of in others, 202
as relation to God, 201-2
theological foundation for, 97
Trinity and, 125-26, 204
universal versus acquired, 203n30
as valued good of contemporary culture, 37-38
worth and, 96, 200-202
divorce, Jesus' teaching on, 166, 166nn17-19
Don Juan (fictional character), 65, 66n4
doubt, versus agnosticism, 74n28
Duns Scotus, John, 81, 137
Edwards, Jonathan, 107-8
emotivism, 32-33
Enlightenment, 28-29, 28n32, 29-30n38, 33-37
envy of God
   versus admiration for God, 54
   ambition and, 90, 100-101
   desire for control and, 50-51
   devotion to good works and, 63
   false divine self and, 123-24
   God as obstacle to freedom and, 104
   God's dignity and, 203
   God's perfection and, 79
   lack of grounds for, 115, 210, 213
   sin and, 53
Epictetus, 177n15
eroticism, 65-66, 66n4
esthetic existence, 34, 65-67, 65-66nn3-4, 146-47, 155-56, 216
ethics
   versus esthetics, 34, 66-67, 66n4
   Jesus' ethical vision and, 164-69, 164nn12-13, 166nn17-19, 167-68nn22-25
   in Judaism, 164nn12-13
Eve (biblical figure), 152, 153
faith, 211
fall, the
   Augustine on, 53-54
   Eve's resentment and, 52n3n6
   human-divine competition and, 152
   as original sin, 51-52
   in *Paradise Lost* (Milton), 44n5
   signs of, 51-52nn4-5
fear of God, 11-12, 84-87
Fee, Gordon D., 160n2
Fénelon, François, 11, 75
Feuerbach, Ludwig, 82, 83
Fish, Stanley, 44n5
Ford, David, 134-35
Ford, Lewis S., 136n18

Fourth Lateran Council, 24, 24n18
freedom
   as ability to do what one wants, 84
   acquired, 186, 187-88, 193-94
   Adler's definition of, 181-82
   Adler's types of, 91, 91n2, 93-95, 99n27, 104, 171, 182, 187
   Christian hope and, 107
   circumstantial, 105-7, 106nn7-8, 108n11, 171-73, 186-90, 186n12
   competitive, 95-96, 171-72
   Descartes on, 21
   from despair, 146n14
   dethronement of God and, 77
   dignity and, 84, 96, 99, 99n27, 107-8, 110
   divine persuasion and, 134-35
   efficient causality and, 136n19
   as a gift, 185-86
   of God, 81, 189n14
   God as competitor for, 46
   God as ground for, 39n65, 186n12, 212
   God as obstacle to, 104
   God's love and, 179-80, 215-16
   God's power and, 130, 137-38
   happiness and, 105-6, 212
   here and now, 186-87
   human serfdom and, 96
   from internal compulsions, 104
   limits of, 102-7
   love for God and, 217
   natural, 91-96, 108-10, 171, 186-90, 186n12
   objective God relation and, 172n4
   perfection of, 113, 182-90, 191
   Plato on, 21
   positive versus negative, 91n2
   as power of new life, 182-85
   salvation and, 184
   self and other and, 94-95
   self-creation and, 92-93
   self-determination and, 92-94, 107, 110, 171-72, 186n12, 187-89
   self-perfection and, 93-94, 171, 187-88
   self-realization and, 91-92, 91n2, 94, 171, 173, 182, 186n12, 187-89
   from sin's tyranny, 175-76, 183-84, 184n8, 184-85n10, 184n8
   Stoic philosophy on, 183
   as triadic relation, 94n11
   trinitarian love and, 206
Freud, Sigmund, 83
Fuchs, Ernst, 184n8
fullness, 18-19, 23, 27, 31, 37-38, 213

Galileo, 21, 82n18

Garrigou-LaGrange, Reginald, 137n22

Gay, Craig M., 12n2

gift giving, 117-18, 131, 185-86

Gillespie, Michael Allen, 22n16, 81n17

God

    admiration for, 54

    as cause of own existence, 140-41

    as competitor for dignity, 46

    as Creator, 116-17, 119

    dignity as relation to, 201-2

    dignity of, 121-23

    fear of, 11-12, 84-87

    foreknowledge of, 140n2

    forms of address for, 160-61, 160n2

    freedom of, 81

    glory of, 122, 122n16, 170

    grace of, 118, 191-92, 212

    as ground for dignity, 39n65, 124, 191,
       200-202, 204, 204n31, 212-13, 216

    holiness of, 121-22

    human dependence on, 129-30, 191-92

    image of, 12-13, 74, 172-73, 175, 195, 197

    inner self of, 87-89

    law of, 176, 176n13, 212

    likeness of, 197

    love and need of, 118-19, 118-19n10

    love of and human dignity, 202-3, 205-6

    omnipotence of, 84-85, 89, 127-30, 129n3, 137

    omnipresence of, 85-87, 89, 139, 139, 140n1,
       142-43

    omniscience of, 86-87, 89, 139, 141, 144,
       148-49

    as perfect being, 80-81

    projection of human qualities onto, 82-83

    providential care of, 148

    remembrance of, 215

    search for, 147

    self of, 123-26

    self-giving of, 213, 215

    self-knowledge of, 140-41

    as superhuman, 78-89, 125

    testing of, 154-55

    as threat to modern values, 39

    See also adoption, divine; defiance of God;
       envy of God; indifference to God;
       persuasion, divine; power of God;
       subservience to God

God-centered self

    freedom and dignity and, 14, 113

    God and self as bound together and, 75n29

Goethe, Johann Wolfgang von, 44-45

good life, 23

grace of God, 118, 191-92, 212

Greek philosophy, 79, 79n8

Gregory of Nazianzus, 215

Gregory of Nyssa, 195

Griffin, David, 134

habit, 22

happiness, 40, 104-6, 118, 212

Harnack, Adolf von, 79n8

Harris, Sam, 59n15

Hartshorne, Charles, 92, 129n3

Hegel, Georg Wilhelm Friedrich, 93, 108-9

Hellenism, 184-85n10

Henley, William Ernest, 46-47, 96

Herder, Johann Gottfried, 30

Herrmann, Wilhelm, 79n8

Hilary of Poitiers, 86

Hillel (rabbi), 166n17

Hitchens, Christopher, 59n15

Hobbes, Thomas, 91, 107-8

holiness, 121-22, 132

Holy Spirit

    divine persuasion and, 135n21, 137

    liberating power of, 187

hope, 211

human condition

    Augustine on, 192-94

    blindness to, 216-17

    Christianity and roots of, 212

    dignity of, 197-98

    Sisyphus as metaphor for, 181

    solution to, 177n15

human nature, 25, 25-26n24, 29, 208-9

Hume, David, 35-36, 91-92

Hutcheson, Francis, 25-26n24, 27n30

Huxley, Thomas, 74

hypocrisy, 56-57, 58, 59, 63

identity

    of humanity, 179n17

    moral space and, 18-19

    relationship with God and, 148

    trinitarian mutual indwelling and, 210

idolatry, 54-55, 56, 58

inauthenticity, 68n8

incarnation, 132, 210

indifference to God

    agnosticism and, 74

    among religious people, 64

    celebrity and, 70-73

    conformity and, 67-70

    defiance and subservience and, 76

    esthetic experience and, 65-67

God of indifference and, 74-75
idea and practice of, 65-74
image of God and, 74-75
versus Stoicism, 64n2
transformation of, 216-17
as unconscious attitude, 65
individualism, expressive, 30
"Invictus" (Henley), 46-47, 96
inwardness
    deification of inner voice and, 29,
      29-30n38
    development of, 19-23, 25-26n24, 27
    moral space of, 22-23
Isaac (biblical figure), 156
Israel, ancient, 54-55
James (disciple), 156
Jeremiah (prophet), 55, 56-57
Jeremias, Joachim, 160n2
Jesus Christ
    versus Adam, 120, 152, 173-76
    as archetype for the world, 116n4
    as archetype of true self, 186-87
    authority and, 155n9
    being crucified with, 174n7
    being in Christ and, 205
    competition transcended in, 208
    death of, 120, 122-23, 122n17, 175
    divine and human natures of, 151-52, 208
    divine dignity and, 123, 125-26
    ethical vision of, 164-69, 164nn12-13,
      166nn17-19, 167-68nn23-25, 187
    in Garden of Gethsemane, 156
    human condition and, 212
    as humans' representative, 136-37
    on hypocrisy, 56-57
    image of ourselves in, 215
    love of, 202
    mutual indwelling and, 209-10
    nature of God revealed through, 13
    new image of humanity and, 13-14, 151, 158
    obedience of, 154n6
    on pagan religion, 48, 48n1
    on resurrection, 162, 162n6
    resurrection of, 175
    sign from heaven and, 155n7
    temptation of, 152-58, 155n8, 156n10
    Trinity and, 150
Jewett, Robert, 174n7, 176n13
Job (biblical figure), 157
John (apostle)
    on freedom, 183
    in Garden of Gethsemane, 156

on love, 58n13, 120, 202
Judaism, ethics in, 164nn12-13, 165-66
Kant, Immanuel
    autonomy and, 155, 191
    as critic of the Enlightenment, 29-30n38
    on grounds of morality, 34-35, 35n57
    on human dignity, 98, 99, 191, 201
    rejection of teleology by, 36-37
    three key questions of, 170
Käsemann, Ernst, 175n11
Kelsey, David H., 179n17
Kierkegaard, Søren
    on admirers versus followers, 60n18
    as critic of default religion, 59-60
    on despair and self, 68n8, 145-46, 145n11,
      146n14, 173, 188
    on dying Jesus, 122n17
    on envy, 54
    on esthetic existence, 34, 65-67, 66n4
    ethical stage of, 145n11
    Fellowship of the Dead and, 66
    fragmented self and, 111
    on human serfdom, 96
    on indifference, 75
    on limits of insight, 105
    on love of self, 215
    on nature of the self, 144
    on pagan religion, 48n1
    on path to self awareness, 146-47
    rejection of teleology by, 36-37
    on self relating to itself, 145, 158, 173, 188
    on soul's wish, 212
    on worldliness or conformity, 68
Kimball, Dan, 37n64
Kinnaman, David, 37n64
La Mettrie, Julien Offray de, 28
Lactantius, 195-96
law, God's, 176, 176n13, 212
law of nature, 25
Leigh, Edward, 122
Lewis, C. S., 44n6, 109, 118-19n10
liberty. *See* freedom
Locke, John
    behaviorism and, 22n14
    development of inwardness and, 21-22
    on freedom, 91
    hedonist theory of morality and, 25-26n24
    on human nature, 25, 27
    on identity and consciousness, 22n16
Lombard, Peter, 197
love
    belief and, 217

Bernard of Clairvaux's stages and, 51-52n5,
    61-63, 214-15
of Christ, 202
creation and, 117
cross and, 115
dignity and, 200-202
distinction among persons and, 208-9
divine adoption and, 202
divine sacrifice and, 119-21
of enemies, 168-69, 168n25
faith, hope and, 210-11
for God and others, 179, 202
God as, 75n29, 119
of God for God's sake, 62-63, 93, 214, 217
God who loves and, 178-79
grace and, 118
liberation and, 179-80
nature of God revealed through, 58n13
need and, 118-19, 118-19n10
of neighbor, 209, 214
power of, 123
of self, 215
self-giving, 213
submission and, 48n2
Trinity and, 124-25
lust, 165-66
Luz, Ulrich
    on discipleship, 153n3
    on Jesus' moral teaching, 164n13, 165-66
    on Jesus' obedience, 155n7
    on Jesus' sonship, 153
    on love of enemies, 168n25
    on nonresistance, 168n24
MacCallum, Gerald C., Jr., 91n2, 94n11
MacIntyre, Alasdair
    on Diderot's moral framework, 35
    on emotivism, 32
    on Enlightenment and teleology, 36-37
    on esthete, manager and therapist, 65n3
    on explaining Christianity, 37-38
    on Kant's moral framework, 35n57
    on Kierkegaard and Kant, 34-35
    modern self and, 12, 33, 211-12
    on sympathy, 36
Marcus Aurelius, 93
marriage, 66, 66n4
Marx, Karl, 45-46, 83, 109-10
me-centered self
    autonomy of, 46
    birth of, 17-18
    in culture set adrift, 32-37
    dread of God's omniscience and

omnipresence and, 86-87
    emotivist, 32-33
    inner world and, 87n28
    inward qualities and outward expression
        of, 12
    limits of human freedom and dignity and,
        102
    pure will and, 76n32
    rebirth of, 211-13
    versus self-centeredness, 31
    superhuman God and, 77
media, celebrity and, 72-73
memory, power of, 194
Miller, Donald, 155n8
Milton, John, 42-44, 44nn5-6, 84, 88, 109, 213
mind, 19-21, 20-21nn9-10
Mirandola, Pico, 97, 97n19, 102
modern self. See me-centered self
monasticism, 23-24
Monson, T. W., 164n12
Moo, Douglas, 175, 176n13
moral space, 18-19, 22-23, 27-28, 31, 37
morality, 32, 33-34
Moses (biblical figure), 153n5
Mozart, Wolfgang Amadeus, 65, 66n4
murder, Jesus' teaching on, 165
nature, 28-31, 30n39
need, love and, 118-19, 118-19n10
Nemesius of Emesa, 196
Newton, Isaac, 82n18
Nicomachean Ethics (Aristotle), 33
Nietzsche, Friedrich, 46, 88-89n29, 155, 191
nominalism, 81n16
nonresistance, 168, 168n24
oaths, Jesus' teaching on, 167
Ockham, William of. See William of Ockham
Oord, Thomas Jay, 136n20
ordinary life, affirmation of, 23-28
Osborn, Robert T., 184n8
Packer, J. I., 163
pagan religion, 48-49, 48n1, 54-55, 79. See also
    default religion
Pannenberg, Wolfhart, 154n6, 183-84, 201-2
Paradise Lost (Milton), 42-44, 44n5, 109. See
    also Milton, John
Paul (apostle)
    on Abba, Father, 160n2, 163, 176-78
    on Adam and Christ, 173-76
    on atonement, 204-5
    on being in Christ, 205
    on creation, 117
    critique of religion by, 57-58

on degeneration after the Fall, 120
on divine adoption, 211
on freedom, 107, 175-76, 183-84, 184n8,
    184-85n10, 185
on God's gift of Christ, 121
on idolatry, 55
on inner "other," 176-77, 176n13
on Jesus' obedience, 154n6
on living by the Spirit, 182
on love, 58n13, 202
on ruling powers, 175n11
perfection, of freedom, 182-90. *See also*
    self-perfection, freedom and
Perkins, William, 24-25
persuasion, divine
    versus coercion, 136
    freedom from sin and, 185
    Holy Spirit and, 135n21, 137
    versus human persuasion, 135-36
    in mainstream Christian theology, 137,
        137n22
    natural affinity and, 134
    power and, 130-32
    process theology and, 134-35, 135n20
    redemption and, 131
    rhetoric and, 132-34
Peter (disciple), 156
Petrarch, 197-98
Pharisees, 155n7
Philo, 93
philosophy. *See* Greek philosophy
Pinnock, Clark, 129
Plato
    on ambition, 23, 90
    development of inwardness and, 19, 21
    on freedom, 93
    on mythic picture of the gods, 79
    natural order and, 26
    on world of forms, 116n4
Plotinus, 79, 93
Plutarch, 71-72n21, 72
polytheistic religions, 78-79
power
    of gospel, 132
    human, 103, 103n1, 128, 130
    love of, 123
    See also power of God
power of God
    arbitrariness and, 84-85
    freedom and, 137-38
    God's omnipresence and, 140
    versus human power, 128, 130

life and freedom and, 13
as noncompetitive, 127-29, 140
process theology and, 136n20
pure, 81
as shared, 129
as threat, 127-28, 130
See also God; power
praise, love of, 71-72, 71n20
pride, 199-200
process philosophy, 129n3
process theology, 134-35, 136n20
projection theory, 82-83
Prometheus
    Augustine and example of, 53
    egocentric God of, 150
    freedom and, 84
    greatness of Zeus and, 88
    Jesus and example of, 155
    literary admiration for, 42-47
    myth of, 40-42, 48
    unbound, 213
Protestant Reformation, 24
Puritans, 24-25
Putnam, Samuel, 77, 89
Rahner, Karl, 184n8, 189n14
rationalism, divine persuasion and, 135n21
reason
    circumstantial freedom and, 106, 106n7
    Descartes's understanding of freedom and,
        21
    dignity and, 194
    human will and, 20
    Kant's inner voice and, 29-30n38
    morality grounded in, 34, 36
    self-control and, 19, 23
    self-love and, 26
    self-preservation and, 25
    utilitarianism and, 28
redemption. *See* salvation
Reformed theology, 137, 137n23
religion, purified, 213-16. *See also* default
    religion
respect, as axis of moral space, 18-19, 23, 27, 31,
    37-38
resurrection, 162, 162n6. *See also* cross
revenge, Jesus' teaching on, 167-68, 167-68n23
Ridgely, Thomas, 121-22
Ritschl, Albrecht, 79n8
ritualism, 56-57
Rolnick, Philip, 119
Rorty, Richard, 110-11
Rousseau, Jean-Jacques, 29, 102, 155

Russell, Bertrand, 107-8
salvation, 131-32, 184, 210, 211
Sartre, Jean-Paul, 92
Satan
 Christ tempted by, 152-56
 the fall and, 152
 Job and, 157
 in *Paradise Lost* (Milton), 42-44, 44n6, 88,
  109, 150, 213
Schelkle, Karl Hermann, 184-85n10
Schöbel, Christoph, 198n22, 200n23
Schopenhauer, Arthur, 88-89n29
self
 buffered, 21n10, 139-40n1
 as complex set of relations, 144-45
 despair and, 145-47, 145nn10-12, 146n14, 188
 divine, 123-26
 as empty, 87-88, 100-101
 false versus true, 174-75
 fragmented, 110-11
 freedom as property of, 185-86
 God's omnipresence and, 139, 143
 human versus divine, 178-79
 image of God and, 172-73, 175
 Jesus as archetype and, 186-87
 love of, 215
 modern versus premodern, 139-40n1, 144n7
 objective God relation and, 172, 172n4
 old versus new, 173-75, 174n7
 the other and, 173-78
 transcendental versus empirical, 95n14
 true versus false, 178
 as will, 22n16, 76n32, 88-89, 172
 See also God-centered self; me-centered
  self
self-awareness, 146-47, 148
self-centeredness, 62
self-creation, 92-93, 109-10
self-determination
 denial of, 107-8
 dignity and, 107
 free will and, 108n11
 freedom and, 91n2, 92-93, 94, 107, 110, 172,
  186n12, 187-89
 "Invictus" (Henley) and, 96
 in *Paradise Lost* (Milton), 213
self-expression, 30, 31
self-knowledge, 148-49, 216
self-perfection, freedom and, 91n2, 93-94, 171,
 187-88. *See also* perfection, of freedom
self-realization, freedom and, 91-92, 91n2, 94,
 171, 173, 182, 186n12, 187-89

self-transcendence, 145n8
self-understanding, freedom and, 105-6
Sermon on the Mount, 57
Shaftesbury, Third Earl of, 25-26n24
Shalkowski, Scott A., 83n21
shame, 199-200
Shammai (rabbi), 166n17
Shelley, Percy, 44n6, 46
sin
 freedom from tyranny of, 175-76, 183-84,
  184n8, 184-85n10, 185
 God's law and, 176, 176n13
 inner "other" and, 176-78
 original, 29, 51-52
 self-liberation from, 183n5
 unoriginal, 53-54
Sisyphus, 181
Sokolowski, Robert, 49
soul, 20, 21, 212
soul mates, 147n16
Soulen, R. Kendall, 203n29
Spurgeon, Charles Haddon, 159
Staniloae, Dumitru, 117, 125, 131
Stoic philosophers, 23, 177n15, 183
Stott, John R. W., 174n7
submission versus subservience, 48n2
subservience to God
 choice of, 213-14
 image of God and, 74
 indifference and defiance and, 76, 203
 lack of inner devotion and, 48
 versus submission, 48n2
sympathy, as philosophical fiction, 36
Taylor, Charles
 on buffered versus porous self, 21n10,
  139-40n1
 on common good, 26
 on deists' view of nature, 27n30
 on Descartes and the mind, 20-21nn9-10
 on development of inwardness, 27
 on explaining Christianity, 37-38
 on expressive individualism, 30n44
 on mimetic view of art, 30n42
 modern self and, 12, 18-19, 144n7, 211-12
 on nature as moral source, 30n39
 on obstacles to happiness, 104
 on ordinary life, 23
 on rejection of God, 46
 on self-understanding, 105-6
 on subjectivism, 22n16
 on Western cultural trends, 37n64
Temple, William, 104

Ten Commandments, 55
theology, of individuality and freedom, 12n2
Tindal, Matthew, 26-27, 27n30, 135n21
Tolstoy, Leo, 68-70, 69n13
Trinity
    dignity and, 125-26, 204
    human mind in image of, 194
    love within, 206
    mutual indwelling within, 209-10
    relationship and, 124-25, 125n23, 150, 201
    as three suns, 178
Trinkaus, Charles, 97n18, 197
Turner, James, 46
United Nations Universal Declaration on
    Human Rights, 98-99
utilitarianism, 28-29
Vawter, Bruce, 52n6
virtue, 25-26n24, 33-34
vocation, 24-25
Voltaire, 64
voluntarism, 81, 81n17
Wagner, Richard, 46
Watts, Fraser, 203n30
Webster, John, 97n19, 201, 201n25
will, God's
    as arbitrary, 81n17, 85-86, 123-24

creation and, 130
versus divine intellect, 81
divine self and, 88-89
human will and, 58, 89
Locke on, 25
in *Paradise Lost* (Milton), 43
pure, 100
submission to, 48n2
will, human
    Augustine on, 20
    Descartes on, 21
    versus desire, 88-89n29
    divine persuasion and, 137
    God's will and, 58, 89
    holiness and, 132
    libertarian versus compatibilist, 108n11
    predetermination of, 108-9
    pure, 22n16, 76n32, 100, 172
    self-determination and, 92, 107-8,
        108n11
    theories of, 88-89n29
William of Ockham, 81, 81n16
Woodhead, Linda, 203n29
Wright, N. T., 162n8
youth, 17n1
Zanchi, Girolamo, 137

Scripture Index

OLD TESTAMENT

Genesis
1:26, 194, 197
3, 51
3—11, 120
18:14, 128

Exodus
20:5, 55

Deuteronomy
6:16, 154
8:3, 153
9:9, 153
24:1-2, 166

Job
1:8, 157
1:9, 157
1:21, 157

Psalms
44:20-21, 86
91:11-12, 154
97:1, 138

Proverbs
16:18, 199

Isaiah
6:3, 121
46:9-10, 55
46:10-11, 85

Jeremiah
7:2-7, 57
10:2-3, 55
10:10-13, 55

Amos
5:24, 56

NEW TESTAMENT

Matthew
1—7, 153, 155,
164, 165, 166,
167, 168
3:17, 153, 160
4:1-11, 152
4:3, 153
4:4, 153
4:6, 154
4:7, 154
4:9, 155
4:10, 155
5—7, 57, 160
5:9, 161
5:16, 161
5:17-48, 164
5:21-22, 165
5:27-30, 165
5:31-32, 166
5:33-37, 167
5:38-42, 167
5:43-48, 168
5:45, 161
5:48, 161
6:1, 161
6:6-8, 161
6:9, 161
6:14-15, 161
6:18, 161
6:24, 58
6:26, 161
6:32, 48
6:32-34, 161
7:11, 161
7:16, 164
11, 160
11:25, 160
11:27, 160
17:5, 160
22:23-33, 162
26:36-46, 156
28:18, 155

Mark
1:13, 152
10:1-12, 166
12:18-27, 162
14:36, 160

Luke
4:13, 156
20:27-38, 162
20:36, 162

John
1:1, 124
1:12-13, 162
3:16, 120
4, 121
8:34, 183
8:36, 183
12:32, 122
14:3, 211
14:8, 209
14:9-10, 209
15:26, 124

Romans
1, 120
2, 58
3—8, 58
5—7, 176
5—8, 174, 212
5:5, 58, 137, 185
5:6-8, 120
5:8, 205
5:12, 175
5:15, 175
5:19, 205
6, 176, 183
6:1, 175
6:3, 205
6:5, 205
6:6, 174
6:6-7, 174
6:7, 183
6:15, 183
6:18, 183
6:20, 183
6:22, 183
7, 58, 176, 182,
187
7:7-8, 176
7:14-17, 176
7:14-25, 176
7:15, 177
7:17, 177
7:18, 177
7:22-23, 176
7:24, 177
7:25, 177
8, 163, 176, 177,
183, 184
8:2, 183
8:3, 177
8:6, 163
8:11, 163
8:14, 163
8:14-15, 177, 205
8:16, 149, 163,
185
8:18-23, 178
8:19, 163, 184
8:19-21, 184
8:21, 107, 137, 163,
213, 216
8:22-25, 184
8:23, 163, 211
8:32, 121

1 Corinthians
1:24, 122
2:8, 122
2:10, 124
9, 184
13:1-3, 57
13:13, 211

2 Corinthians
1:22, 211
5:14-15, 182
5:17, 186
8:9, 122

Galatians
2:20, 182, 205
4:6, 160
5:16-17, 182
5:22-23, 187
6:15, 186

Ephesians
1:4, 205
1:4-5, 117
1:5, 205
1:13-14, 205
2:1-3, 174
2:6, 205
3:16-17, 185
3:18-19, 202
4:22-23, 174
5:1-2, 205

Philippians
1:21, 182

Colossians
3:5, 55
3:9-10, 174
3:10, 175

Hebrews
1:1-3, 124
2:14, 152
4:13, 86
5:8, 154

James
1:8, 58
4:8, 58

1 Peter
3:18, 120

1 John
3:1, 159, 202
3:1-10, 159
3:2, 163, 178
4:8, 124
4:10, 120
4:19, 58